JCMS Annual Review
of the European Union
in 2009

Edited by

Nathaniel Copsey
and
Tim Haughton

General Editors: Jim Rollo and Daniel Wincott

WILEY-BLACKWELL

This edition first published 2010

Blackwell Publishing was acquired by John Wiley & Sons in February 2007. Blackwell's publishing program has been merged with Wiley's global Scientific, Technical and Medical business to form Wiley-Blackwell.

Registered Office
John Wiley & Sons Ltd, The Atrium, Southern Gate, Chichester, West Sussex, PO19 8SQ, United Kingdom

Editorial Offices
350 Main Street, Malden, MA 02148-5020, USA
9600 Garsington Road, Oxford, OX4 2DQ, UK
The Atrium, Southern Gate, Chichester, West Sussex, PO19 8SQ, UK

For details of our global editorial offices, for customer services, and for information about how to apply for permission to reuse the copyright material in this book please see our website at www.wiley.com/wiley-blackwell.

ISBN 978-1-4051-9703-8
ISSN 0021-9886 (print) 1468-5965 (online)

Set in 11/12.5 Pt Times by Toppan Best-set Premedia Limited
Printed in Singapore

2010

CONTENTS

Editorial: 2009, a Turning Point for Europe?

NATHANIEL COPSEY
Aston University
TIM HAUGHTON
University of Birmingham

The year 2009 was a momentous one for the European Union that brought a long-awaited conclusion to the near decade-long period of institutional reform that had begun in December 2001 with the Laeken Declaration's commitment to a more democratic, transparent and effective Union. With the entry into force of the Lisbon Treaty in December 2009, a death knell was rung for the European Communities,[1] and the European Union assumed full responsibility for the European integration project. Equipped with a permanent Chairperson for the European Council, titled, naturally, 'President', to match the authority of the Presidents of the European Parliament and the European Commission and acting in concert with the new European foreign minister, or more properly, High Representative for Common Foreign and Security Policy, it was hoped Europe would be more likely to speak with one voice in global affairs.

This process of redesigning and recalibrating Union structures and procedures was originally necessitated by the decision of the Member States to open the EU's doors to include the states cut off from western Europe by the power politics of the cold war. The great eastward enlargements of 2004 and 2007 had, of course, been made possible by the central European revolutions of 1989 and the year 2009 marked the 20th anniversary of these changes that had set Europe on its path to ever-closer Union. Much of what the revolutionaries of 1989 had hoped to accomplish had been achieved: the states of central Europe had become democracies, market economies, had 'returned to

[1] With the exception of Euratom.

Europe', and a significant part of the gap in living standards between east and
west had been closed. Yet by 2009, the uncertainty and fluidity that marked
the first phase of post-cold war European history appeared to be over as new
divisions in the European continent between Member States, candidate countries and neighbours became ever more entrenched. The ruling of Germany's
Constitutional Court on the Lisbon Treaty in June 2009 also appeared to
preclude the possibility of any deeper European integration for the time
being, citing, albeit ambiguously, the Union's democratic deficit. Thus the
grand idea of an ever-closer and wider European Union spanning the whole
continent appears for the moment to have run its course. It is not certain what
will follow in its place.

The year 2009 did not begin well for the European Union. Although
January marked the entry of Slovakia into the euro area and the inauguration
of Barack Obama as president of the United States, millions of EU citizens
began the year in the cold as the perennial conflict between Russia and
Ukraine over gas prices flared up once again. At the beginning of 2009, the
global financial crisis that had entered a particularly virulent stage following
the failure of Lehman Brothers in September 2008, appeared to have brought
the European economy to the brink of the abyss with the German economy
contracting by 3.8 per cent in the first quarter of the year alone (Eurostat,
2009). An economic crisis comparable to that of the Great Depression of
1929–33 was widely forecast at the turn of the year. In the event, the European economy bounced out of recession far sooner than expected with the
French and German economies returning to growth in the second quarter of
the year. Although agreements struck by the G20 appeared to rescue the
financial architecture of capitalism, the financial earthquake had unleashed an
economic tsunami. The cost of bank bail-outs and government stimulus
packages designed to mitigate the extent of the downturn saddled the citizens
of some European Union Member States with large levels of debt which they
looked likely to be paying off for several decades. This in turn looked likely
to reduce still further the trend economic growth rate of many EU Member
States. The full effects of the economic crisis of 2008–09, including its impact
on the solidarity of the euro area, will not be fully felt for several years, but
2009 may come to be seen as a turning point in the history of European
capitalism, and the year in which the centre of gravity of the world economy
returned to Asia for the first time since the Industrial Revolution.

Throughout the year, the Lisbon Treaty bumped and stumbled its way
towards final ratification. Once Irish voters had dutifully endorsed the treaty
at the second time of asking in October after they had secured some promises
on tax, abortion, defence and the retention of one commissioner per Member
State, all eyes turned to the Czech Constitutional Court and the country's

contrarian, eurosceptic president, Václav Klaus. Klaus, who had enjoyed annoying MEPs in a speech in February when he likened the EU and its institutions to Soviet-era dictatorships and could not contain his glee in June 2008 when the Irish had voted no in the first referendum, tapped into deep-seated Czech concerns by raising the spectre of the post-war Beneš decrees and suggesting that ethnic Germans (or rather their descendants) might use the Charter of Fundamental Rights to claim back their confiscated property. When the Czech Constitutional Court finally issued its verdict, however, with reluctance and the promise of an opt-out from the Charter, Klaus signed the treaty.

More significant for the future development of the European Union, however, was the verdict of the German Constitutional Court in June 2009 (*Bundesverfassungsgericht*, 2009). Whilst it ruled that there were 'no decisive constitutional objections to the Act Approving the Treaty of Lisbon' passing through the *Bundestag*, the Court's decision could be interpreted as placing a brake on further European integration because it does not believe that the European Parliament can be regarded as sufficiently representative to make decisions as *European* decisions on the political direction of the Union. The Court stated that the 'principle of electoral equality does not apply to the European Parliament' since the relative weighting of each European citizen's vote for their representatives in the European Parliament is not identical, which of course compensates for the differences in population between, say, Malta and Germany. As such, the EP cannot be regarded as meeting 'the principle of democracy [. . .] which is accepted by the developed democratic states'. It concludes, therefore, that there cannot be said to be 'independent people's sovereignty of the citizens of the Union in their entirety'. Whilst this decision could be seen at the very least as a rebuff to the European Parliament, and perhaps a brake on deeper European integration, it must be balanced against Germany's commitment in the Basic Law (constitution) to 'establishing a united Europe'.

Despite the Treaty's limitation and its suboptimal institutional arrangements, Lisbon provides the EU with at least an improved constitutional framework to deliver, for example, as Monar notes in this volume, on the Stockholm objectives in the field of justice and home affairs. Nonetheless, as many contributors to the Annual Review stress, the treaty's success in bringing about a more efficient and effective Union will depend on a quality absent in the wording of the treaty: political will.

The eye-catching provisions of the Lisbon Treaty created two new posts, a President of the European Council and a High Representative for Foreign and Security Affairs. As it began to look as if it was a question of when rather than if Lisbon would be ratified many names were floated including Jean-Claude Juncker and Tony Blair. The choice of Herman van Rompuy and Catherine Ashton raised many eyebrows and provoked much debate. As Tony Barber argues in his contribution to the Annual Review, 'EU leaders left themselves open to the criticism that they had been too unambitious and allowed political horse-trading to triumph over merit'. Although neither had the political profile on appointment to stop the traffic in Washington and Beijing, both of them have the ability and personal characteristics to grow into their roles. Nevertheless, they face major challenges. Ashton, for instance, is charged with launching the European External Action Service and will have to juggle her role as the Council's lead on foreign affairs with her position as a Vice-President of the Commission. Moreover, the EU has not been able to project itself on the world stage. As Allen and Smith note in their contribution to this volume, a survey of the EU's external political and security activities in 2009 highlights that the EU 'struggles to "punch its weight" in the world'. Indeed, EU leaders were reminded of the roles and responsibilities of a major world power on the day that the Lisbon Treaty came into force (1 December) when President Obama announced that the US was looking for Europeans to respond positively with both hard and soft power instruments to his long awaited and much anticipated decision to increase US troop levels in Afghanistan.

Perhaps it was symbolic that the Lisbon Treaty was finally ratified almost 20 years to the day that the Berlin Wall fell. On a cold, wet night in Berlin the iconic event of 1989 was commemorated by significant figures associated with the heady days of the collapse of communism. Two months earlier, Germany's chancellor Angela Merkel, who was a citizen of East Germany in November 1989, had led her party to victory in the German federal elections. The success of the Free Democrats at the ballot box enabled the formation of a centre-right government bringing to an end the grand coalition, which had governed the EU's largest Member State since 2005.

Two decades after the semi-free elections in Poland which ushered in the first post-communist democratic government, June's elections to the European Parliament showed the best and worst of European democracy. Fewer than half of the EU's 375 million citizens turned out to cast their vote. Moreover, among the ranks of the army of MEPs elected to represent citizens was a significant brigade from the far right including the British National Party, Jobbik in Hungary and the Party for Freedom in the Netherlands. Prior to the election much publicity had been received by Declan Ganley (who had run the no campaign in the first Irish referendum on the Lisbon Treaty in June 2008) and his pan-European Libertas Party, but his challenge proved to be a damp squib. The winners of the elections were the centre-right forces of the European Peoples Party (EPP), although their number was depleted soon after by the creation of the European Conservatives and Reformists Group led by the British Conservatives, the Polish Law and Justice Party and the Czech Civic Democrats promising to push an anti-federalist agenda in the EP. Nonetheless, the former Polish prime minister and member of the EPP, Jerzy Buzek, was elected President of the European Parliament. The victory of the centre-right in the EP elections tied to those of similar political colour being in power in Berlin and Paris, ensured Barroso would continue for a further term as Commission President.

Last year's editorial was entitled 'The Gathering Storm'. In 2009, the European Union managed to weather the storm, although it required the unwelcome donning of waterproofs and the hasty construction of new shelters, but dark clouds continued to lurk menacingly. As we write this editorial, for instance, question marks have been raised over the future cohesion of the euro area as Greece struggles to cope with the harsh winds of economic retrenchment. Moreover, the coming into force of the Lisbon Treaty occurred in the same month as the Copenhagen summit designed to provide a co-ordinated response to the non-metaphorical threat of climate change. Neither the EU, nor indeed much of the rest of the world for that matter, emerged from Copenhagen bathed in glory. Nonetheless, the location of the climate change conference reminds us of what the European Union can achieve: it was after all at summits in the Danish capital in 1993 and 2002 that decisions were taken to lay out the conditions for membership to the aspirant Member States in the former communist bloc and latterly to admit eight of those states into the club.

***

This is our second issue of the *JCMS* AR as editors and we have continued our policy of commissioning contributions from practitioners and commentators from outside the academic world. Following last year's contribution 'Delivering a "Europe of Results" in a Harsh Economic Climate' by Commission President Barroso (2009), and given the importance of the financial and economic crisis for developments in the EU during 2009, we decided to commission our State of the Union address article from a key player in EU economic policy-making. We are honoured and delighted that this year's State of the Union address comes from the President of the European Central Bank, Jean-Claude Trichet. In his article, Mr Trichet explains the response of the ECB to the global economic and financial crisis over the past couple of years. Our second commissioned article comes from the Brussels bureau chief of the *Financial Times*, Tony Barber, who offers an insight into the process of choosing Van Rompuy and Ashton as the new President of the European Council and High Representative on Common Foreign and Security Policy, respectively. His analysis highlights 'the sheer difficulty of brokering the necessary compromises among 27 nations ruled by governments of varying political complexions'.

Kalypso Nicolaïdis, Professor of International Relations at Oxford University, and a member of the Reflection Group on the future of the European Union kindly accepted our invitation to give the *JCMS* AR Lecture at the 2010 UACES Conference in Bruges, Belgium, entitled 'Europe: 2.0' and, following on from Vivien Schmidt's (2009) call to 'Re-envision the European Union', joins our series of articles that not only diagnose the current problems facing the European Union but suggest possible solutions to them. Nicolaïdis argues that 'sustainability is borderless, that distributed intelligence is centreless and that post-cold war mindsets must make way for the world-wide-web world'. Although she sees Europe as standing on the brink, she argues that the era of institutional wrangling needs to come to an end, allowing us to shift our attention to building sustainable integration which involves radically shifting our attention from 'discrete inter-governmental to public inter-societal bargains, and from short-term inter-national bargains to long-term inter-generational bargains'.

We would like to thank all the contributors to this issue of the *JCMS* AR for their efforts and efficiency in producing such excellent copy on time. Two long-standing contributors to the Annual Review, Debra Johnson and Amy Verdun, stood down this year. We extend our thanks to them for their insightful contributions over the years and welcome on-board two rising stars, Dermot Hodson from Birkbeck College, London and Richard Connolly from the University of Birmingham. We would also like to thank the outgoing editors of the *JCMS* over the past year – Jim Rollo, Dan Wincott and Charlie Lees – as well as UACES and the staff at Wiley-Blackwell. We look forward to working with the incoming *JCMS* editors, Michelle Cini and Amy Verdun, and hope our relationship will be just as productive.

References

Barroso, J. (2009) 'State of the Union: Delivering a "Europe of Results" in a Harsh Economic Climate'. *JCMS AR*, Vol. 47, s1, pp. 7–16.

Bundesverfassungsgericht (2009) 'Decision of 30 June 2009'. 30 June 2009. Available in English at «http://www.bundesverfassungsgericht.de/entscheidungen/es20090630_2bve000208en.html».

Eurostat (2009) 'Flash Estimates for the First Quarter of 2009'. Available at «http://europa.eu/rapid/pressReleasesAction.do?reference=STAT/09/70&type=HTML».

Schmidt, V. (2009) 'Re-Envisioning the European Union: Identity, Democracy, Economy'. *JCMS AR*, Vol. 47, s1, pp. 17–42.

JCMS 2010 Volume 48 Annual Review pp. 7–19

State of the Union: The Financial Crisis and the ECB's Response between 2007 and 2009*

JEAN-CLAUDE TRICHET
President of the European Central Bank

Introduction

In the global financial turmoil that started in 2007 and erupted into a financial crisis in 2008, the European Central Bank (ECB) has confirmed its capacity to take bold action to foster financing conditions and enhance its credit support to the euro area economy, while remaining fully aligned with its primary mandate of safeguarding medium-term price stability. The ECB has also been co-operating closely with other central banks worldwide: the network of global central bank co-operation has been as dense as the integration in the global financial system itself.

This article reviews and explains in detail how both the ECB and the Eurosystem – the latter comprising the ECB and the 16 national central banks of the euro area countries – responded to the financial tensions in 2007 and the intensification of the crisis in 2008 and 2009. In this sense, the article is backward looking. The cut-off date for data used in this article is February 2010. More recent developments are not covered, in particular, the adjustment programme for Greece negotiated by the International Monetary Fund and the European Commission, in liaison with the ECB, and the Securities Markets Programme, which was adopted by the ECB in response to severe tensions in some segments of the debt securities market in early May 2010.

* I would like to thank W. Modery and F.P. Mongelli for their support in drafting this article and P. Mercier and P. Moutot for their comments.

Journal compilation © 2010 Blackwell Publishing Ltd, 9600 Garsington Road, Oxford OX4 2DQ, UK and 350 Main Street, Malden, MA 02148, USA

For the purpose of this article, it is useful to distinguish between three periods, each with specific challenges:

1. the period of *financial turmoil,* which started on 9 August 2007;
2. the period of the full-blown *financial crisis,* which set in on 15 September 2008;
3. the period marked by the first steps in the gradual *phasing-out of non-standard measures* towards the end of 2009.

Obviously, the considerations on the third phase can only be tentative, as in February 2010 this phase was ongoing and the economic and financial environment remains characterized by a continued high degree of uncertainty.

I. The Financial Turmoil Starting on 9 August 2007

For the European Central Bank the global financial turmoil started on a precise date: 9 August 2007. On this day, severe tensions made themselves felt in the interbank market. Confidence evaporated and trading became seriously impaired. Short-term money market rates, such as the euro overnight index average (EONIA), and spreads surged significantly, both in the euro area and in other major economies, such as the United Kingdom and the United States (see Figure 1). Had it been left unaddressed, this situation would have caused a systemic liquidity threat to the financial system as a whole. The situation brought to the fore the underlying imbalances and severe weaknesses in the financial system that had been building up for some time. There were two main factors behind these developments: massive external and domestic imbalances worldwide, both in the real economy and financial systems, and the very rapid emergence of insufficiently regulated and supervised financial instruments, financial markets and non-bank financial entities. The complexity of new financial products had made it increasingly difficult to rate properly the risks contained in financial innovations, especially when distorted by bad risk management, adverse incentives and moral hazard. As long ago as in 2006 and early 2007, the BIS, the ECB and other central banks had, on a number of occasions, warned financial market participants to prepare themselves for a general reassessment and re-pricing of risk.[1]

The ECB's response to these unfavourable developments was bold and fast. On 9 August 2007 it provided €95 billion of overnight credit, against collateral, to euro area banks at the then prevailing main refinancing rate. This operation, which was the first of four very large overnight fine-tuning

---

[1] See, for instance, the front-page article in the *Financial Times* of 29 January 2007, which reported: 'Trichet warns markets of a re-pricing of risks'.

Figure 1: Money Market Spreads in the Euro Area, United Kingdom and United States (*in basis points*)

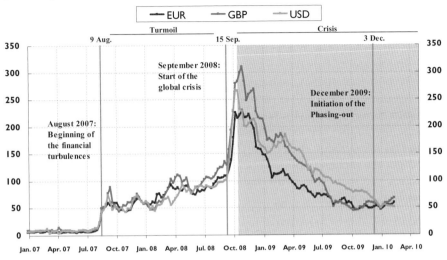

Notes: Spreads are the difference between the 12-month unsecured Euribor/Libor and secured Overnight Index Swap rates and are commonly used as measures of market perceptions of potential insolvency of counterparties, i.e. the higher the spread, the greater the risk of default by a counterparty. The shaded area refers to the period when the ECB conducted its operations by means of a fixed rate tender procedure with full allotment. Data are given as weekly averages.
Sources: Bloomberg and ECB calculations.

operations, was conducted at a fixed rate and the entire demand was accommodated, prefiguring what the ECB would do one year later.[2] As a result, tensions in the short-term segment of the euro area money market abated to a significant extent.[3]

In the following months the ECB lengthened the average maturity of its liquidity provision through the adoption of supplementary refinancing operations with maturities of three and six months. It also began to provide US dollar liquidity against euro-denominated collateral, on the basis of a swap agreement with the US Federal Reserve System. The ECB borrowed US dollars from the Federal Reserve and passed them on to the banking sector, at conditions agreed with the Federal Reserve, thus addressing a potential US dollar liquidity shortage in Europe resulting from a less than fully

[2] See Mercier (2009) for an account of the Eurosystem's liquidity management during the initial 18 months of the crisis.
[3] This liquidity injection did not, however, change the overall amount provided during the maintenance period, as the ECB provided larger amounts of credit at the beginning of each reserve maintenance period and smaller amounts of credit at the end (a procedure known as 'frontloading'). See also Trichet (2009a,b).

functioning transatlantic interbank market. Moreover, the ECB conducted special tender procedures at the end of 2007 to counter the major funding concerns of banks over the year-end period.

Two features of the ECB's response during the financial turmoil stand out:

- First, all measures were taken within the existing operational framework of the Eurosystem. This framework proved sufficiently flexible and robust to align short-term money market rates with the ECB's main refinancing rate. In this respect, the relatively broad collateral framework and the large list of counterparties in the main refinancing operations were particularly helpful. These favourable elements reflect the diversity of the national frameworks that had prevailed in the euro area countries before EMU;
- Second, the monetary policy operations kept the short-term money market interest rates in line with the level determined by monetary policy decisions.

In the event, the EONIA remained very close to the main refinancing rate. Still, volatility in money market rates remained significantly higher than before August 2007, and money market spreads at longer maturities also remained elevated. Hence, we were a long way from a return to normality.

II. The Crisis Period From 15 September 2008 to 3 December 2009

On 15 September 2008 the collapse of a major US financial institution transformed a large-scale crisis of confidence in the financial markets of the advanced economies into a global financial and economic crisis. Information asymmetries, together with heightened liquidity and counterparty risks, became overwhelming. This led to a virtual breakdown of the money market, with spreads soaring to abnormally high levels both inside and outside the euro area (see Figure 1). Financial intermediaries tried to restore liquidity buffers, shedding risk and tightening lending conditions. This resulted in large-scale 'deleveraging'. Credit spreads surged and financial activity in a large number of financial markets collapsed. This severe intensification of financial market tensions was accompanied by a free fall in global trade and a rapid and synchronized deterioration of economic conditions in most major economies of the world.

In response to these developments, central banks around the globe took prompt and resolute action. In a co-ordinated move, both exceptional and historic in nature, the Bank of Canada, the Bank of England, the ECB, the Federal Reserve System, Sveriges Riksbank and the Swiss National Bank announced reductions in policy interest rates on 8 October 2008. On this occasion, the ECB lowered its key rates by 50 basis points (see Figure 2),

Figure 2: ECB Interest Rates and Money Market Rates
(percentages per annum)

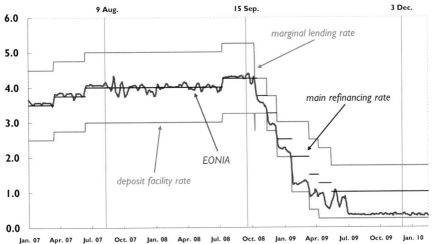

Notes: In addition, the Governing Council of the ECB reduced the interest rate on the deposit facility by 50 basis points on 8 October 2008 and narrowed the corridor of standing facilities by 100 basis points around the interest rate on the main refinancing operation on 9 October 2008. The EONIA rate is given in weekly averages.
Source: ECB.

taking into account subdued inflationary pressures in a context where the intensification of the financial crisis had weakened the economic outlook and significantly diminished upside risks to price stability. In the following months, further rate cuts followed. Overall, between October 2008 and May 2009, i.e. within a period of only seven months, the main refinancing rate of the Eurosystem was reduced by 325 basis points to 1 per cent, a level not seen in the countries of the euro area in recent history.

At the same time, the functioning of the financial system – in particular the money market – was severely hampered, and the transmission of the substantially reduced key ECB interest rates to money market and bank lending rates impaired (ECB, 2009). Dysfunctional money markets had weakened the ability of monetary policy to influence the outlook for price stability by interest rate decisions alone (ECB, 2010). Therefore, to bring the spreads down and ensure a proper transmission of monetary policy impulses, the Governing Council adopted a number of non-standard measures and allowed the EONIA rate to be positioned closer to the deposit rate. In fact, during the 2008/2009 crisis, the deposit facility rate played a more prominent role as regards the dynamics of the EONIA rate and very short-term money market rates than in normal times.

Figure 3: Phasing-In/Out of the Eurosystem's Enhanced Credit Support

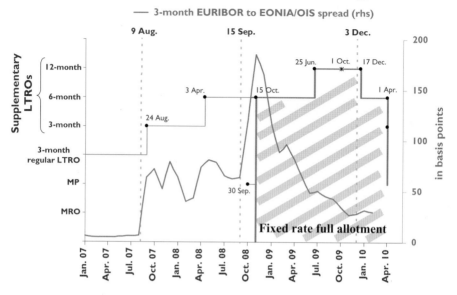

Notes: Left-hand scale: the thick line represents the domain of the fixed rate full allotment across operations of various maturities and over time. The thin line represents the maximum maturity of the operations. The dots represent the introduction/phasing-out of the various operations. Right-hand scale: 3-month EURIBOR–EONIA swap spread.
Sources: Bloomberg and ECB.

These non-standard measures were tailored to the specific financial structure of the euro area, in which banks are the primary source of credit to the economy. In the euro area a much larger share of corporate financing is provided by banks (whereas the financing structure in the United States is such that a larger share of financing is market-based). Thus, banks play a pivotal role in the transmission of monetary policy to the economy of the euro area. What we have called the ECB's 'enhanced credit support' comprises the following key measures:

• First, since October 2008 the Eurosystem has been providing unlimited central bank liquidity to euro area banks at a fixed rate (i.e. the main refinancing rate) and against adequate collateral in all refinancing operations (see Figure 3). The primary aim of these non-standard measures is to support the short-term funding of banks in order to alleviate the potential negative impact of liquidity risk on the availability of credit to households and companies across the euro area economy;
• Second, the list of assets accepted for use as collateral has been extended until the end of 2010 (Cheun et al., 2009). This measure has enhanced

banks' access to liquidity during the crisis. In particular, it has allowed many banks to refinance a larger share of their balance sheet with the Eurosystem;

- Third, the Eurosystem provided liquidity for longer periods. Specifically, it lengthened the maximum maturity of refinancing operations to up to one year. These longer-term refinancing operations (LTROs) have extended banks' liquidity into the traditionally less liquid segment of the money market, thus prolonging the rollover date and reducing the refinancing requirements of banks in the short term;[4]

- Fourth, in order to address euro area banks' needs to fund their US dollar assets, the Eurosystem has continued to provide liquidity in foreign currencies, most notably in US dollars. In addition, the ECB agreed with the central banks of several European countries outside the euro area to improve the provision of euro liquidity to their banking sectors. This measure has been particularly valuable in supporting banks faced with a massive shortfall in US dollar funding in the aftermath of mid-September 2008;

- Finally, in order to support the long-term refinancing operations of the financial sector, in May 2009 the ECB initiated a measured, but significant, programme to purchase euro-denominated covered bonds issued in the euro area. Such covered bonds – known as 'Pfandbriefe' in Germany, 'obligations foncières' in France and 'cédulas' in Spain – are long-term debt securities that are issued by banks to refinance loans to the public and private sectors, often in connection with real estate transactions. The covered bond market represents a major source of funding for banks in large parts of the euro area. This market nearly collapsed when the financial crisis intensified. The total sum allocated to the programme (€60 billion) represents around 2.5 per cent of the total outstanding amount of covered bonds at the end of 2008 (according to the European Covered Bond Council), a sum which may appear relatively modest. In fact, the covered bond market is the largest and most active segment of the fixed income market in the euro area – even exceeding the corporate bond market – with the exception of the public sector bond market.

The response of the ECB has been particularly effective, as inflation expectations in the euro area have remained broadly stable (see Figure 4). The impact on money markets of the ECB's decisive, yet steady-handed, interest rate cuts has led to a corresponding decline in nominal and real yields at two and three-year maturities (see Figure 5). This reflects, in part, private

[4] The outstanding amount of LTROs increased from €150 billion in June 2007 to over €600 billion by the end of 2008. Over the same period, the total amount of outstanding liquidity almost doubled, peaking at €857 billion on 2 January 2009, more than 9 per cent of euro area GDP and nearly 4 per cent of total euro area MFI financial assets.

Figure 4: Break-Even Inflation Rates (BEIRs)
(percentages per annum; daily data)

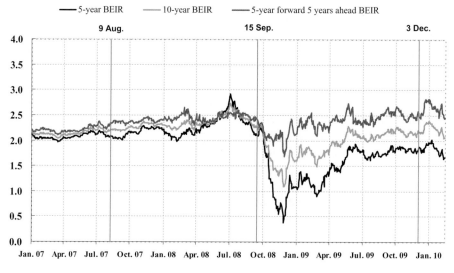

Source: ECB.

Figure 5: 2-Year and 3-Year Bond Yields: Nominal and Real
(percentages per annum; daily data)

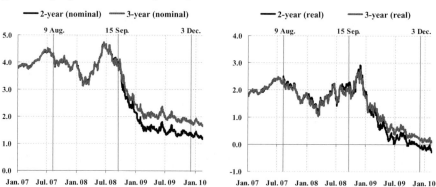

Notes: Nominal yields are based on the triple A euro area yield curve, published by the ECB. Real yields are based on index-linked government bonds.
Sources: MTS and ECB.

Figure 6: MFI Interest Rates on Short-Term Loans
(percentages per annum)

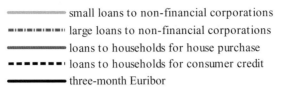

small loans to non-financial corporations
large loans to non-financial corporations
loans to households for house purchase
loans to households for consumer credit
three-month Euribor

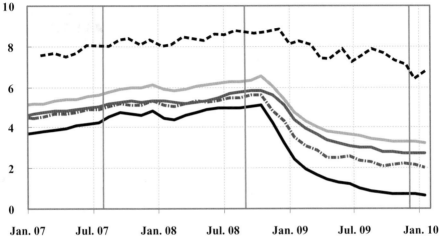

Sources: ECB and Reuters. Last observations: January 2010.

expectations of continued low policy rates for some time to come. At the same time, expectations regarding euro area inflation remained well anchored in line with price stability. By implication, real rates at such maturities fell substantially, pointing to significant monetary easing in the euro area.

Moreover, the Eurosystem's exceptional policy measures supported the flow of credit to the economy through both demand factors (owing to the very low level of interest rates) and supply factors (notably by alleviating funding pressures in the banking sector). Providing central bank liquidity to banks in unlimited amounts at a fixed rate exerted significant downward pressure on money market rates, as it ensured that banks had broad and deep access to liquidity, thereby increasing their ability to lend to the real economy and placing downward pressure on bank lending rates. Consequently, interest rates on short-term loans declined steadily (see Figure 6). Likewise, overall financial market volatility decreased substantially.

At the same time, the purchase of covered bonds by the ECB has contributed to the revitalisation of the covered bond market and to the decline of covered bond spreads.[5]

Equally importantly, the Eurosystem's non-standard measures have bought time for banks in the process of deleveraging and building up of capital buffers. These processes should help banks in the euro area to restart loan growth as early as possible under the circumstances.

III. A Gradual Phasing-Out Initiated on 3 December 2009

Without the ECB's non-standard measures in response to the crisis, a breakdown in money markets would have occurred. The refinancing of many bank assets might have been impeded, risking a massive and disorderly deleveraging by credit institutions. This might have altogether frozen the bank-lending channel, rendering the ECB's monetary policy ineffective. Such a breakdown, had it been protracted, would have turned the financial crisis into a profound and long-lasting economic depression.

The ECB's extraordinary policy measures have been a response to extraordinary circumstances. From the start, the Governing Council emphasized that these measures would not be maintained forever and that they would have to be gradually phased out once the underlying rationale had faded away and the situation had normalized.

Continued very abundant liquidity in an environment of accommodative interest rates may ultimately lead to excessive risk-taking and a misallocation of resources. This, in turn, may have adverse effects on economic growth and the sustainability of asset price developments. The 2008/2009 crisis has graphically illustrated the fact that the economic fallout from bursting bubbles can be considerable. At the same time, gradualism is warranted in phasing out non-standard measures, given the continued high uncertainty surrounding the overall financial market situation.

In summer 2009 the ECB announced the overall framework that would guide its exit considerations, which was based, in particular, on the following key elements (Trichet, 2009d):

- First, the ECB's exit strategy is embedded in its monetary policy strategy, with a focus on the medium term. This is essential for fulfilling the ECB's mandate to maintain price stability in the euro area. Accordingly,

---

[5] Preliminary empirical analysis suggests that, when comparing covered bond yields with a risk-free benchmark, it appears that German covered bond spreads have declined to below pre-2008 levels, whereas covered bond spreads in other euro area countries have reached their pre-Lehman levels.

in order to counter any threat to price stability over the medium term, the liquidity provided will be absorbed when necessary. At the same time, in the absence of such risk, non-standard measures could be maintained to the extent that they are needed in order to support the flow of credit to the economy;

• Second, the ECB has designed its non-standard measures with exit considerations in mind: in fact, with the exception of the covered bond purchase programme – which is itself relatively modest in scope – all operations are repo transactions, i.e. the liquidity is provided in exchange for collateral and for a defined period. This allows a relatively easy and 'natural' phasing-out of a number of measures upon maturity, once the overall situation has normalized, unless there are good reasons to extend them. In addition, outright purchases for which an exit would require either unwinding or offsetting operations have indeed been carefully calibrated, whereby the offsetting operations fully reabsorb the additional liquidity provided through purchase operations;

• Third, with its operational framework the Eurosystem is well equipped to facilitate the unwinding of non-standard measures when the need arises. In particular, the framework permits short-term interest rates to be changed, while keeping some non-standard measures in place, should continued credit support be needed. Additionally, given its independent status, the ECB can carry out any action it deems necessary to deliver on its mandate to maintain price stability in line with the Treaty on the functioning of the European Union.

It is against this background that the Governing Council, on 3 December 2009, announced that it was initiating a gradual phasing-out of those non-standard measures that were not needed to the same extent as in the past. At the same time, the Governing Council made clear that the ECB's enhanced credit support to the banking system would be continued, while taking into account financial market conditions and avoiding distortions associated with maintaining non-standard measures for too long.

With the benefit of hindsight, the first steps in the phasing-out of non-standard measures were announced at a time of improving financial market conditions. This picture changed in the first few months of 2010, when developments related to Greece accelerated and severe tensions in certain segments of the financial markets emerged abruptly in early May. To address these issues, the Greek authorities negotiated an economic and financial adjustment programme with the International Monetary Fund and the European Commission, in liaison with the ECB. As already indicated, these more recent developments are not discussed in this article.

IV. Some Lessons from the Crisis in 2008/2009

As of February 2010, the euro area economy, having avoided a depression and having displayed modest growth since the third quarter of 2009, is projected to post moderate growth in 2010. At the same time, the international environment is still uncertain and could present new challenges in the period ahead. The ECB stands ready to act within a posture of credible alertness.

The 2008/2009 crisis has clearly demonstrated the absolute necessity to reform financial regulation and supervision in such a way that market participants' incentives are aligned with the risks that they take. It must be clear that whoever acts bears both the risk and the consequences. This crisis has also shown that we have to work very intensively on the issue of systemic risks at the level of the global financial system. Systemic risk is the threat that developments in the financial system can cause a seizing-up or breakdown of this system and trigger massive damages to the real economy.[6] Such developments can stem from the failure of large and interconnected institutions, from endogenous imbalances that accumulate over time, or from a sizeable unexpected event. A seizing-up of the financial system – or large parts of it – is what we experienced in September 2008, triggering an economic free fall, a surge in unemployment and a massive increase in public debt.

The 2008/2009 crisis has also demonstrated that price stability is a necessary though insufficient precondition for financial stability. At the same time, financial stability helps a central bank to foster price stability by ensuring an orderly functioning of the transmission mechanism. In this respect, regular in-depth analysis of developments in monetary and credit aggregates and their interaction with financial trends is essential. In particular, by giving importance to money and credit developments in its two-pillar monetary policy strategy, the ECB's monetary analysis has proven invaluable in difficult times. It has provided a channel through which elements pertaining to possible risks to financial stability can be taken into account. In particular, our monetary pillar serves not only to detect risks to price stability but also to detect cases in which excessive money and credit growth may lead to risks of asset price misalignments. Once such misalignments reverse, this can pose serious risks to price stability and the economy[7].

The ECB and the Eurosystem, which responded decisively to the financial crisis, can be counted on to remain a reliable anchor of stability and confidence.

---

[6] For a detailed discussion of this concept, see Trichet, 2009e.
[7] See also Stark, 2008; Papademos, 2009; Trichet, 2009c. For more information on the new areas of research that we are pursuing in this regard, see Alessi and Detken, 2009; De Santis *et al.*, 2008; Gerdesmeier *et al.*, 2009; Moutot and Vitale, 2009.

References

Alessi, L. and Detken, C. (2009) '"Real-Time" Early Warning Indicators for Costly Asset Price Boom/Bust Cycles: A Role for Global Liquidity'. ECB Working Paper No. 1039.

Cheun, S., von Köppen-Mertes, I. and Weller, B. (2009) 'The Collateral Frameworks of the Eurosystem, the Federal Reserve System and the Bank of England and the Financial Market Turmoil'. ECB Occasional Paper No. 107.

De Santis, R.A., Favero, C.A. and Roffia, B. (2008) 'Euro Area Money Demand and International Portfolio Allocation: A Contribution to Assessing Risks to Price Stability'. ECB Working Paper No. 926.

ECB (2009) 'Recent Developments in the Retail Bank Interest Rate Pass-Through in the Euro Area'. Monthly Bulletin, August 2009, pp. 93–105.

ECB (2010) 'The ECB's Monetary Policy Stance during the Financial Crisis'. Monthly Bulletin, January 2010, pp. 63–71.

Gerdesmeier, D., Roffia, B. and Reimers, H.-E. (2009) 'Asset Price Misalignments and the Role of Money and Credit'. ECB Working Paper No. 1068.

Mercier P. (2009) 'The Liquidity Management of the Eurosystem during the Financial Turmoil: August 2007 to February 2009'. Forum Financier, No. 2–3, pp. 96–104.

Moutot, P. and Vitale, G. (2009) 'Monetary Policy Strategy in a Global Environment'. ECB Occasional Paper No. 106.

Papademos, L. (2009) 'Financial Stability and Macro-Prudential Supervision: Objectives, Instruments and the Role of the ECB'. Speech of 4 September 2009.

Stark, J. (2008) 'The Contribution of Monetary and Financial Statistics to the Conduct of Monetary Policy'. In A Strategic Vision for Statistics: Challenges for the Next Ten Years (Frankfurt a.M.: ECB), pp. 43–52.

Trichet, J.-C. (2009a) 'The ECB's Enhanced Credit Support'. Keynote address at the University of Munich, 13 July 2009.

Trichet, J.-C. (2009b) 'The Financial Crisis and our Response so Far'. Keynote address at the Chatham House Global Financial Forum, 27 April 2009, New York.

Trichet, J.-C. (2009c) 'Credible Alertness Revisited'. Intervention at the symposium on 'Financial Stability and Macroeconomic Policy' sponsored by the Federal Reserve Bank of Kansas City, Jackson Hole, Wyoming, 22 August 2009.

Trichet, J.-C. (2009d) 'The ECB's Exit Strategy'. Speech at the ECB Watchers Conference, Frankfurt, 4 September 2009.

Trichet, J.-C. (2009e) 'Systemic Risk'. Clare Distinguished Lecture in Economics, University of Cambridge, 10 December 2009.

JCMS 2010 Volume 48 Annual Review pp. 21–54

The JCMS Annual Review Lecture
Sustainable Integration: Towards EU 2.0?*

KALYPSO NICOLAÏDIS
University of Oxford

> 'For everything to remain the same,
> everything has to change.'
> Tancredi Falconieri in *Il Gattopardo*,
> Giuseppe Tomasi di Lampedusa

Introduction

Many in Europe today feel that we are hovering on the brink of chaos. We have managed collectively to disrupt the fragile equilibrium of our ecosystem, in place since the dawn of humanity. The storms of global capitalism strike with unprecedented force in every corner of the globe, leaving much human debris in their wake. And nuclear Armageddon seems only marginally less implausible than it was half a century ago. However, today's general malaise is but a glimpse of what is to be expected in 20 years – looming wars over resources like oil, water and clean air, hunger or disease on an unprecedented scale, masses of refugees fleeing man-made and natural disasters, exploding inequalities and global imbalances as the world population rises towards the nine billion mark. On our continent itself, the view ahead to 2030 is no less gloomy: the aspirations of today's youth swamped by inter-generational debt, the young

* The views expressed in this article have greatly benefited from the discussions held in the Gonzales Reflection Group from December 2008 to May 2010. I would like to thank its members, its chairman, its assistants and the secretariat for the insights shared over this period. I warmly also thank my Oxford colleagues who provided invaluable feedback and intellectual companionship throughout this process, and for their special roles Brad Blitz, Pavlos Eleftheriadis, Lars Hoffmann, Peter Hall, Hartmut Mayer and Claudia Schrag. I would also like to thank all the organizations and individuals who graciously volunteered to work with the Reflection Group during this period, especially UACES and Policy Network, as well as OSI, ULB, EUISS, TEPSA, EPC Sciences-Po, ISTAME, BEPA, CFIA, Princeton, Eurobarometer, FIIA and the Navarino Initiative. Last but not least, I would like to thank the editors of this special issue, Nathaniel Copsey and Tim Haughton, as well as David Dawneway, Gabi Maas, Anand Menon, Simon Saunders, Peter Taylor and Ziga Turk for their input. A succinct version of this article was published in Nicolaïdis, 2010b,c.

swamped by the old, industries swamped by Asian competition. For the first time in our recent history, our children may be worse off than ourselves! The pessimists in our midst see the horsemen of the apocalypse galloping towards us at a breakneck speed. The optimists reply that it could be worse.

'We can still step back from the brink and become agents of change rather than its victims. The EU is no longer a choice but a necessity.' This is the message that a group of 'wise men' attempted to substantiate last June in *Project Europe, 2030*, a report which spelt out for the European Council the critical choice that we face – survival vs renewal – and its concrete implications for the Union, its leaders and its citizens (González Marquez *et al.*, 2010).[1] In this article, I offer my own, sceptical, variation on this universal call for action. My argument could be dubbed 'Europe 2.0 – with caveats'.

Risorgimento is hardly a new idea in Europe. The dilemmas we face today are perhaps not unlike those facing the Prince of Salina. Tancredi's words (quoted above) were, after all, a warning – a warning that the Prince ignored – although he knew that he would have to grant change to Italy's new masters if his family was to hold on to its influence. Yet the Prince was unwilling to change. Life in Sicily was too pleasant: thrilling hunting, delicious food, fine wines, magnificent palaces, beautiful women . . . and the island was too irredeemably set in its ways anyway. Life in the EU is not too bad either when contrasted with most parts of the world. Like Don Fabrizio, we know what we have to do to continue to flourish, but we are too comfortable, selfish or cowardly to act. And like him, if we do not decide urgently to act for the long term, our children will pay the price.

The *Project Europe 2030* report argues that for today's 'choice' for Europe to succeed it must mobilize the efforts of every level of society, and not only the princes of this world. Europe must be driven by a political vision, a shared project that asserts anew an answer to the question: why Europe? And why the EU in its 21st-century political incarnation? EU aficionados and insiders, including the readership of *JCMS*, may feel justifiably impatient with the periodic return of the *raison d'être* question, and equally critical of self-aggrandizing pronouncements. Many of the good things produced and nurtured by European integration – peaceful cohabitation between *frères-ennemis*, the freedom to move across borders and the democratic anchor offered to scores of weak states during and after the cold war – are taken for granted these days. They should not be. They still need to be nurtured.

---

[1] The same message can also be heard from all manner of speeches, pamphlets and reports currently circulating around Europe's deliberative sphere in the wake of the financial crisis. See for instance, Tsoukalis *et al.* (2009); Fabry and Ricard-Nihoul (2010); Fondation Robert Schuman (2010).

Nevertheless, all these accomplishments can be seen as those of the EU's adolescence, the first phase of a journey, as we enter a second, mature, era of European integration, that of EU 2.0. Will this be a story we can tell?

Many would argue that after 50 years of expansion and consolidation on the European continent, the next 50 years ought to be about consolidating Europe's global role and our capacity to contribute to the responsible governance of our planet in the 21st century. But how? For the pragmatic among us, EU mark 2 does not require new grand institutional or constitutional plans. Instead it should aim to put the integration process at the service of the coming generations and make it sustainable in the broadest sense of the word. For this, European leaders and societies must be ready to pay the costs. Jean-Claude Trichet in this volume demonstrates that such a prospect is not utopian.

Sustainable integration can be defined as an ethos and a practice for EU action. The concept is increasingly present in various areas of EU policy-making but needs to be generalized. It consists of systematically assessing short-term actions against the benchmark of long-term goals while at the same time eschewing the kind of teleology geared at resolving once and for all the question of the nature of the EU as a polity. This requires in turn grounding the various variants and myths of Global Europe (Manners, 2010) on solid home ground. In short, the sustainability agenda contributes to moving the pervasive conflict over 'ends' from polity and identity to policy and outcome.

Many concepts and issue areas are part of the sustainable integration mix, albeit discussed under different agendas, from sustainable development and the relation between environmental, economic and socio-political sustainability to socio-economic resilience, human ecology, institutional robustness, federal durability, sustainable security, renewable energy, resistance to unexpected shocks or policy viability. Sustainable integration does not privilege one level of governance over another: a sustainable *EU* supports a more sustainable *Europe*, more sustainable European economies and welfare states. Indeed, the idea of sustainability is intimately bound up with flexibility in the ways each component contributes to the whole and vice versa. When it comes to individuals and groups, sustainability is grounded in principles for collective action like empowerment, emancipation and responsibility. And the value of collaboration over both individualism and hierarchy is of course the hallmark of the 2.0 revolution on the web.

Crucially, such an emphasis on sustainability is predicated on the idea that the EU's unique comparative advantage must be better exploited: its future-friendliness is the silver lining of its democratic shortcomings. With its indirect form of accountability, the EU machinery can go on pretty steadily as individual governments fail. So it can overlook voter or shareholder short-termism and focus instead on the business which voters care less about: the interests of those not yet born and preventative action which if successful is invisible. At a time of unprecedented inter-generational divides, such a shield is precious for Member States and may become increasingly valued by citizens themselves.

EU 2.0 is about recognizing that sustainability is borderless, that distributed intelligence is centreless and that post-cold war mindsets must make way for the worldwide web world. In today's Europe as with Salina's 19th-century Sicily, I argue that the real object of change is change itself. Change is accelerating. Division of labour must make way for flexible partnerships, conservation calls for revolution and the foundations of integration must be re-examined through the lens of sustainability.

I lay out my argument in three steps: past, future and present. First, I try to take seriously the otherwise self-serving prognosis that we Europeans *stand at a critical juncture in our history* and take on ambient declinism by substantiating what I mean by sustainable integration. Second, I unpack this imperative and turn to the prescriptive mode by suggesting a set of guidelines for action towards a 'sustainable EU'. Finally, coming back to the here and now, I lay out some of the obstacles in the third part of this article, along with my own bias: the EU will only be sustainable as a political project if its leaders and citizens abandon the equation of integration with oneness, top-down policy design and simple hierarchical structures, all anachronistic in a 2.0 world.

I. Echoes of our Pasts: The Advent of EU 2.0?

Historical turning points, like the polities they encompass, are socially constructed. Like mini-Hegel clones, we are often prone to historical hubris, perceiving radical change in our times so that we may bask in the excitement. Apocalyptic benchmarks give us something to hold onto, but they are short-lived. Ten years ago, the new millennium heralded the end of everything: the end of history, the end of geography, the end of territory, the end of the state and even the end of time . . . ten years later, endism may have ended but heroic narratives are still with us. While we should not dismiss their mobilizing power, we need to take them in our stride.

Our Tocquevillian Moment

There are certainly many ways to characterize this moment. After the French and Dutch 'no' to the Constitutional Treaty, I suggested that Europe's seeming malaise was akin to a modern day 'Tocquevillian moment', in which a doomed era was ending without being replaced by the benefits of a new one (Nicolaïdis, 2005). A century and a half ago, the democratic aristocrat Alexis de Tocqueville, passionately concerned with the fate of Europe, anatomized democracy in America for hints of what to hope for (or not) on his own continent. While many of his contemporaries hoped for a liberal restoration, passively bemoaning the loss of a gentler era – Talleyrand's *douceur de vivre* – and the ills of their times – centralization, bureaucracy, atomization of society – Tocqueville argued that the transition from aristocratic to democratic regimes was inevitable. Witness to the pan-European upheaval of the 1840s, he saw these ills as growing pains, an expression and a function of the gap between rising expectations of the masses clashing with old regimes apparently incapable of reform. Though appropriately sceptical about the possible emergence of a truly democratic engaged citizenship on the old continent, he could clearly see that the in-betweenness of his era was unsustainable.

I believe that likewise, the EU has been going through an era of *in-betweenness* which is now ending. Its 20-year addiction to institutional reform, the almost continuous renegotiation of its founding pact, the democratic prevarication of its elites, and the obsession with process goals over policy outcomes, all speak to the agonies of political mutation. The EU, fired up by the end of the cold war, has been poised between introversion and extroversion, precisely because it is unable to bridge its technocratic-aristocratic past and an uncertain but irrevocable future where citizens would enjoy the power of their collective veto over the grand (and not so grand) designs of their political masters. As heightened expectations for the EU could neither be fulfilled nor ignored, and today's European peoples turned polling stations into their barricades, their leaders have wavered between democratic denial and democratic atonement (Nicolaïdis, 2007b). Scholars of federalism have stressed the idea that the EU has been mired in a Calhounian situation 'in which the invidious question of competence attribution cannot be disentangled from the equally vexing one of institutionalizing democratic accountability via popular sovereignty' (Glencross, 2009). Until a new generation embraces the instruments of participatory democracy including the democratic power potential of the Internet, the clumsy dance will continue (Saurugger, 2010). More broadly, the global financial crisis has created an unprecedented demand for more effective global governance in our emerging post-post cold war. So we may be left with a pre-crisis treaty for a post-crisis world, but treaties after all are only what the parties make of them.

To make the message starker, we can imagine the echoes of Europe's pasts like three tidal waves of 20, 50 and 200 years breaking simultaneously on our shores from various distances, leaving us to interpret the wavelength created by their untimely merging. Will they merge to amplify each other's downward momentum; or will they level off together, combining their momentum to sustain European integration?

To be sure, beyond 20 years of post cold-war, the second wave of 50 years could be seen as the artificial product of anniversaries, of thoughtless anthropomorphizing around metaphors of 'mid-life crisis'. And yet, a plausible case can be made that the first half-century of European integration has been a *longue marche* from market-making to polity-making, from the EU-as-space to the EU-as-actor, from continental consolidation to embryonic global projection. Copenhagen 2009 then is a *rendez-vous manqué*. As the EU knocks at the door of the global theatre, others relegate it backstage.

That is of course because although *the EU* may be an international actor in the making, *Europe* is a continent in relative decline. By any standards, we are coming to the end of five centuries of western global dominance, especially as we witness the closing of the extraordinary industrial gap of the last 200 years between the west and Asia (Zakaria, 2008). In the 1800s, Asia was home to three-fifths of the world population and three-fifths of global product, which shrank to one-fifth of both in 100 years. Today, it is recovering its 'normal' share. Europe's share of world population is down to 7 per cent from 25 per cent a century ago, and its share of GDP down to a fifth. But these figures would only be evidence of decline if we reasoned in zero-sum terms. In fact, the rise of others' wealth can benefit us if the peace between us is sustainable. What the figures do mean is that the EU's mission is to grant weight to a continent that is without doubt but a province of a non-European world.

However, the last 200 years are, of course, also about a much greater conflict, that between a planet with finite resources and a human species with infinite aspirations. 'In such a war – a war we are waging against our very life-support systems – we have no hope of winning. Our best hope is to, as quickly as possible, call off the war, regroup, and fundamentally restructure our society around the acceptance of our planet's finite nature – around limits' (Allen, 2009). So the question is: will the EU help Europeans regroup?

Decline, Settlements, Equilibria and Cycles

The idea of Europe 2.0 is both a diagnosis as to where we are and a way of framing prescriptions for the future. It can be contrasted with two alternative stories.

The first story is that of *Phoenix-Europe*, in which the EU is faced with a stark choice in contemplating the brink of chaos: death vs rebirth. Mere survival won't do. Either the EU disintegrates, or it braces itself for a 21st-century renaissance. But are we really faced with so stark a choice other than in rhetorical terms? In truth, the complexity of EU politics makes it unamenable to bold revolutions – all the more given the shared character of EU leadership, which is in my book one of its most commendable traits. There is no one fork in the road, but thousands of micro-decisions and indecisions, constrained by inertia, customs and path-dependency (Pearson, 2004). In contrast to Phoenix-Europe, 'EU 2.0' purports to encapsulate a confluence of trends and serve as a motto for action, a desirable bias in favour of sustainability. Born with the dawn of ecology, sustainability is becoming the name of the game in Europe across realms. No one can be seen to vote against such a state of mind but any policy or corporate action with short-term costs and long-term benefits is bound to elicit a brouhaha.

An EU 2.0 is not, however a simple variant of a second story, that of *Equilibrium-Europe*. It is true that with the Treaty of Lisbon, and arguably before its adoption, the EU had reached a constitutional settlement of sorts, ranging from issues of market liberalization and flanking policies to the balance between small and big states, the division of labour among EU institutions, and between them and the Member States (Moravcsik, 2006; Magnette and Nicolaïdis, 2003; Menon, 2008). The EU has developed a complex mix of forms of governance suited to the various requirements of policy areas (Boerzel, 2010). And its normative sustainability has been fine-tuned through 50 years of mutual accommodation between its legal and political systems (Maduro, 2010). This is why in fact we had little need for our protracted and costly constitutional debates, as demonstrated by the resilience of EU decision-making post-enlargement and pre-Lisbon (Dehousse *et al.*, 2006); and why the EU is all the more unlikely to engage in further treaty reform in the near future – with the significant and contested exception of economic governance.

Nevertheless, it would be misguided to equate such a settlement with a prognosis of equilibrium. What we have today is an unstable equilibrium at best, limited to the constitutional realm. Even if its institutions are not in need of reform, endogenous or exogenous forces may mean that the EU can no longer be sustained only by incorporating new tasks into its mission – albeit necessary ones like an energy Union. Perhaps we have reached the limit of bicycle theory to enter a world of tightrope walking.

As mentioned in the introduction, the EU 2.0 agenda has much to do with flexibility. In a modern federal vision, we do not need to choose between the one and the many, and fix the 'optimal level' for dealing with various issues. Rather, the determination of who does what and how should be flexible enough to allow it to adapt to changing circumstances on the demand or supply side of the governance equation (Nicolaïdis and Howse, 2001; Menon and Schain, 2006). Proportionality should trump subsidiarity. It can be argued that the EU has now entered the cyclical logic of all federal constructs, including by starting to re-nationalize certain policies, for example, competition and agriculture (Donahue and Pollack, 2001). However, it is also an insecure federal contract in which both centralizing or decentralizing moves are not yet seen as normal cycles of federalism, but rather interpreted by opponents and proponents as existential moves. The key to a durable EU system of governance, including its monetary union, will be to hold in check *at the same time* the two main sources of instability usually associated with federal systems, namely state shirking and federal over-reach (Kelemen, 2010).

In such a context, a constitutional settlement today does not make the EU immune to gradual or abrupt decline. Most prominently, it is nothing new to argue that the EU is not underpinned by a stable transnational societal bargain. But the combination of unequal vulnerabilities across Member States to financial crises, the looming demographic trends and radically changing work patterns are making this disequilibrium increasingly unsustainable. The current dilemma can be summed up by the quip that if we are not careful, the fallout from the crisis will be not 'the death of capitalism' but 'the death of social democracy' in Europe. Witness the alienation of the 'no camp' of those feeling left out, including those threatened by the increase in competition brought about by the single market, the opening up of the welfare state to foreign access and the denial of access to public services.

Underlying such a social legitimacy deficit lies the continued fundamental asymmetry of the European socio-economic project between the protective-solidarist functions upheld by the (welfare) state and the competition function upheld by the EU. This unholy division of labour, while it may make sense in many ways, risks being further exacerbated as the EU increasingly takes on the function of a 'budget police' in the euro area. In last year's *JCMS*, Ferrera provided a brilliant analysis of the challenge at hand as one of targeting the optimal balance between two fundamental imperatives: openness to allow for the freedom to move across borders vs closure to create enough sense of *we-ness* among people to sustain feelings of solidarity which underpin redistributive justice at the national level (Ferrera, 2009). In this realm, the EU strategy of accommodation has been to impose minimal duties on access to welfare-state provisions for non-nationals, while limiting transnational redistribution to the realms of agriculture and regions, not individuals (Tsoukalis, 2005). This logic may have become unsustainably lopsided, at least on the continent.

While all our capitalist economies must reverse the deadly combination of privatization of gains and socialization of losses highlighted by the 2008 economic crisis, such an imperative may be more demanding in Europe than anywhere else. This is why the EU must play its part in addressing it. But the management of the post-crisis will be harder than the management of the crisis itself, as we will be lacking the sense of urgency and desperation that can make sacrifices acceptable. Against the rise of nationalism, populism and benign Euroscepticism which characterizes the political atmosphere of a majority of Member States today, the challenge of sustainable integration is daunting.

Sustainable Europe-Sustainable EU: Making Sense of Sustainable Integration

In a 2.0 Europe, I argue, we will need to shift our attention radically from discrete inter-governmental to public inter-societal bargains, and from short-term inter-national bargains to long-term inter-generational bargains. In other words, we will need to move from arguing over more vs less integration, more social vs more market, more regional vs more global, more centralized vs more decentralized, to a prior question: what will it take to make European integration sustainable?

Sustainability is not a sexy, heroic, revolutionary idea – we are not facing dichotomous, make-or-break choices in the EU, but rather choices of degrees and of emphasis. At the same time, it is an all-encompassing concept which we can generalize beyond its original source in the environmental domain (Dresner, 2008). An ethic of sustainability applies to our global but also local ecosystems, biodiversity and our landscapes, to the way economic growth is fostered and measured, to political responsibility and to the societal foundations for the huge transformations ahead in our ways of life. Indeed, we are starting to see many signs of this emergent way of thinking whose threads need to be connected. Most obviously, we can read much of the economic debate in Europe today in terms of sustainable integration (Barroso, 2009). Can *this* crisis management prevent the recurrence of *future* crises? Can we increase European growth and competitiveness in a sustainable way, asks the Commission's Agenda 2020, when forecasters predict that the rest of the world will grow 3 percentage points faster than us? Can we shift our growth paradigm from a competitive race to the bottom to a qualitative prosperity strategy (Friedrich Ebert Stiftung, 2010)? What would a durable stability and growth pact look like? Can sustainability be measured?

We must also connect sustainability to the most important insights of the so-called 2.0 revolution. That is, that survival is about the capacity to reinvent oneself or one's organization: if we are facing a decade of transition in which radical adaptation must happen in any case – in how we work, produce, consume, learn and live – let's at least gain from the pain and reinvent the EU in the process.[2] More specifically: flexibility must apply not only to levels of governance as discussed above but to its content; complex systems are always dynamically evolving and rarely in equilibrium; stability is a derivative concept referring to how such systems allow for entry and exit. Greater connectivity, community collaborative networks are much more efficient than hierarchies at generating value. Resilience and robustness are usually not built in from the start but are a result of adaptive learning on the part of network participants themselves on how to stop the propagation of disruption. Contingency plans and mechanisms are always a good idea. Structures of incentives that fail to internalize externalities (such as unregulated free markets) are bound to be destabilizing. And distributed intelligence trumps central command. James Martin's cathedrals of cyberspace will be cathedrals of the mind, far more intricate than those of stone (Martin, 2006). Likewise, global actors will increasingly be challenged to harness the power of networks (Slaughter, 2004). And in such edifices, the wisdom of the crowds is not the demagogy of a new priesthood but the great lesson of the Internet age. There are caveats as always and the 2.0 world certainly has its dark sides, empowering individuals and groups bent on destroying value created by others.

Fascinatingly, the same kind of lessons emerge from the much longer view. Why do civilizations endure? Those dedicated to understanding why societies decline or collapse, while others are sustainable, assess the amount of adaptative capital they possess and that can be mustered to face endogenous and exogenous shocks (Diamond, 1998; Toynbee, 1948; Burke and Ashton, 2005; Porritt, 2005; Friedman, 2008; Rees, 2002). They observe that successful societies, like successful organisms, are only sustainable when they are in dynamic equilibrium with the larger system in which they are embedded, whether dynamically symbiotic or cautiously parasitic. This equilibrium is possible because they have evolved by developing feedback mechanisms to contend with extreme or cyclical change in their home systems including catastrophic risks. One of the best predictors of breakdown of these virtuous dynamics is the systematic detachment of elites from their host populations and the isolation of communities from their neighbours. As a result, we witness an ever-increasing mismatch of resources and demand, leading to what some have called (in its most extreme variant) the Medea hypothesis: life will kill itself, contrary to the rosy self-sustaining picture of a Gaia-earth.

In social terms then, sustainability is about the embeddedness of freedom of movement within the social contract of different states and communities at the

---

[2] I am grateful to Richard Lambert for this formulation.

regional and global level (Polanyi, 2001 [1957]). Socio-economic resilience rests with the ability of a social and economic system to withstand 'shocks' which can cause propagation of change in highly disruptive ways – coming from rogue bankers, volcanoes or shoe bombers. But there is a silver lining. The massive increase in communications generated by the Internet has allowed unprecedented access to information from experiments being carried out elsewhere in the world today or in other times, from which we have the ability to learn. We are the first to be able to map, measure and manage the impact of various factors on the systems that sustain us. The threat and the promise may be global, but each part of the global must develop its own way to resist political entropy in order to agree eventually on how to endure together. The EU is a resilient enough machine that will not disintegrate overnight. Instead, as we stand between a considerable *acquis* and radically new *realities*, to stagnate carries risks of its own, including that the system may be too vulnerable to unforeseen catastrophic events.

Sustainability calls for identifying difficult trade-offs – if high growth is unsustainable on the ecological front and low growth equally untenable on the social front, true sustainability is about changing those very parameters: there are indeed 'green reasons for growth' and 'social limits to growth'. Strategies and policies should resist aiming for the optimal, but must adjudicate between overshooting and undershooting in either realm. This is what the debate should be about.

To start along this path, we need to develop an early warning system, indicators of long-term unsustainability. This does not require predictive feats – we all know that there is nothing harder to predict than the future! Rather, we need to spell out the concrete implications of long-term trends (NIC, 2008). Foremost among these, for instance, is a well-known predicament: Europe is getting old – in 20 years' time and going on current trends, EU countries will face a gap of 70 million working-age adults.[3] The inverse age pyramid simply makes our welfare and pension systems unsustainable. It is a matter of fact that such prospects call for only three categories of solutions: more babies, more foreigners or longer working lives. All of these require change.

In this perspective, unsustainability can be summarized with a more generalizable ageing metaphor: Europe's progressive loss of its power of attraction. The unsustainability warnings will likely apply increasingly across the board: *vis-à-vis* future migrants who will not materialize by magic the day we need them to plug the demographic hole; *vis-à-vis* investors, who will look for dynamism elsewhere on current growth and productivity projections; *vis-à-vis* candidate countries like Turkey who might one day decide

[3] I am grateful to Rainer Munz for providing the Reflection Group with evidence to support this claim.

that accession is not worth the aggravation; *vis-à-vis* neighbourhood coun-
tries for whom convergence will generate fewer and fewer pay-offs; *vis-à-vis* foreign and European researchers and entrepreneurs who find better conditions in the US today, in the BRICs tomorrow; *vis-à-vis* Muslim migrants, who represent our privileged links with their countries of origin, as Europeans flunk the test of integration; and *vis-à-vis* other regions around the world who want to see the EU as a laboratory for governance and not a patronizing bully.

If sustainable growth is a *sine qua non* of our power of attraction, support for networks of social innovators, research universities and green city plan-ners as well as humane management of illegal migration must surely be on our policy list. Tomorrow's knowledge society will require the constant injection of new talent, much of which may come from people born outside of Europe. Sustainable growth embedded in sustainable communities will also require that we radically change our understanding of the value of older people and their work, so that either staying or leaving work after a given age becomes a choice rather than an obligation.

Can politicians make such 'sustainability decisions' and still win elec-tions? The sustainability agenda is not going to be easy, but Don Fabrizio's complacency will not do.

II. Shadow of our Futures: The Choice for Sustainable Integration

What is to be done? This article does not purport to provide a policy blue-print for a sustainable EU. Rather it presents a set of guidelines for action, a possible typology for the numerous proposals and 'agendas' on the table today emanating from think tanks, academia and EU institutions. These guidelines are focused on what the EU does *as the EU* directly. But they also relate to what Member States do as partners in the EU, or ultimately, to the actions of individuals and groups in European societies. They are mainly common sense, and already inspire a great deal of action. But they also present tensions and trade-offs which I believe must be made more visible in our European politics. And they all relate to what I see as the EU's existing, or at least potential, comparative advantage. I have structured them around three broad 'dramatic' categories: (1) the strategic imperatives which define the play – the treatment of time and space; (2) the plot of the play itself – the internal, regional and global pacts that need to be struck; (3) and the actors – defined through their standards of behaviour or what could be called a political ethics around which Europeans can converge to inspire their action.

Strategic Imperatives (the Action)

To start with, sustainability requires two systemic enablers, two classic dramatic imperatives which relate to the unity of time and space. In EU jargon, these should be 'mainstreamed'.

Time

This must be our starting point: rarely in history have we had such strong inter-generational divides in Europe. We are in the process of bequeathing daunting legacies to Europe's next generation in terms of climate change, debt, welfare, pensions and so on. European countries invest less in research and education than most other developed countries, our universities are losing their ranks under the weight of clientelism and closed-shop practices, risk-taking investors are discouraged. Our societies have for too long indulged in the cult of emergency (Aubert and Roux-Dufort, 2004). We are living on borrowed time and borrowed time: public debt in the euro area is now at 78.7 per cent which means that a 2010 European baby already owes €21,585.[4] And indeed, from every corner of Europe, from activists to industrial barons, from the jobless to the planners, from Copenhagen to Athens, we hear the imperative: *it is urgent to think long-term! We owe it to ourselves not to owe our children.*

Thankfully, the future is the EU's comparative advantage. This is the silver lining of its lack of short-term accountability, indeed of the indirect nature of its democracy. As Tocqueville famously noted, democracy is about the here and now – the past and the future are an elite concern. Since prevention succeeds when nothing happens (hard to sell to an electorate), and since future generations do not vote, a less democratically constrained set of institutions – especially the Commission, whose mission is to uphold the common good – should be expected to be particularly future-friendly. Sustainable integration implies that EU governance be legitimate and effective *over time* rather than as a function of electoral cycles.

Only at the EU level can we truly engage in a patient, systematic and intelligent rebalancing between today's and tomorrow's political imperatives. The task may be never ending, but 'we must conceive of Sisyphus as a lucky man' said Camus.[5] Serious change needs time: the financial crisis and reactions to it have amply shown that governments overestimate what they can change in the short term and underestimate what they can change in the long term. The EU can help lower their discount rate (Trichet, this volume).

---

[4] I thank Jean Dominic Guliani for pointing this figure out and his broader insights.
[5] I am grateful to Mario Telo for his inspired Sisyphus metaphor.

There is no single answer as to when to act for the long term at horizon 2030 – the art of back-casting must become second nature to the EU. In some cases, long-term vision calls for *big bang* action: acting immediately because we are at a tipping point or because every year we wait, divergence from the objective increases. This is obvious in the realm of economic co-ordination for sustainable growth. In other cases, we must prepare the preconditions for *delayed* action further down the road when the technologies or mindset are ripe – as with investment in training for green growth employment. This is also true for enlargement or setting up a sustainable immigration policy in Europe grounded on the idea of citizenship of residence to encourage non-coercive circular migration.[6] But thirdly, in many areas we may be in between and must use the *window of opportunity* open in the next five years to set ourselves on a desirable path, which may otherwise diverge irrevocably. The window may characterize many issue areas, from upholding Europe's lead on green innovation and 'clean nuclear', to building digital Europe, the knowledge economy or a new Energy Community (Delors *et al.*, 2010; Sapir, 2009).

Generally, long-term structural policies must more systematically include in-built flexibility, on the assumption that they will need to change; immigration policies are a case in point. Short of radical moves like giving children the right to vote, we can take steps to increase the EU's future-friendliness.[7] For every action the EU takes, I suggest making an impact assessment of 'non-Europe 2030'. And in order to be better equipped to think about long-term strategy, we also need to create an effective network between national forecasting units in our Member States – a European forecasting network capable of connecting with its sister institutions, like the NIC, around the world.

Space

Our changing strategic equation concerns space as well as time. Sustainability requires fluid boundaries between policies within and policies without. Europeans were the first to invent the very idea of *globality* 200 years ago, thereby extending their reach around the globe, for better or for worse (Postel Vinay, 2005). Since the beginnings of the EU, born of the ashes of global war and global colonialism, we have been cautious, acting externally in a reactive manner for the most part. Europe's virgin birth in the wake of decolonization implied an enforced introversion. And indeed, EU foreign policy tends to this day to be conducted as a domestic affair itself, condemned to

---

[6] I am grateful to Brad Blitz, Alex Betts and Rainer Muenz for enlightening discussions on this topic.
[7] I am grateful to Philippe Van Parisj for persuading me that the child vote is not a crazy idea.

fulfilling the rival internal goals of the various parties engaged in turf wars and institutional point scoring – a logic referred to as 'internal functionality' (Bickerton, 2009). But with EU 2.0, acting globally can no longer be a residual concern, an external outlet for our internal rivalries. Instead, the global picture must inform all our actions.

This does not mean lowering our domestic ambitions: on the contrary. In fact, acting global starts at home. Most obviously, our global ambitions cannot be served without sustainable growth throughout the EU. In general, EU institutions and European leadership must systematically consider each internal policy implication of our external objectives, and each global dimension of our domestic action – starting with energy, security and migration policies. We will fail in tomorrow's Copenhagens if we do not put our house in order. Indeed, a lot can be done on global environmental governance through the incremental externalization of our own practices, starting with the emission trading system (King and Walker, 2008). Is there any doubt that the EU's long-term asymmetric dependency on Russia is a direct function of our domestic energy policies and our failure to systematically apply competition rules in this field? Should the tools and competences for tackling internal and external threats be so distinct from each other? Does it make sense to deal with Europe's Muslim neighbourhoods *within* and *without* as different universes? Acting by example outside our borders rather than preaching to others requires [8]exacting standards for our domestic enforcement of the rule of law, labour and minority rights, or effective regulations. Such consistency between the internal and the external requires ongoing vigilance – it is, in fact, an old and exacting theme going back to the days when Duchêne pointed to the imperative of domesticating foreign policy as Europe's new contribution to the world (Duchêne, 1972). Each decision taken at the EU level should contain such a 'synergy rationale', and the new external action service must dedicate a special unit to enforcing it.

Three Interlocking Bargains (the Plot)

We now turn to the plot itself. What kind of action needs to take place in order to sustain integration under the above-mentioned imperatives related to time and space? The idea that long-term political coexistence is based on bargains between different groups of actors, and that these bargains need to be renewed periodically in order to sustain the social compact, is pervasive. Indeed, the notion of bargain covers different realities. There are iterated small sectoral bargains, the stuff of daily politics, political compromises and horse-trading. Then there are foundational or constitutional 'grand bargains', which usually contain packages of issues that benefit or cost different parties differently

(Moravcsik, 1998). The form that they take (treaty reform; new sets of laws; general frameworks) matters less than the extent to which they reflect a value-creating trade among parties. Because the EU is founded on consensus rather than majoritarian politics, its Member States either forge compromise deals or agree to disagree. More often then not, compromise between actors mirrors compromises between ideological stances (social vs Christian democrats), or between competing principles (say, multilateralism vs regionalism, conditionality vs partnership). As a result, our long-term plot for sustainable integration calls for devising subtle strategies of accommodation between equally compelling principles (see Meunier and Nicolaïdis, 2006). In short, I advocate thinking in terms of new bargains or pacts at three levels, namely internal, regional and global. These do not need to be struck in a big bang at one moment in time, but European decision-makers must ask whether the policies they now choose will have entrenched these bargains 20 years from now. And while a lot is up to Member States themselves, the EU can nudge in multiple ways.

Internal

For prosperity to be the well of sustainability that it should be, we need fundamentally to rethink how to measure and generate it (Stiglitz *et al.*, 2009). Can the EU become the engine of a sustainable social green-growth economy? As discussed earlier, the current economic and financial crisis may well have tipped the lopsided socio-economic contract in the EU beyond the sustainability threshold. If so, a renewed bargain should progressively be struck at the Union level between the economic, social and ecological dimensions of our development, if our leaders are ready to accept the electoral sacrifice they imply (Barroso, 2009; Commission, 2010). Give and take must take *inter alia* three forms:, (1) between social-market economies and Anglo-Saxon economies, the former committing to refrain from economic nationalism, the latter accepting more intervention to deal with the negative social side-effects of market integration (including through more EU-level redistribution or most likely through core minimal standards, greater tax co-ordination and enhanced corporate responsibility) (Monti, 2010; Herzog and Nicolaïdis, 2007); (2) between surplus and deficit countries (fiscal and trade), the former consuming more and accepting a more viable exchange rate for the euro; the latter committing to shed state capture by particularistic interest; (3) between those committed to *green* growth, through sustaining Europe's precarious global lead in green technological innovation and the proponents of nuclear power (Barroso, 2009; Climate Change Foundation, 2010).

More radically, some would argue that socio-economic sustainability requires nothing less than a complete transformation of capitalism (Joerges, 2006). In part, sustainable capitalism is about change in corporate governance structures as shareholder control no longer exists, and change in regulatory cultures to stem regulatory capture and incompetence. It is also about a better distribution of risk between socio-economic groups, regions and countries. Europe is home to the most risk-averse societies on earth (Laidi, 2010). Communism called for redistributing modes of production, social democracy for redistributing revenue, liberalism for redistributing power. Sustainable systems call for redistributing risk. Under such conditions, simple changes, for instance to the length of a working life, will not only benefit European society as a whole at some indefinite stage in the future but also individuals right now who will be cared for while taking care themselves.

Regional

Sustainability also rests on security, broadly defined – the freedom from fear dear to Judith Shklar. Can the greater Eurospheres which include and transcend the EU to its south and east generate sustainable security rather than insecurity in a 20-year horizon (Oxford Research Group, 2006)? Such a goal arguably calls for a second pact beyond the borders of the EU, between greater inclusiveness through mobility and less EU-centric polity-building in the Eurasia – Euromed regions. On the first count, the EU will need in particular to rethink radically its approach to free movement of people origi-nating from neighbourhood countries, and devise ways of encouraging cir-cular movement for the benefit of all sides – including through a European blue card and the portability of rights, for example, mobility packs which can encourage the return of people acting as bridge builders across the region (Wilson and Popescu, 2009). On the second count, the regions in question could progressively break with the association between more EU convergence and more EU access – simply engineering unreflexive EU policy export (Bechev and Nicolaïdis, 2010; Korosteleva, forthcoming; Whitman and Wolff, 2010). This would mean following a decentred path – sensitive to local priorities, empowering local actors and building a polity together with the countries willing to enter a true spirit of partnership. As the EU becomes increasingly provincialized in an emerging world order of rising powers, its geostrategic interest may very well be to be a part, indeed a driver of a wider strategic community, stretching from 'Gibraltar to Kars'. A regional geopo-litical vision is crucial for the EU's future, including in its relations with Turkey, and cannot remain hostage to the hard constraints of regulatory and technical convergence.

Global

Finally, the plot will continue to unfold at the global systemic level, where sustainability must rest on redefining the complex links between global order and global justice (Foot *et al.*, 2004). We can be quite sure that in 20 years, the world will not only have several centres but also that its centre of gravity will have shifted – to Asia and the global south, to new public and private actors, to transnational institutions (Gnesotto and Grevi, 2006). But we cannot tell how this 2030 multipolar world will accommodate new patterns of globalization, residual US military unipolarity, traditional balance of power dynamics, a range of ad hoc bilateral alliances, regional groupings, power fragmentation, and competition over scarce resources, as well as probably broad areas of chaos. Sustainable integration is thus about global resilience: given these massive uncertainties, what will it take for Europe to remain a relevant pole and help accommodate the revisionist urge of rising states to change the rules of the game devised under the previous balance of power? What will it take to define and negotiate the terms of a truly sustainable global governance pact for the more crowded world of the future?

Such a pact, I would argue, will need to reflect better at the global level the need to balance the logics of openness and closure which we find within the EU itself or in the Eurosphere. Ultimately, this line is about who is responsible for providing 'human security' within the circumscribed boundaries of our communities (Kaldor, 2007). Clearly, Europeans should strive for a world in which interdependence is nurtured rather than a world of chaos or new hierarchies, isolated poles and rival states or regions – in short, an interpolar world (Grevi, 2009; Telò, 2009). A new 'global grand bargain' involving the engineering of 'nothing less than a new international system' (Hutchings and Kempe, 2008; Howorth, 2010) is only likely to emerge piecemeal and contested, but if it does, it must rest on renegotiating what we mean by global justice, in particular in determining 'who adjusts' to shocks in our system (surplus or deficit countries; carbon producers or consumers; nuclear or non-nuclear states; ultimately the poor or the rich . . .). The EU should not only strive to be a responsible power itself (Mayer and Vogt, 2006), but also to help make the idea of *responsible interdependence* as widely shared as possible among nations. Let us not shy away from the difficult questions which will underpin a sustainable global order: should we not be responsible stakeholders in the global climate as consumers, not only producers (Helm and Hepburn, 2009)? When does responsibility give us a licence to act without the consent of all? If enabling local actors is a pre-condition, who decides how and when? Can different degrees of responsibility justify new patterns of hegemony? And who defines what 'fairness' means and the mechanisms by which the protection of some does not end up hurting others more?

A Political Ethics (The Actors)

The final branch of our dramatic tryptic brings us to the actors themselves. Ultimately, sustainable integration will rest on its legitimacy, its capacity to generate ongoing passive support and sporadic mobilization among the greater public. Others have demonstrated how democracy and efficiency, input and output legitimacy, a Europe of participation and a Europe of results are intrinsically linked (for an overview, see Schmidt, 2009). In the same spirit, I have argued with Robert Howse that democratic legitimacy is likely to come as much from patterns of behaviour as from formal structures of representation (Howse and Nicolaïdis, 2009). To paraphrase Dahrendorf, we can live with flaws in European democracy as long as we have European democrats. In this spirit, the sustained legitimacy of governance arrangements beyond the state will depend on the prevailing political ethics, to the extent that such an ethics reflects and shapes widely shared social norms. There is no one 'right' blueprint here, nor is there any reason why the conversation over the principles that should underpin such a political ethics should be restricted to Europe. I would highlight five: recognition, solidarity, empowerment, decentring and ownership.

Recognition

Surprisingly, Europe, home to the highest density of nation-states on earth, continues to resist a philosophy of difference. After 50 years of 'ever closer Union', European officialdom needs to change the story from engineering convergence to recognizing and exploiting complementarities through integration. And European citizens need to grapple with the fact that managed mutual recognition is the key to a sustainable single market, founded on the tolerance for 'foreign' workers, the exploitation of complementarities, the enforcement of fair competition and the adoption of common minimal standards. But recognition is a broader ethos of integration underpinned by trust and tolerance, the ethical frontier of sustainability (Nicolaïdis, 2007a, 2010a). Similarly, multilingualism must be lovingly nurtured, provided we adopt English as a European lingua franca as advocated by Philippe Van Parisj. The same basic concepts underpin plans for a Europe-wide renewable energy grid that could exploit the complementarities between windy northern Europe and sunny southern Europe, all-nighters in the south and early birds in the north (Climate Change Foundation, 2010). And in discussing the economic governance of the euro area, sustainability implies that states must decide more clearly where they need to converge, and where freedom to act is necessary for diversifying risk and enabling trial and error innovation.

Solidarity

Ultimately, recognition must apply to the social struggles and sacrifices by those at the periphery of our societies and our Union to be part of the whole. In this post-crisis era, we need to ask anew what is the glue that holds us together, as ethics and pragmatism meet in Europe's rekindled debate over solidarity under conditions of extreme diversity (Van Parijs, 2004). Surely the vast differences in socio-economic status between different Member States of the EU, as well as between individuals across Europe, deeply undermine the call for otherwise exploiting our differences. But incantations that solidarity must inform all relations between individuals, regions, generations and states will remain wishful thinking unless we focus on sustaining the virtuous circle linking solidarity, responsibility and competitiveness. As the crisis of the euro demonstrates once again, solidarity will not be sustained or indeed have much impact if not conditioned on a deep sense of collective and individual responsibility on all sides and on a concern for sustaining growth. EU policies must be assessed on their contribution to this core virtuous circle. The underlying ethos is that simple, and as old as humanity: rational solidarity is not a zero-sum game but also benefits those who practise it; diffuse reciprocity over the benefits of solidarity enhances economic stability over time; it also operates as a signalling device to generate outside trust in the system as a whole; and it functions as a trigger for increased responsible behaviour on the part of its beneficiaries. In sum, a sustainable union must practice what Lampedusa's Prince called 'profitable altruism'.

Empowerment

Our Union has suffered from the widespread perception that it was only about 'markets not individuals'. Redressing this distorted perception is not just a matter of shifting paradigms: markets serve people if managed properly. It is also about recentring the European project around citizens, workers, consumers, entrepreneurs, researchers, innovators, right holders, border crossers, volunteers and members of communities. Politically, empowerment is about fostering a new and active European citizenship for the 21st century. On the socio-economic front, individual talent must be nurtured through everything the EU does: more and smarter investment in education, culture, research, creativity and innovation, lifelong learning and training at work; resolute action against entrenched corporatism and the vested interests which often stand in the way of new ideas and practices, including in many European universities (Commission, 2009; Lambert and Butler, 2006).

More generally, empowerment is a philosophy of governance which sees the EU as a shared infrastructure, an enabler of activity for its citizens, firms and governments.[8] In such a world, power, authority and competence (and concomitantly the subsidiarity guidelines) should not be understood as a zero-sum game: the Union takes it, others lose it; or local governments keep it against EU encroachment. On the contrary, the Union acts as a 'power multiplier' at all levels: to empower individuals against states with directly enforceable rights, consumers against firms who abuse their dominant power, firms against protectionist states, and its Member States on the global scene.[9] In our networld, the EU can only be a global enabler if it ensures that those who are in charge in cities, districts, regions, countries and transborder areas are enabled by the collective to act effectively by governing in partnership while still taking responsibility (Committee of the Regions, 2009). The EU Commission in particular needs to make empowerment its foremost imperative, moving from a culture of control to one of trust for instance when funding universities, research or industrial innovation. EU institutions can help strengthen citizens' involvement in calling public authorities to account on their true commitment to the rule of law.[10] And the same philosophy can apply when acting outside our borders. There is little doubt that both internally and externally, transparency is key to empowerment and that the Internet can serve as a powerful tool in this regard (Ghani and Lockhart, 2008). Leaders not only need to *convey* that this is the logic driving the EU, but must also *act* in accordance with such a principle: no action without empowerment!

Decentring

Decentring follows from empowerment but takes this logic one step further. It is about acknowledging that the Union is a sophisticated, complex and messy system of shared governance requiring several hubs and not one, from national capitals hosting summits, as opposed to Brussels, to networks of local representatives shaping EU governance. But of course, decentring is not

---

[8] I am grateful to Rem Koolhaas for substantiating this metaphor.

[9] I am grateful to Lykke Friis for this expression.

[10] In this spirit, concrete steps could be taken. The office of the Ombudsman is spearheading a campaign to encourage the European and national parliaments to organize annual hearings of citizens on the application of EU law – say on free movement of people. The same logic can be taken one step down to support direct citizen-led enforcement by watchdog voluntary groups targeting corruption, clientelism and bad governance in old and new Member States especially with regards to the distribution of EU funds. I am grateful to Nikiforos Diamandouros and Alina Pippidi for our discussions on this topic.

only a strategy for governance within. As mentioned above, it needs to apply to the EU's external relations including through co-development and fluid movement of people; conditionality over processes that empower local actors rather than standards designed in Brussels; decentralizing decisions to EU country delegations; locating management away from Brussels; and new kinds of status for partner countries linked to shared polity building rather than simple convergence (Bechev and Nicolaïdis, 2010).

Ownership

Finally, a political ethics is about collective ownership of the Union. Sustainability cannot be accomplished without changing the tone of our political game. If governments continue to treat the EU and its institutions as alien or hostile when it suits them, they should not be surprised to see them rejected. If they continue to treat their peoples as needing to be re-elected *à la Brecht*, they should not be surprised at their sense of alienation. The Union deserves better than to be treated as a convenient scapegoat for unpopular or difficult decisions – scapegoats can play useful roles, but not when at the same time people are expected to identify with them (the IMF is not a union of peoples). Member States, regional and local authorities have to accept once and for all that they *are* Europe and say it. For its part, the Commission has to play the role entrusted to it – it should not set itself out as the European government nor should it shy away from its responsibilities, even when this involves confrontation with the Member States. Politicians and citizens alike must take ownership of this Union of ours and accept that it is an imperfect and fragile exercise in shared leadership and that blaming the EU for the pains of adaptation, or its citizens for blaming the EU, is a dangerous game. The EU does not need to be loved but *sustained* by more diverse forms of participation connecting e-democracy, culture, festivals, referendums and transborder exchanges. Let us start with the annual holding of a mega-Agora Europe, the Woodstock of European politics.

III. History of our Presents: Europe's Demons and Sacred Cows

If the EU possesses the kind of comparative advantage which lends itself to the prescriptive ambition exhibited above, why is there a sense that we may not be on the right track? What are the obstacles to attaining the mundane but nevertheless highly desirable steady state of sustainable integration? The path to sustainable integration is bumpy indeed, paved as it is with misguided realist temptations and useless utopias. Many have dissected and attempted to explain EU failings in the pages of *JCMS* in the last few years. The EU will not instantaneously get rid of its pathologies: grandstanding at the very top unduly inflating citizens' expectations, apathy at the bottom, the pervasiveness of double standards and hypocrisy, the popularity of blame-thy-neighbour rhetoric, the rigidity of its bureaucracy, the pervasiveness of self-destructive turf battles, the old habits of bullying on the part of big states, socio-economic rigidities, generalized risk aversion, normative dissonance and of course the infamous lack of political will. All this capped by the lure of transcendentalism – when heads of state make overly ambitious common declarations and then blame Brussels for failing to deliver on them.[11] And because the EU machinery tends to focus on process rather than substance, its decision-makers can continue to feel that progress is being made when nothing is actually happening.

I will not assess all these pathologies here. Instead, I will focus on what I see as crucial cognitive and political barriers to progress on the road to sustainable integration, which can be captured in the mytho-zoological pantheon of old demons and sacred cows. Perhaps more than others, the world of politics is prone to the fear of cognitive dissonance, prone to use the cognitive material with which it is familiar. Hence the obsession with oneness in much of the EU instead of that of plurality, complexity, polycentricity and complementarity, which ought to characterize our world of networks and managed conflict.

This diagnosis brings us back to the fundamental ethos of a 2.0 world, that is a world not defined by top-down management and self-contained organizing units of groups or individuals, but rather a world in which value emanates from distributed intelligence. In Euro-parlance, unless and until the EU turns unity in diversity into more than a pretty motto, sustainable integration will remain a mirage.

What is the EU? A People, State, Power, Territory and the Cult of Onenesss

Statism is certainly the EU's mother of all demons. The state-centric paradigm still pervades the thinking on governance among its elites. To be clear, most of contemporary European history has been about state building: sovereign-state building, then nation-state building in the 17th–19th century, democratic-state building in the 19th century, welfare-state building in the 20th century and now 'Member State building'. Indeed, the construct of the nation-state with its defined territory, people and government has been Europe's greatest export to the world – for better or worse. And while

---

[11] For a brilliant, yet sober analysis see Menon (2008). See also the proceedings of the conference, 'Why the EU Fails', SIIA, Helsinki, December 2009, «http://www.upi-fiia.fi/en/event/241».

globalization is testing its resilience, churning out failed states and propping up globalized states, we can be sure that the nature of the state is undergoing major transformation (Clark, 1999; Obinger *et al.*, 2010). So EU Member States *qua states* and their attachment to what remains of their sovereignty are not the problem – states are generally a good thing. The problem instead is the propensity to wish for the EU itself the attributes of statism – one people, one territory, hierarchical governance, single leadership, majoritarian voting, one voice – when it is not, and should not be, a state.

So the EU is a schizophrenic power, proud to be a 'different kind of actor' in world politics yet yearning to look like other states on the block adorned with the traditional paraphernalia of statehood. Vivien Schmidt conveys this duality in her expression of 'regional state'. To be sure, many nationals in Europe can only countenance one European polity if it looks just like them: a Republican France, a regionalized Spain, a federal Germany writ large. Euro-Rhineland is alive and well in the 2009 EU pronouncement of the German Supreme Court. In short, one way or another an ever closer union has long been akin to an ever 'cloner' Union, cloning the state at a higher level of aggregation. This pathology, understandable as it may be, is the ultimate obstacle to sustainable European integration.

In fact, we do have a counter-narrative to inspire a non-state-centric understanding and management of the EU, which can be found under many different labels, from constitutional pluralism to post-national, cosmopolitan or transnational variants (Menon, 2008; Habermas, 1998; Ferry, 2005; Eleftheriadis, 2009) – although even the guardians of the post-national temple have been found to lapse into the temptation of 'othering' (in this case the US) in order to foster a 'European identity' (Habermas and Derrida, 2003). I have argued that the EU must be understood as a demoi-cracy in the making, that is as a community of others engaged in a highly demanding exercise of mutual recognition not only of their cultural idiosyncrasies but also of their various political systems and societal bargains (Weiler, 1999; Nicolaïdis, 2004). While the extent to which the bigger Member States uphold the anti-hegemonic spirit which presided over the creation of the EU will be key, there are reasons to be pessimistic on this front (Bunse *et al.*, 2006).

On the external front, the obsession with oneness inspires talk of the EU as a superpower encapsulated by the aspiration for a single European army. But if the EU is not a state in the making, it should not strive to become a classic 'superpower' or claim to redefine the nature of diplomacy in the 21st century while practising 19th-century diplomacy. This means to aim to affect the regional and global rules of the game rather than expand its sphere of influence, including through using the leverage of the (still) biggest market in the world (Leonard, 2005; Nye, 2004; Moravcsik, 2010).

Who Speaks for the EU? The Mantra of a Single Voice

There is no more powerful mantra in the EU lexicon than the call for 'one voice'. If we could find a way to have only one of us pick up the infamous Kissinger call, we would achieve international greatness and easily shape those regional and global pacts. Instead, the story goes, we might provide a single phone number, but the voice at the other end will redirect the caller, 'press 1', 'press 2'. . . In truth, why should this not be the case? How can we profess a belief in 'strength and diversity' and yet not accept that the failed pursuit of 'one voice' is more often than not counterproductive?[12]

The most intuitive set of arguments here are arguments *from necessity*. In other words, since the EU is not a state but an aggregation of states, let us orchestrate its polyphony as best we can. EU institutional actors who represent it in the outside world – such as the Trade Commissioner, the High Representative or the President of the EU Council – do not have the 'arbitrary power' of national heads of state but reflect different ways of aggregating interests across Member States. And while one could argue that any large heterogeneous democratic polity (like, say, the US) will be prone to divisions plainly visible to the outside, the EU stands in a class of its own. The actors that compose it are all free to act as individual external actors on the international scene – this is a not a prerogative attributed to the same extent to the US Congress, or individual US states. Each EU Member State in turn has its own national geostrategic interests, historical traditions and political sensitivities – *vis-à-vis* ex-colonies or the ex-Soviet Union; *vis-à-vis* the US or Muslim states; in terms of trade interests or resource dependencies. These differences need to be exploited, not denied.

Which brings us to another set of arguments, those arising *from desirability*. In short, the European ship can be seaworthy no matter how mismatched its parts (Leibfried *et al.*, 2009). Sometimes, of course, it is useful simply to be able to rely on plain old division of labour, to have different European leaders speak for Europe with different accents and sensitivities – with so many arenas, comparative advantage should be exploited in diplomacy as well as in trade. Indeed, it could be argued that Europe's internal diversity makes it more attuned to the needs of a 'new peoples' diplomacy'.[13] Moreover, it may be plainly counterproductive for the EU to speak with 'one voice'. UN corridors are full of stories of how once EU Member States have reached a common position they are no longer capable of give-and-take with others with dire consequences for its justice and human rights agenda (Gowan and Brantner, 2008). Not only are they collectively rigid

[12] I am grateful to Anand Menon for our discussions on this issue.
[13] I am grateful to Richard Whitman for sharing his thoughts on this issue.

and therefore unfriendly to the UN system, but their joint position may be much more polarizing than if they were defending a range of compatible options. The most radical version of this argument is that differences in positions among Europeans can sometimes be positively empowering for the EU as a whole. One example could be the Janus-faced diplomacy pursued around Kosovo, and the utility of having held different national positions when Russia sought to use Kosovo as a precedent in the Georgian context. In the end, a sustainable EU foreign policy will have to become smarter at combining one voice, orchestrated polyphony and even, when need be, constructive cacophony.

What Sells the EU? The Delusion of the European Model

Oneness, however, is also about the message itself, not only the messenger. Europe-as-a-model is an old and familiar trope even while reincarnated as EU-as-a-model for regional and global governance. Are those who see parallels between the old *mission civilisatrice* and EUniversalism suffering from post-colonial stress disorder? Can we not argue that today's idea and practice of the EU as a model, with its hands-off and non-coercive character and the involvement of Member States that historically have been at the receiving end of the 'Soviet model', has precious little to do with the *mission* of yesteryear?

Admittedly, the rest of the world seems to see the EU in contradictory terms: as a highly attractive example of regional integration, which too often squanders its soft power potential through lapses into patronizing.[14] The EU's great comparative advantage is its predilection and capacity for negotiation among a plethora of actors. Others see this; but they also see this advantage being used unwisely. As a result, the message of the EU as a normative leader is contested everywhere even while Europe's 'check appeal' continues to bolster it. So the hope here is that its leaders learn to project a more self-reflective stance, an understanding of the EU as a *laboratory* – a place where experiments can lead to failures as well as successes – and as a *tool box* – providing a range of 'governance tools' from which others can pick and choose – whether spanning varieties of capitalisms, or different rule of law traditions or alternative governance mechanisms. Only by acknowledging its experimental and multifaceted nature can the EU be a credible inspiration for regional and global governance, and provide a non-colonial vocation for Europe in its engagement with new regional and rising powers.

[14] I am grateful to Tobias Lenz and Juri Viehoff for our discussions on this issue.

Why the EU? The Obsession with a European Narrative

These dilemmas with regards to our attitude to the outside world bring us back full circle to the inside story. If only, we hear in many European corners, we could come up with a single European story, a narrative about why we must stick together across the continent. To be sure, Europeans do seem to share a certain inclination for reiterating their commitment to universal political principles and purposes, such as freedom, peace, the rule of law, prosperity, solidarity, fundamental rights and social justice (Garton Ash, 2007). These common principles are arguably the object of a 'soft consensus' on the EU 'namely, as a market founded on democratic values' (Medrano, 2010).

But beyond these vague principles, solace cannot be found in the sacred cow of narrative hegemony. In reality, if there are many equally acceptable ways of belonging and feeling allegiance to any political community, this is all the more the case when the political entity at issue is the EU. Indeed, the EU rests on practices of interpretation and negotiation reflecting strong – yet reasonable – disagreements between its many component parts on the norms and goals that underpin the process of integration (Nicolaïdis and Pélabay, 2009). We need to embrace the prevailing narrative diversity about the EU both within and across European countries. Vivien Schmidt has identified four broad EU narratives, namely 'pragmatic', 'normative', 'principled' and 'strategic' (Schmidt, 2009). Actually, the EU gives rise to many more variants as an object of scorn or desire – attracting labels from an artificial construct, or even an identity threat, ethical hazard, a giant supermarket to a community of values, a humanist polity, a cosmopolitan order, a legal community or a democratic anchor (Lacroix and Nicolaïdis, 2010). Taken together, all these stories are part of a bigger multifaceted whole, part of a logic we can only wish for, a logic of reflexive appropriation, decentring and mutual learning. If we can amplify the echoes between them and hear them together in a new kind of political polyphony intended to take the competing visions of Europe seriously, we may start to turn 'unity in diversity' into the core normative basis for sustainable integration.

Conclusions

This article is part manifesto, part research agenda – although I readily grant that it is too long for the former and too short for the latter. Thankfully, European studies have become firmly embedded in global and comparative *problematiques* while being increasingly characterised by exuberant methodological and theoretical pluralism (Egan *et al.*, 2010; Jørgensen *et al.*, 2006; Warleigh-Lack and Phinnemore, 2009). The sustainable integration frame opens up many questions which can be explored through a range of conceptual lenses. How do we know it when we see it? What are the actors and factors which impede or support it? How are they likely to evolve in the next decades? What is the relationship between legitimacy, democracy and sustainability? How does a sustainable EU affect sustainable European states and vice versa? How are the various pieces of the sustainability agenda related across issue areas? Who are the winners and losers of sustainable policies? What kinds of institutional features best serve sustainability?

We can venture a few broad hypotheses. First, that sustainable integration is a tall but not impossible order. With our European weather and wealth some of us have it too easy, so like Don Fabrizio, we do not try hard enough. For others, tomorrow is simply an unaffordable luxury. But we can. Crisis, as we all know, has the power to bring out the best in all of us. As this momentous year reminds us once again, the EU continues to accumulate a wealth of experience, from its mistakes at least as much as its success. While it would be a tremendous hubris to believe that today's EU has all or even most of the answers, when it comes to problems that transcend our individual national capacities to act, it is the best we have! While it is urgent to think long-term, we must act now, while the window of opportunity is still open. And future-friendliness is the EU's comparative advantage.

Second, the time may be ripe to call for EU 2.0. The ideal underpinning the EU does not need to be grand in order to be great. A sustainable EU 2.0 should be our collective ambition for horizon 2030. We need to translate the new 'web philosophy' on the power of networks and distributed intelligence to the governance and policies of the EU itself. Only if we embrace this new modernity can we aspire to help shape a world of responsible interdependence in the 21st century reflecting the aspiration – within and outside Europe – for greater fairness, solidarity and justice. Europe can still embody the power of a simple idea – that the ties that bind sustain peace – but that this must be a *global* ideal for Europe requiring *new* modes of co-operation.

Third, this is also why the story we tell must reflect perceptions and priorities from outside. Outside Brussels an EU 2.0 would be an EU that relies much more radically on decentred action, decision-making and power throughout Europe. And outside Europe: after 200 years of western dominance, we are now but a province of a non-European world where we must strive to make a difference as a post-colonial power and a global mediator. Perhaps, then, we can once again aspire to be the inspiring project we once were in a language that speaks to new generations.

Ultimately, if we seriously aspire to change the world, we Europeans must first change ourselves. The Lisbon Treaty is but a beginning, necessary but insufficient. We will not instantaneously get rid of our European patholo-gies, nor slay our sacred cows. And because it *is* remote and complex, the EU will likely remain remote and complex in the eyes of its citizens. But these facts of life should not stifle its ambitions. Obscure EU, complicated EU, infuriating EU, quiet EU can be a power multiplier making its *raison d'être* the empowerment of others, individuals and nations, insiders and outsiders, born and not yet born. In short, if the rising powers in this world want to brush us aside prematurely, as they seemed to in Copenhagen 2009, let us not get mad, let us get even! We must put our common house in order if we are to keep it in orbit. Only on solid foundations will the European Union be able to move down the road of sustainable integration. The journey requires political courage and collective ambition, solid pragmatism and a clear sense of the ideals worth fighting for. Let us, once again, echo Beethoven's call to seize fate by the throat. Together. Now.

References

Allen, D. (2009) 'The Speech Obama Needs to Give (. . . in which he Renounces Industrial Civilization)'. Energy Bulletin, 12 October.

Aubert, N. and Roux-Dufort, C. (2004) *Le culte de l'urgence: la société malade du temps* (Paris: Flammarion).

Barroso, J.M. (2009) 'State of the Union: Delivering a Europe of Results in a Harsh Economic Climate'. *JCMS AR*, Vol. 47, No. s1, pp. 7–16.

Bechev, D. and Nicolaïdis, K. (2010) *Mediterranean Frontiers: Borders, Conflict and Memory in a Transnational World* (London: I. B. Tauris).

Bickerton, C. (2009) 'Legitimacy through Norms: The Political Limits to the Euro-pean Union's Normative Power'. In Whitman, R. (Ed.) *Normative Power Europe: Empirical and Theoretical Perspectives* (Basingstoke: Palgrave).

Boerzel, T. (2010) 'European Governance: Negotiation and Competition in the Shadow of Hierarchy'. *JCMS*, Vol. 48, No. 2, pp. 191–219.

Bunse, S., Magnette, P. and Nicolaïdis, K. (2006) 'Big versus Small: Shared Leadership and Power Politics in the Convention'. In Mazzucelli, C. and Beach, D. (eds) *Leadership in the Big Bangs of European Integration* (Basingstoke: Palgrave Macmillan).

Burke, T. and Ashton, J. (2005) 'Climate Change and Global Security'. *Open-Democracy*, 16 May.

Clark, I. (1999) *Globalization and International Relations Theory* (Oxford: Oxford University Press).

Climate Change Foundation (2010) *Roadmap 2050: Practical Guide to a Pro-sperous, Low Carbon Europe* (Brussels: CCF/Rotterdam: OMA).

Commission of the European Communities (2009) 'Preparing Europe for a new renaissance: a strategic view of the European Research Area'. First Report of the

European Research Area Board – 2009. Available at «http://ec.europa.eu/research/erab/pdf/erab-first-annual-report-06102009_en.pdf».

Commission of the European Communities (2010) 'Europe 2020: a strategy for smart, sustainable and inclusive growth'. *COM*(2010) 2020.

Committee of the Regions (2009) *Supporting Sustainable Cities and Regions* (Brussels: CoR Publications).

Dehousse, R., Deloche-Gaudez, F. and Duhamel, O. (2006) *Elargissement: comment l'Europe s'adapte* (Paris: Presses de Sciences-Po).

Delors, J. *et al.* (2010) *Towards a New European Energy Community* (Paris: Notre Europe).

Diamond, J. (1998) *Guns, Germ and Steel: A Short History of Everybody or the Last 13,000 Years* (London: Vintage).

Donahue, J.D. and Pollack, M.A. (2001) 'Centralization and its Discontents: The Rhythms of Federalism in the United States and the European Union'. In Nicolaïdis, K. and Howse, R. (eds) *The Federal Vision* (Oxford: Oxford University Press).

Dresner, S. (2008) *The Principles of Sustainability* (London: Earthscan).

Duchêne, F. (1972) 'Europe in World Peace'. In Mayne, R. (ed.) *Europe Tomorrow* (London: Fontana/Collins), pp. 32–49.

Egan, M., Nugent, N. and Paterson, W. (2010) *Research Agendas in the EU Studies: Stalking the Elephant* (Basingstoke: Palgrave).

Eleftheriadis, P. (2009) 'Pluralism and Integrity'. Oxford Legal Studies Research Paper No. 43/2009, 9 October.

Fabry, E. and Ricard-Nihoul, G. (eds) (2010) *Think Global – Act European* (Paris: Notre Europe).

Ferrera, M. (2009) 'The JCMS Annual Lecture: National Welfare States and European Integration: In Search of a "Virtuous Nesting" '. *JCMS*, Vol. 47, No. 2, pp. 219–33.

Ferry, J.M. (2005) 'Europe, la voie Kantienne: essai sur l'identité postnationale'. *Éditions du Cerf, Collection 'Humanités'*.

Fondation Robert Schuman (2010) 'L'etat de l'Union 2010'. Rapport Schuman sur l'Europe.

Foot, R., Gaddis, J.L. and Hurrell, A. (eds) (2004) *Order and Justice in International Relations* (Oxford: Oxford University Press).

Friedman, T. (2008) *Hot, Flat, and Crowded: Why We Need a Green Revolution – and How it can Renew America* (New York: Farrar, Straus and Giroux).

Friedrich Ebert Stiftung Foundation (2010) 'Paving the Way for a Sustainable Prosperity Strategy'. Friedrich Ebert Stiftung Foundation, Division for International Dialogue.

Garton Ash, T. (2007) 'Europe's True Stories'. *Prospect*, No. 131, pp. 36–9.

Ghani, A. and Lockhart, C. (2008) *Fixing Failed States: A Framework for Rebuilding a Fractured World* (Oxford: Oxford University Press).

Glencross, A. (2009) *What Makes the EU Viable? European Integration in the Light of the Antebellum US Experience* (Basingstoke: Palgrave Macmillan).

González Márquez, F. *et al.* (2010) 'Project Europe 2030'. A Report to the European Council by the Reflection Group on the Future of the EU 2030, European Council, 9 May.

Gowan, R. and Brantner, F. (2008) 'A Global Force for Human Rights? An Audit of European Power at the UN'. European Council of Foreign Relations Publications.

Habermas, J. (1998) *The Postnational Constellation* (Cambridge, MA: MIT Press).

Habermas, J. and Derrida, J. (2003) 'Nach dem Krieg: Die Wiedergeburt Europas'. *Frankfurter Allgemeine Zeitung*, 31 May.

Gnesotto, N. and Grevi, G. (2006) *The New Global Puzzle: What World for the EU in 2025?* (Paris: EU Institute for Security Studies).

Grevi, G. (2009) 'The Interpolar World: A New Scenario'. Occasional Paper No. 79, EU Institute for Security Studies, June.

Helm, D. and Hepburn, C. (2009) *The Economics and Politics of Climate Change* (Oxford: Oxford University Press).

Herzog, P. and Nicolaïdis, K. (2007) 'Europe at Fifty: Towards a New Single Act'. *OpenDemocracy*, June.

Howorth, J. (2010) 'The EU as a Global Actor: Grand Strategy for a Global Grand Bargain?' *JCMS*, Vol. 48, No. 3, pp. 455–74.

Howse, R. and Nicolaïdis, K. (2009) 'Towards a Global Trade Ethics'. In Eagleton-Pierce, M., Jones, E. and Nicolaïdis, K. (eds) *Building Blocks towards a Global Trade Ethics* (Oxford: GTE Programme), WP Series, July.

Hutchings, R. and Kempe, F. (2008) 'The Global Grand Bargain'. *Foreign Policy Online*, November.

Joerges, C. (2006) 'Constitutionalism in Postnational Constellations: Contrasting Social Regulation in the EU and in the WTO'. In Joerges, C. and Petersmann, E.-U. (eds) *Constitutionalism, Multilevel Trade Governance and Social Regulation* (Oxford: Hart), pp. 491–527.

Jørgensen, K.E., Pollack, M.A. and Rosamond, B. (2006) *Handbook of European Union Politics* (London: Sage).

Kaldor, M. (2007) *Human Security* (Cambridge: Polity Press).

Kelemen, D. (2010) 'Built to Last? The Durability of EU Federalism'. In Meunier, S. and McNamara, K.R. (eds) *Making History: European Integration and Institutional Change at Fifty* (Oxford: Oxford University Press).

King, D.A. and Walker, G. (2008) *The Hot Topic* (London: Bloomsbury Publishing).

Korosteleva, E.A. (forthcoming) 'Rocking the Boat? Security Dilemmas for the Contested Neighbourhood'. *European Security*, special issue.

Lacroix, J. and Nicolaïdis, K. (2010) *European Stories: Intellectual Debates on Europe in National Contexts* (Oxford: Oxford University Press).

Laidi, Z. (2010) 'Europe as a Risk Averse Power: A Hypothesis', Garnet Policy Brief 11, February, pp. i–xvi.

Lambert, R. and Butler, N. (2006) *The Future of European Universities: Renaissance or Decay* (London: Centre for European Reform).

Leibfried, S., Gaines, S. and Frisina, L. (2009) 'Through the Funhouse Looking Glass: Europe's Ship of States'. Transtate Working Papers 90, University of Bremen.

Leonard, M. (2005) *Why Europe will Run the 21st Century* (London: Fourth Estate).

Maduro, M. (ed.) (2010) *The Past and Future of EU Law: The Classics of EU Law Revisited on the 50th Anniversary of the Rome Treaty* (Oxford: Hart).

Magnette, P. and Nicolaïdis, K. (2003) 'Grands et petits Etats dans l'Union européenne : réinventer l'équilibre' ('Large and Small Member States: Reinventing the Balance'). *Notre Europe, Research and European Issues*, May.

Manners, I. (2010) 'Global Europa'. *JCMS*, Vol. 48, No. 1, pp. 67–87.

Martin, J. (2006) *The Meaning of the 21st Century: A Vital Blueprint for Ensuring our Future* (London: Random House).

Mayer, H. and Vogt, H. (eds) (2006) *A Responsible Europe? Ethical Foundations of EU External Affairs* (Basingstoke: Palgrave).

Medrano, J.D. (2010) 'Europe's Political Identity: Public Sphere and Public Opinion'. In Lacroix, J. and Nicolaïdis, K. (eds) *European Stories*.

Menon, A. (2008) *Europe: The State of the Union* (London: Atlantic Books).

Menon, A. and Schain, M. (eds) (2006) *Comparative Federalism: The European Union and the United States in Comparative Perspective* (Oxford: Oxford University Press).

Meunier, S. and Nicolaïdis, K. (2006) 'The European Union as a Conflicted Trade Power'. *Journal of European Public Policy*, Vol. 13, No. 6, pp. 906–25.

Monti, M. (2010) 'A New Strategy for the Single Market: At the Service of Europe's Economy and Society'. A Report to the President of the European Commission.

Moravcsik, A. (1998) *The Choice for Europe: Social Purpose and State Power from Messina to Maastricht* (Ithaca, NY and London: Cornell University Press and Routledge).

Moravcsik, A. (2006) 'What Can we Learn from the Collapse of the European Constitutional Project?' *Politische Vierteljahresschrift*, Vol. 47, No. 2, pp. 219–41.

Moravcsik, A. (2010) 'Europe: The Second Superpower'. *Current History*, March.

National Intelligence Council (2008) 'Global Trends 2025: A Transformed World'. Available at «http://www.dni.gov/nic/PDF_2025/2025_Global_Trends_Final_Report.pdf».

Nicolaïdis, K. (2004) 'We, the Peoples of Europe . . .'. *Foreign Affairs*, Vol. 83, No. 6, pp. 97–110.

Nicolaïdis, K. (2005) 'UE: un moment Tocquevillien'. *Politique étrangère*, 3.

Nicolaïdis, K. (2007a) 'Trusting the Poles? Constructing Europe through Mutual Recognition'. *Journal of European Public Policy*, Vol. 14, No. 5, pp. 682–98.

Nicolaïdis, K. (2007b) 'Our Democratic Atonement: Why we Need an Agora Europe'. *The People's Project? New European Treaty and the Prospects for Future Negotiations*, Brussels, European Policy Centre, December.

Nicolaïdis, K. (2010a) 'Kir Forever? The Journey of a Political Scientist in the Landscape of Recognition'. In Maduro, M. (ed.) *The Past and Future of EU Law*.

Nicolaïdis, K. (2010b) 'Project Europe 2030: Reflection and Revival'. *OpenDemocracy*, 11 May.

Nicolaïdis, K. (2010c) 'EU 2.0?' *OpenDemocracy*, 17 June.

Nicolaïdis, K. and Howse, R. (eds) (2001) *The Federal Vision: Legitimacy and Levels of Governance in the United States and the European Union* (Oxford: Oxford University Press).

Nicolaïdis, K. and Pélabay, J. (2009) 'One Union, One Story? In Praise of Europe's Narrative Diversity'. In Phinnemore, D. and Warleigh-Lack, A. (eds) *Reflections on European Integration* (Basingstoke: Palgrave Macmillan), pp. 175–93.

Nye, J. (2004) *Soft Power: The Means to success in World Politics* (New York: Public Affairs).

Obinger, H., Starke, P., Moser, J., Bogedan, C., Obinger-Gindulis, E. and Leibfried, S. (2010) *Transformations of the Welfare State: Small Countries, Big Lessons* (Oxford: Oxford University Press).

Oxford Research Group (2006) 'Sustainable Security for the 21st Century'. Available at «http://www.sustainablesecurity.org».

Pearson, P. (2004) *Politics in Time: History, Institutions, and Social Analysis* (Princeton, NJ: Princeton University Press).

Polanyi, K. (2001 [1957]) 'The Economy as Instituted Process'. In Granovetter, M. and Swedberg, R. (eds) *The Sociology of Economic Life* (2nd edn) (Boulder, CO: Westview Press), pp. 31–50.

Porritt, J. (2005) *Capitalism as if the World Matters* (London: Earthscan).

Postel Vinay, K. (2005) *L'Occident et sa bonne parole: nos représentations du monde de l'Europe coloniale à l'Amérique hégémonique* (Paris: Flammarion).

Rees, W.E. (2002) 'Globalization and Sustainability: Conflict or Convergence?' *Bulletin of Science, Technology and Society*, Vol. 22, No. 4, pp. 249–68.

Sapir, A. (ed.) (2009) *Europe's Economic Priorities, 2010–2015 – Memos to the New Commission* (Brussels: Bruegel).

Saurugger, S. (2010) 'The Social Construction of the Participatory Turn: The Emergence of a Norm in the European Union'. *European Journal of Political Research*, Vol. 49, pp. 471–95.

Schmidt, V. (2009) 'Re-envisioning the European Union: Identity, Democracy, Economy'. *JCMS AR*, Vol. 47, No. s1, pp. 17–42.

Slaughter, A.-M. (2004) *A New World Order* (Princeton, NJ: Princeton University Press).

Stiglitz, J., Sen, A. and Fitoussi, J.-P. (2009) 'Report by the Commission on the Measurement of Economic Performance and Social Progress'. Available at «www.stiglitz-sen-fitoussi.fr».

Telò, M. (2009) *The European Union and Global Governance* (Abingdon: Routledge).

Toynbee, A. (1948) *Civilization on Trial* (Oxford: Oxford University Press).

Tsoukalis, L. (2005) *What Kind of Europe?* (Oxford: Oxford University Press).

Tsoukalis, L., Cramme, O. and Liddle, R. (2009) *An EU 'Fit for Purpose' in the Global Age: Can we Rise to the Challenge?* (London: Policy Network).

Van Parijs, P. (ed.) (2004) *Cultural Diversity versus Economic Solidarity* (Brussels: De Boeck Université, Bibliothèque scientifique Francqui).

Warleigh-Lack, A. and Phinnemore, D. (eds) (2009) *Reflections on European Integration* (Basingstoke: Palgrave).

Weiler, J.H.H. (1999) *The Constitution of Europe: Essays on the Ends and Means of European Integration* (Cambridge: Cambridge University Press).

Whitman, R. and Wolff, S. (eds) (2010) *The European Neighbourhood Policy in Perspective* (Basingstoke: Palgrave).

Wilson, A. and Popescu, N. (2009) *The Limits of Enlargement-Lite: European and Russian Power in the Troubled Neighbourhood* (London: European Council on Foreign Relations).

Zakaria, F. (2008) *The Post-American World* (New York: W.W. Norton & Company).

JCMS 2010 Volume 48 Annual Review pp. 55–67

The Appointments of Herman van Rompuy and Catherine Ashton

TONY BARBER
Financial Times Bureau Chief, Brussels

Introduction

On 19 November 2009, heads of state and government of the European Union named Herman van Rompuy as the first full-time President of the European Council and Baroness Catherine Ashton as the EU's new High Representative for Foreign Affairs and Security Policy. In the three weeks leading up to the dinner in Brussels at which the leaders announced their decisions, the selection of van Rompuy had become a virtual certainty. The choice of Ashton, however, took aback even the nominee herself, who made no secret of her surprise that she had suddenly been elevated to one of Europe's highest-profile political posts (Palmer, 2009).

Each appointment drew praise and criticism, though not in equal quantities. Van Rompuy, a Flemish Christian Democrat who had served as Belgium's prime minister since December 2008, was regarded by Europe's political and bureaucratic elites as a shrewd, thoughtful politician deeply committed to the ideal of European integration and well-suited to the task of forging a consensus among national leaders sitting in the European Council. His multilingual skills and economic policy expertise were attractive qualities, and many were impressed by his apparent success over the previous 11 months in calming tensions between Belgium's francophone and Flemish-speaking communities. In addition, policy-makers in many parts of the EU – 20 of whose 27 countries have populations of less than 17 million – found it reassuring that he was from a small Member State and therefore unlikely to ride roughshod over the interests of their nations. There were some misgivings, however, about van Rompuy's relative lack of experience of international affairs at the highest level.

Ashton, a former treasurer of Britain's Campaign for Nuclear Disarmament and former chairwoman of Hertfordshire health authority, was widely recognized as having performed competently after she replaced Peter Mandelson as EU Trade Commissioner in October 2008. Nevertheless she was a little-known personality even in her own country, she was not a foreign policy specialist or a talented linguist, and she appeared significantly less well-qualified for the job of High Representative than her predecessor, Javier Solana, who had served as Spain's foreign minister for three years and Nato secretary-general for four years before he took up the EU post in 1999. Moreover, the circumstances of Ashton's appointment raised concerns that it had been inspired less by an appreciation of her abilities than by pressure from political party groups in the European Parliament, and by the need of other EU leaders to repay Britain's Labour government for its reluctant decision to sacrifice the ambitions of Tony Blair, the former prime minister, to become the first full-time European Council President. In choosing van Rompuy and Ashton, EU leaders left themselves open to the criticism that they had been too unambitious and allowed political horse-trading to triumph over merit – even if it was true, as Chancellor Angela Merkel of Germany pointed out, that 'characters can grow into jobs'.[1]

I. Raising the EU's Global Profile

The 19 November appointments were the high point of a six-month transition period in which the EU renewed and reshaped its institutions by holding elections to the European Parliament, deciding who should be European Commission President for the five years from 2010 to 2015, and adopting the Lisbon Treaty on institutional reform. The structure and membership of the new 27-member Commission, which eventually took office in February 2010, was also mapped out in the closing months of the year. Each of these developments played its part in the decision to nominate van Rompuy and Ashton for the two high-level jobs.

Yet the appointments were also the culmination of a much longer phase of diplomatic negotiation and political struggle over the EU's future whose origins lay in the collapse of European communism in 1989–91, the onset of globalization and the increasing weight in the world political and economic order of countries such as Brazil, China, India, Russia, South Korea and

[1] *Deutsche Welle* online, 20 November 2009.

South Africa. The EU, having started life in the 1950s as a coal and steel community and proceeded by fits and starts to the creation of a common agricultural policy, a single market and a single currency, contained 15 members at the turn of the millennium. Its decision to go ahead with its biggest ever enlargement by adding 12 more countries, all but two from central and eastern Europe, strengthened the perception that the Union needed a substantial modernization of its decision-making procedures. Moreover, the spread of globalization and the emergence of new, unconventional security threats – dramatized by the 11 September 2001 attacks on the United States – deepened the conviction of European policy-makers that the EU could no longer afford to stand on the margins of world politics (Hix, 2005, p. 397). As EU leaders put it in the Laeken Declaration: 'Now that the cold war is over and we are living in a globalized, yet also highly fragmented world, Europe needs to shoulder its responsibilities in the governance of globalization. The role it has to play is that of a power resolutely doing battle against all violence, all terror and all fanaticism, but which also does not turn a blind eye to the world's heart-rending injustices' (European Convention, 2001).

One step had already been taken with the establishment in the 1997 Amsterdam Treaty of the post of foreign policy High Representative, an action reflecting the EU's concern that the 1991–95 wars of the Yugoslav succession had exposed severe weaknesses in the unity and effectiveness of European foreign policy (Peterson, 2008, pp. 213–14). A second, more wide-ranging initiative was the establishment of a Convention on the Future of Europe, which met from February 2002 to July 2003 under the chairmanship of Valéry Giscard d'Estaing, the former French president. The convention produced a draft constitutional treaty for the EU which proposed the appointments of a full-time European Council President for a two-and-a-half year term, renewable once, and a Union foreign affairs minister who would simultaneously serve as a Commission vice-president (Avery, 2009).

Agreement on the full-time Presidency, intended partly to displace the traditional system of six-monthly rotating national presidencies, was not easily reached. The leading advocates of the change were the 'ABC' trio – Prime Minister José María Aznar of Spain, Blair and President Jacques Chirac of France. As representatives of large EU states, they were disturbed by the prospect that, after the forthcoming round of enlargement, the Council would be led too often by small countries such as Cyprus, Latvia and Malta that lacked the resources to give the EU the dynamic international presence it required. Conversely, smaller states and those with a less intergovernmentalist vision of the EU were concerned that a powerful full-time presidency would curtail their influence and hobble progress towards deeper

European integration. As a compromise, it was decided to retain the rotating
Presidency but to exclude foreign affairs from its competency.

The attempt at redesigning the EU's institutions came to a shuddering
halt in May and June 2005 when voters first in France and then in the
Netherlands rejected the draft constitutional treaty. The 'No' votes had little
to do with the proposals to equip the EU with a full-time Presidency and a
foreign minister, but the rejections forced the abandonment of the treaty and
its replacement by a new document, ultimately to be known as the Lisbon
Treaty, signed in December 2007 (EUR-Lex, 2008). Among the changes
was the substitution of the title of High Representative for that of Foreign
Minister, an alteration aimed at removing any impression, however misguided, among the European public that the EU was heading in the direction
of a pan-European government.

EU leaders were determined, however, to preserve the substance of the
foreign minister's job. In particular, they left intact the proposal that the High
Representative should become a more powerful figure by taking over three
areas of responsibility – those handled by Solana, those of the foreign minister
of the country holding the rotating Presidency, and those of the EU External
Relations Commissioner, who from November 2004 to December 2009 was
Benita Ferrero-Waldner of Austria. Moreover, as suggested by the European
Convention, the High Representative would simultaneously hold the post
of Commission Vice-President. It was widely remarked during Ferrero-
Waldner's tenure of office that EU policy-making had often been rendered
incoherent by the rivalry between two separate foreign policy bureaucracies in
her Commission office and Solana's office in the Council of Ministers (Grant,
2009a). The incoherence was apt to spread when a country in domestic political
turmoil and possessing little or no experience of managing EU affairs held the
rotating Presidency, a point of which national governments were to become
acutely aware during the Czech Republic's six-month term in the first half of
2009 (Grant, 2009b).

The political and institutional shortcomings of the EU's common foreign
and security policy were exposed in episodes ranging from the US-led invasion
of Iraq in 2003, which produced a Franco–German alignment with Russia in
opposition to a coalition led by Britain, Italy and Spain, to the EU's troubled
efforts to form a strategic partnership with Moscow. It appeared to many
commentators that the EU was an 'awkward foreign and security policy actor,
unable to formulate a cohesive identity or credible capabilities with which to
project itself on the world stage' (Dover, 2007, p. 237). The fundamental
problems were the division of responsibilities between the Council and the
Commission, the persistence of national over European interests, and the
frequent tendency of EU activities in the fields of conflict prevention and

peace-building to clash with other policies in areas such as energy and trade (EPLO, 2009).

Unfortunately, the Lisbon Treaty did not put forward clear-cut solutions to these problems. It provided no clarity on how the High Representative was to share responsibilities with other high-level decision-makers, notably the Council President and the Commission President. It left undefined the structure of the future External Action Service, which the High Representative was to lead, and it skirted the issue of how the EAS was to interact with the tried and tested diplomatic services of Member States, especially those of Britain, France and Germany. It fell to Ashton, a foreign policy novice, to make a stab at clearing up the confusion (Martin, 2009).

II. Picking the Winners

The elections to the European Parliament, held on 4–7 June 2009, delivered a convincing victory for centre-right parties in the six largest EU countries – Britain, France, Germany, Italy, Poland and Spain – and ensured that the European People's Party would remain comfortably the largest party group in the new assembly. Its success reinforced the EPP's determination not merely to secure a second five-year term as Commission President for José Manuel Barroso, the centre-right former Portuguese prime minister, but also to achieve its long-standing goal of winning the post of full-time Council President for a senior representative of the EPP family (Hughes, 2008, p. 13). The EPP held the upper hand because 20 of the EU's 27 Member States were ruled by centre-right parties or coalitions.

However, the EPP's first objective proved easier than the second to attain. The EPP had thrown its weight behind Barroso's reappointment even before the June elections. By contrast, the socialists, the assembly's second largest group, had been too divided to settle on a single candidate. Socialists and other critics of Barroso succeeded in delaying his reappointment when the new legislature convened in July, but only until 16 September, when his candidacy was approved by 382 votes to 219 with 117 abstentions. There were rather more obstacles in the path of securing the full-time Council Presidency for the EPP. In the first place, the job did not exist because the Lisbon Treaty, which established it, had not yet been approved by all 27 Member States. Everything depended on the outcome of an Irish referendum on the Treaty, to be held on 2 October, and on the political calculations of President Václav Klaus of the Czech Republic, who was a bitter opponent of the Treaty but whose signature was required to complete the process of Czech ratification. Secondly, EPP strategists faced the difficulty that the British government was intent on promoting the chances of Blair, hardly a dyed-in-the-wool socialist but a representative of the centre-left nonetheless. The British appeared confident – perhaps too confident – that President Nicolas Sarkozy of France and several other national leaders, notably in Ireland and in central and eastern Europe, looked on Blair's candidacy with sympathy. Lastly, the EPP did not, until October, have a preferred candidate of its own. Various names were aired – including Prime Minister Jean-Claude Juncker of Luxembourg, Prime Minister Jan Peter Balkenende of the Netherlands and Wolfgang Schüssel, the former Austrian chancellor – but none stood out from the crowd.

Ireland's approval of the Lisbon Treaty by a crushing margin of 67.1 per cent to 32.9 per cent, reflecting a 20 per cent swing to the 'Yes' camp since the failed referendum of June 2008, transformed the outlook by making it all but certain that the Treaty would finally come into force. Klaus put a small spanner in the works by demanding guarantees that the Treaty would not be used as a pretext for claims on Czech property from Sudeten Germans expelled from Czechoslovakia in 1945 or from their descendants. These guarantees were duly provided at the European Council of 29–30 October in the form of a protocol that granted the Czech Republic the same exemptions to the Treaty's Charter of Fundamental Rights as those pre-viously extended to Britain and Poland. Klaus then signed the Treaty on 3 November. This set the stage for two weeks of delicate diplomatic contacts between Prime Minister Fredrik Reinfeldt of Sweden, holder of the EU's six-month rotating Presidency, and the EU's 26 other national leaders over whom to select as the full-time Council President and the new High Representative.

Even before Reinfeldt initiated these contacts, however, it was evident that Blair's prospects were rapidly fading. There were several reasons for the objections to Blair. Some European leaders had bitter memories of his co-operation with George W. Bush, the former US president, in launching the invasion of Iraq, an episode that had deeply divided the EU at a time when it was trying to strengthen its ability to speak with a common voice on foreign policy. Britain's self-exclusion from core EU projects such as monetary union and the Schengen border-free travel regime were another factor. The govern-ments of Belgium, Luxembourg and the Netherlands distributed a paper to other Member States in early October which set out their position that the full-time Council President should be 'someone who has demonstrated his commitment to the European project and has developed a global vision of the Union's policies, who listens to the Member States and the institutions, and who is sensitive to the institutional balance that corresponds to the

Community method'.[2] It was apparent that Blair, in the opinion of the Benelux trio, did not fit this description.

No less important was the view of many EU national leaders that the Presidency should go to a politician from a small or medium-sized country rather than a big Member State such as Britain, France or Germany. A majority of leaders were unhappy at the thought that a charismatic, independent-minded 'chief executive' such as Blair might gain the Presidency instead of a lower-profile, consensus-building 'chairman'. Blair, an instantly recognizable figure on the world stage, might have overshadowed not only most national heads of government but even the Commission President and the High Representative, thereby disrupting what was meant to be a carefully constructed balance of power in the EU's institutions. The differences between the British government and most of its EU partners on Blair's candidacy crystallized in the final week of October. In an eye-catching remark on 25 October, David Miliband, the British foreign secretary, argued in favour of Blair by referring to the EU's supposed need for a high-profile Council President who would 'stop the traffic' in Beijing, Moscow and Washington.[3] Two days later, Juncker made plain that he regarded Blair as unsuitable and floated the possibility that he might put forward his own name for the Presidency.[4] Juncker's move smacked more of an attempt to disrupt Blair's campaign than a serious effort at self-promotion. However, it is worth bearing in mind that Luxembourg's rank as the 26th largest EU country had not stopped Juncker's name from repeatedly cropping up in connection with the Presidency over the previous 18 months, not least in Germany, where he had supporters in the chancellery as well as the influential *Bundestag* foreign affairs committee.[5]

Blair's fate was sealed at a dinner in Paris on 28 October at which Sarkozy and Merkel, who had consistently stressed that they would unite behind the same candidate, discussed van Rompuy's presidential credentials. After telephoning the Belgian premier to say that they had him in mind for the job, they received the reply that he was 'ready to go'.[6] On 29 October, only hours before the start of a European Council in Brussels, socialist party leaders in mainland Europe drove home the message that Blair's candidacy had collapsed by informing Prime Minister Gordon Brown of Britain that they had struck a deal with the EPP under which a centre-right leader would become the first full-time Council President and a centre-left politician would inherit Solana's position. The socialists had

---

[2] *EUobserver*, 6 October 2009.
[3] *The Guardian*, 25 October 2009.
[4] *Le Monde*, 27 October 2009.
[5] *Der Spiegel* online, 19 October 2009.
[6] *Le Soir*, 6 November 2009.

drawn up a shortlist of six candidates for foreign policy High Representative: Frank-Walter Steinmeier, Germany's outgoing foreign minister;
Miguel Ángel Moratinos, Spain's foreign minister; Elisabeth Guigou, a
former French EU affairs minister; Alfred Gusenbauer, a former Austrian
chancellor; Adrian Severin, a former Romanian foreign minister; and
Miliband. This list was at once alluring and deceptive. Steinmeier, who had
suffered a crushing defeat in September at Merkel's hands in Germany's
parliamentary elections, but who was then quickly selected as the Social
Democrats' leader in the *Bundestag*, had no interest in the job of EU High
Representative. Moratinos was ruled out partly because Spain was due to
assume the EU's rotating Presidency in January 2010, guaranteeing Madrid
a prominent place in the EU's Lisbon Treaty structures from the start, but
also for the more practical reason that Joaquín Almunia, the EU's Spanish
monetary affairs commissioner, was due to be appointed to a different high-
level job in the new Commission.[7] Guigou was ruled out because Sarkozy
was intent on securing the post of EU Internal Market Commissioner for
Michel Barnier, a fellow Frenchman. No one regarded Gusenbauer or
Severin as credible candidates. In effect, Europe's socialist hierarchs were
telling Brown that the job was Miliband's for the taking, if he wanted it.

Miliband, however, stated that he saw his future in British politics, not in
an EU foreign policy post that many considered he would have filled with
distinction. Miliband's decision presented the British government with the
choice either of continuing to press Blair's presidential credentials – by now,
a doomed endeavour – or of finding a suitable candidate for High Representative. Ultimately, the British government put up little resistance to the demise
of Blair's candidacy, partly because they did not regard van Rompuy as
utterly unacceptable. In contrast to Jean-Luc Dehaene and Guy Verhofstadt,
two former Belgian prime ministers whom Britain had rejected as Commission President in 1994, and 2004, respectively, van Rompuy was viewed in
London as less likely to promote far-reaching schemes of EU integration sure
to generate a great deal of controversy in British politics, especially ahead of
the 2010 general election.[8] As far as concerned a British candidate for High
Representative, however, the influence of the EU's socialist parties was once
again substantial. Before EU leaders gathered for the 19 November dinner,
Brown met his centre-left European comrades and floated the names of Geoff
Hoon and John Hutton, each a former Labour defence minister. The response
was unenthusiastic. The appointment of a woman was deemed necessary to

---

[7] Almunia was officially confirmed in February 2010 as Neelie Kroes' replacement as Competition
Commissioner.
[8] *NRC Handelsblad*, 19 November 2009.

strengthen female representation in the new Commission. Ashton was nominated – to the consternation of those onlookers who doubted both her foreign policy skills and her ability to emerge from the shadow of Barroso, her superior in the future Commission hierarchy.

III. Learning the Ropes

Van Rompuy was widely credited with making a promising start in his job. In December, January and early February he made a point of visiting all 27 Member States with a view to forming a consensus on the EU's new ten-year economic reform programme, known as the Europe 2020 strategy. He also held regular weekly meetings with Barroso and struck up a working relationship that was constructive, if marked by some jostling for influence over the EU's economic agenda. The 2020 plan was duly discussed at an informal European Council that van Rompuy convened in Brussels on 11 February. The event was overshadowed to a large extent by the Greek sovereign debt crisis, and van Rompuy played a central role in drafting the EU statement that promised 'determined and co-ordinated action, if necessary, to safeguard financial stability in the euro area as a whole' (Council, 2010a). His main focus in these early months was, however, on the need for the EU to find new sources of economic growth in order to sustain the prosperity required to pay for the European social model, with its generous array of state-supplied public services. In public speech after speech, he referred to the goal of at least doubling Europe's annual growth rate from the level of 1 per cent to which it had sunk as a result both of the financial crisis that exploded in 2007 and of longer-term weaknesses in Europe's public finances, labour markets, capacity for business innovation and education systems. His aim was partly to raise public awareness of the economic challenges ahead, partly to concentrate the minds of EU national leaders on the need for a co-ordinated response, and partly to set the tone for how he intended to carry out his presidential duties. 'The role of the permanent president is to enhance a shared sense of direction. Nothing more, nothing less', he said in February (Council, 2010b). In this period it was striking that he refrained from high-profile interventions in foreign policy. But he commented that he intended in time to make his presence felt in this area, too.[9]

Ashton's early months in her job were less smooth, partly because she found herself the target of repeated sniping from critics, and partly because she was caught in the middle of a battle for influence over the structure of

[9] Conversation with author. Brussels, 12 February 2010.

the EAS among the largest Member States and between national governments and the Commission. At an informal EU foreign ministers' meeting
in Córdoba, one minister spoke publicly of 'huge frustration among the
Member States that the whole issue would be steered by the Commission'.[10]
The suspicions of national governments were aroused when, in one of
its first administrative moves, Barroso's new Commission transferred two
sections of the Directorate-General for External Relations – those dealing
with international climate change talks and with energy issues – to the new
Directorate-Generals for climate action and energy, respectively. The action
appeared intended to protect the Commission's control over these policy
areas and keep the EAS at arm's length. Member States, by contrast, regarded
it as important that the EAS should have a body of experts in such matters
under its auspices, enabling it to weld foreign policy in the traditional sense
of high diplomacy with the external dimensions of internal EU policies such
as climate change and energy security. Similar tensions arose over control
over the EU's multibillion euro development aid programmes, as well as the
role of the EAS *vis-à-vis* the Commission in relations with countries
approaching EU membership and those in Europe's neighbourhood, such as
Ukraine and the other five former Soviet republics grouped in the EU's
Eastern Partnership initiative.

Behind the tensions lay a sense among Member States that Barroso was
deploying his greater political experience and knowledge of the EU bureaucracy to outmanoeuvre Ashton. The most egregious example was Barroso's
appointment of João Vale de Almeida, a fellow Portuguese and his former
chef de cabinet, as ambassador to Washington in place of John Bruton, a
former Irish prime minister.[11] Although Barroso was technically within his
rights to make the appointment, since the EAS was not yet up and running, the
action smacked of an attempt to give the EU's most prestigious ambassador-
ship to a trusted ally who would be seen in Washington as having a direct
private line to the Commission President rather than being beholden to
Ashton as head of the new diplomatic service. Meanwhile, Ashton's personal
abilities were under constant scrutiny. Her first foreign policy speeches were
thin on substance, she appeared hesitant and vague on detail at her confirmation hearing in the European Parliament, and she was regarded in Germany as
having been taken too closely under the wing of the British Foreign Office.[12]
To some extent, however, her difficulties were attributable to her lack of a
fully staffed private *cabinet* when she took up her job at the start of December

---

[10] *European Voice*, 11 March 2010. The minister was Michael Spindelegger of Austria.
[11] *EurActiv*, 23 February 2010.
[12] *Guardian.co.uk*, 28 February 2010.

2009. In the view of one EU ambassador, she would have done better to wait two months and benefit from Solana's advice and experience before she assumed her new responsibilities.[13]

Conclusions

The methods by which the EU appoints its highest-level representatives are not always a pretty sight. The clash in 1998 over whether Wim Duisenberg of the Netherlands should be the European Central Bank's first president, and if so for how long, was perhaps the ugliest example of the past 20 years, but even Barroso's reappointment as Commission President in the summer of 2009 left something to be desired. The process that led to the nominations of van Rompuy and Ashton said much about the fitful progress of EU integration since the euro's launch in 1999 and the grand enlargement of 2004–07. On the one hand, van Rompuy and Ashton were chosen behind closed doors, with next to no public input, by an 'electorate' – the 27 EU national leaders – that was even smaller than the College of Cardinals that picked the successor to Pope John Paul II in 2005. A last-minute attempt by Poland's government to dispel the cloud of secrecy, by inviting candidates for the full-time Council Presidency and post of High Representative to appear for 'job interviews' in front of EU leaders, might have added a modest degree of transparency, but the proposal was in the event quickly brushed aside.[14] On the other hand, the selection process underlined the steadily rising influence in EU affairs of the party political groups in the European Parliament, a trend likely to be confirmed in coming years as the assembly wields the new powers conferred on it by the Lisbon Treaty. This influence stemmed partly from the fact that the new High Representative, as a Commission vice-president, required confirmation by the Parliament. But it also reflected a calculation by EU leaders that to involve the two main party groups would underpin the political legitimacy of the leaders' choices. EU heads of government and state were nonetheless careful to keep close control over the nomination of the Council President. Their choice of van Rompuy underlined their desire for more efficient management of Council business in the newly expanded Union, as well as their preference for a figure who would not challenge their control over the pace and direction of EU integration. Overall, a certain contradiction was evident in the appointments of van Rompuy and Ashton. Numerous EU politicians had undoubtedly hoped, in the years leading up to the Lisbon Treaty's ratification, that the two posts would make Europe a stronger actor on the world stage. But

[13] Conversation with author. Brussels, 6 March 2010.
[14] *EUobserver*, 10 November 2009.

when push came to shove, the sheer difficulty of brokering the necessary compromises among 27 nations ruled by governments of varying political complexions meant that the EU ended up with consensus-builders of relatively low profile, unlikely to contest the principle of national sovereignty that remains at the heart of so much EU decision-making.

It is open to question whether the choice of two personalities other than van Rompuy or Ashton would have made much difference to the way that the EU tackles its challenges at the dawn of the Lisbon Treaty era. The problems facing the EU are far too profound for two mere individuals and the bureaucracies at their disposal to solve. Put simply, the two overriding challenges are the need to strengthen Europe's economic performance and the need to show that the EU can stabilize its immediate neighbourhood on the basis of advancing economic prosperity, the rule of law and democracy. Low economic growth rates, the crisis of the public finances, the fragility of the banking system and the slow pace of the EU's structural economic reforms are problems that van Rompuy can make no more than a modest contribution to solving. Likewise, Ashton will be no miracle-worker in handling dossiers such as the dysfunctional condition of Bosnia-Herzegovina, the growing independent-mindedness of Turkey and the political and economic instability of Ukraine. Answers to these questions, if there are any, will begin with national EU governments and their willingness to intensify their co-operation both with each other and with the EU institutions. The Lisbon Treaty, so EU leaders assure their publics, provides the instruments for enhancing European economic policy co-operation and projecting the EU's influence more effectively across the globe. What the treaty does not contain, however, is that vital ingredient for success – political willpower.

References

Avery, G. (2009) 'Europe's Foreign Service: From Design to Delivery'. European Policy Centre Policy Brief. Available at «http://www.epc.eu/TEWN/pdf/959676591_Europe's%20foreign%20service.pdf».

Council of the European Union (2010a) 'Statement by the Heads of State or Government of the European Union'. Brussels, 11 February. Available at «http://www.consilium.europa.eu/uedocs/cms_data/docs/pressdata/en/ec/112856.pdf».

Council of the European Union (2010b) Speech by Herman van Rompuy at the European Parliament. Brussels, 24 February. Available at «http://www.consilium.europa.eu/uedocs/cms_data/docs/pressdata/en/ec/113028.pdf».

Dover, R. (2007) 'The EU's Foreign, Security and Defence Policies'. In Cini, M. (ed.) *European Union Politics* (2nd edn) (Oxford: Oxford University Press).

EUR-Lex (2008) 'Consolidated Versions of the Treaty on European Union and the Treaty on the Functioning of the European Union'. Official Journal of the European Union, C115, 9 May.

European Convention (2001) 'Laeken Declaration on the Future of the European Union'. Available at «http://european-convention.eu.int/pdf/LKNEN.pdf».

European Peacebuilding Liaison Office (EPLO) (2009) 'The EU as a Global Force for Good: Peace at the Heart of the European External Action Service'. EPLO Policy Paper. Available at «http://www.toledopax.org/uploads/EPLO_CITpax_The_EU_as_a_Global_Force_for_Good_September_2009.pdf».

Grant, C. (2009a) 'Making a Success of the EAS'. Centre for European Reform blog. Available at «http://centreforeuropeanreform.blogspot.com/2009/05/making-success-of-eas.html».

Grant, C. (2009b) 'Is Europe Doomed to Fail as a Power?' Centre for European Reform Essay. Available at «http://www.cer.org.uk/pdf/essay_905.pdf».

Hix, S. (2005) The Political System of the European Union (2nd edn) (Basingstoke: Palgrave Macmillan).

Hughes, K. (2008) 'Shaping Lisbon's Legacy: The EU's Very Discreet Debate on who Will Make Foreign Policy'. Friends of Europe (Les Amis de l'Europe), Brussels.

Martin, G. (2009) 'Europe Gets a "Diplomatic Service"'. The European Institute, Vol. 10, No. 3, Article 5.

Palmer, J. (2009) 'Ashton Underlines EU's Significant Moment'. The Guardian, 20 November. Available at «http://www.guardian.co.uk/commentisfree/2009/nov/20/cathy-ashton-european-union».

Peterson, J. (2008) 'The EU as a Global Actor'. In Bomberg, E., Peterson, J. and Stubb, A. (eds) The European Union: How Does it Work? (2nd edn) (Oxford: Oxford University Press).

The Czech Presidency

VÍT BENEŠ
Institute of International Relations, Prague
JAN KARLAS
Faculty of Social Sciences, Charles University/Institute of International Relations, Prague

Introduction

The Czech Presidency of the EU Council was not the subject of high expectations. Many observers across Europe were concerned about its possible negative consequences for the performance of the Union. First of all, the overall potential of the Czech Republic as a medium-sized and new Member State was limited. In addition, the government that prepared, and initially also executed the Presidency, was led by the centre-right Civic Democratic Party (Občanská demokratická strana, ODS), which has been generally perceived as a Eurosceptic party. Moreover, Czech President Václav Klaus is regarded as a particularly Eurosceptic actor. When the government of Prime Minister Mirek Topolánek lost the vote of no-confidence in March 2009 and a caretaker government was established, the fears of a weak and unconstructive leadership were replaced by worries of no leadership at all. Yet the six months of the Czech chairmanship were also not short of serious challenges including, among others, the uncertain fate of the Lisbon Treaty, the global financial crisis and the gas crisis.

To what extent was the Czech Presidency effective? We consider an EU Presidency effective if it supplies the demand stemming from the existing policy issues and problems adequately (for a similar notion of effectiveness see Schout and Vanhoonacker, 2006). An effective Presidency, therefore, makes a suitable selection and application of its four main possible functions consisting of administration, agenda-management, mediation and representation.

We argue that the effectiveness of the Czech Presidency could be characterized as mixed. While it provided the EU with a useful service on a number of occasions, it also did not avoid wasting opportunities. In the following analysis we subsequently deal with the actions and performance of the Presidency in the most crucial areas. We will start our account with institutional issues and then proceed to the single market and the global financial crisis. Subsequently, we will concentrate on energy and environment and external relations.[1] The conclusion will reflect on some general implications of the Czech Presidency.

I. Set-Up of the Presidency: Programme and Domestic Context

The Topolánek government started with the preparation of Presidency priorities right after its formation in January 2007, perceiving the Presidency as a unique opportunity to shape the course of the EU and its policies.[2] At the same time, it was believed that the event would attract attention and (if successful) improve the image, reputation and influence of the Czech Republic in the EU. The overall co-ordination of the Presidency issues was vested in the deputy prime minister for European Affairs Alexander Vondra[3] and his office, while the ultimate decision-making power was reserved for the governmental committee for the EU consisting of all the government ministers.

The bureaucratic apparatus devoted much energy to the process of the formulation of Czech priorities. This preparatory phase produced ambitious priorities (Lehtonen, 2009) covered by the motto 'Europe without Barriers', which indicated the Presidency's interest in removing obstacles of any kind between Member States and keeping Europe competitive and open to the world. It was received well since it fitted into the ethos of European integration generally and of the single market in particular. The main priority areas were formulated in the form of three 'Es': Economy, Energy and the European Union in the World, embodying a focus on the single market and the global financial crisis ('Economy'), external energy security ('Energy') and three external relations priorities: EU enlargement, the Eastern Partnership and transatlantic relations ('EU in the World'). The neo-liberal approach to economic issues and the concern with EU relations with eastern Europe coincided well with the preferences of Sweden as one of the other two

---

[1] Compared to other areas, justice and home affairs was marked by less dramatic developments in the first half of 2009 and the Czech Presidency also did not include this field among its most crucial priority areas. For a discussion of JHA developments see Monar's contribution to this volume.

[2] In contrast to President Klaus, who described the institution of the EU Presidency as unimportant.

[3] Vondra was replaced in the caretaker government by Štefan Füle as minister for European Affairs who subsequently became Enlargement Commissioner.

Member States of the Presidency 'Troika'. The convergence of views between the Czech Presidency and France, the other Member State of the Troika, however, was less apparent.

With the stated intention of attracting 'the attention of the national audience as the main and only target' (Governmental press release, 9 September 2008), Czech leaders initiated a provocative communication campaign prior to the Presidency. But the 'presentation' (such as the ambiguous slogan *Evropě to osladíme* which can mean 'we will make it sweet for Europe' or 'sweet' in a more ironic sense, i.e. making it difficult) inevitably crossed Czech borders and received widespread attention from the European media. In addition, in January 2009 a controversial Entropa sculpture depicting stereotypes of European nations was installed in the headquarters of the Council of the EU and provoked much criticism, especially from countries such as Bulgaria who felt the sculpture had gone beyond a provocative joke and was merely offensive.

The bleak domestic context undermined the whole Presidency. The government responsible for the preparation and conduct of the Presidency stood on shaky foundations thanks to the 2006 election stalemate and reliance on party defectors for its majority in parliament. Furthermore, the governing and opposition parties failed to conclude a 'toleration' agreement for the Presidency period.[4] The course of events escalated on 24 March when the Czech Chamber of Deputies (lower house of the parliament) issued a vote of no-confidence in the Topolánek government. Following the Chamber's decision, a caretaker government led by Jan Fischer was established on 8 May. No matter how we assess the performance of the Czech Presidency as an institution, the performance of the Czech political elites could perhaps be described as a 'failure' due to the subordination of the country's EU responsibilities to their immediate domestic political interests.

II. Institutional Issues

Concerning the Lisbon Treaty, the Presidency found itself in a relatively undemanding situation. Given the rejection of the Treaty in the Irish referendum in June 2008, it did not face the complicated task of implementing the Treaty in practice. Yet the Lisbon Treaty was, at the same time, still on the table. Hence, the Presidency also did not have to deal with the similarly difficult task of treaty renegotiation. What is more, the basic agreement on the Treaty's adoption in Ireland had already been made under the French

---

[4] In contrast to Slovenia where the political parties reached an agreement to avoid major domestic disputes during the Slovenian Presidency held in the first half of 2008 (Kajnč, 2009).

chairmanship at the European Council in December 2008.[5] Under such circumstances, the only task for the Presidency was therefore to ensure an
agreement on the legal implementation of the Irish guarantees and to facilitate
the beginning of the process of forming the new Commission.

With regard to both issues, the Czech Presidency ended up with adequate
outcomes. Despite claims about a tension between the Czech and Irish governments,[6] Irish Foreign Minister Martin stated that 'the relationship with the
Czech presidency is going well'.[7] Indeed, at its June summit the European
Council endorsed the precise formulation of the Irish guarantees. The resulting agreement satisfied the Irish government but simultaneously did not
require a re-ratification of the Treaty by other Member States.

Second, on the Czechs' watch President José Manuel Barroso – whose
nomination was actively supported by the Czech Presidency[8] – was backed
by the June European Council as the Commission President designate for a
further term.

The satisfactory performance of the Czech chairmanship in institutional
issues was, to some extent, made possible by Klaus' decision to leave the
ODS just a month before the start of the Presidency. In spite of the fall of
the Topolánek government, the Fischer government was also able to lead
the negotiations and thus to help secure the outcome on both institutional
issues.

III. Single Market and Economic Policies

The economic part of the initial Presidency programme reflected a set of
neo-liberal ideas articulated by ODS. Before it assumed the EU helm, the
Czech government highlighted the progress in strengthening the single
market as its top priority. In the end, the Czech chairmanship undertook a
large amount of work on economic legislation, though the concrete results
should probably be classified as rather mixed.

The Presidency achieved its greatest success in the field of economic
legislation in March 2009 with the deal on the reduced rates of VAT. The
existing VAT Directive required the Member States to keep the value of the
tax at least at 15 per cent, but also enabled them to maintain a 5 per cent tax

---

[5] At this summit, the EU agreed on holding the second referendum in Ireland in the second half of 2009
and on a rough package of guarantees for Ireland; see Dinan (2009).
[6] In its mid-term the Presidency was criticized precisely for little progress on the Irish guarantees
(Kaczynski, 2009). Similarly, another mid-term assessment of the Presidency argued that 'the Czechs have
not been able to provide neutral guidance or sound advice for Ireland when it comes to finding a solution'
(Lehtonen, 2009).
[7] *EUobserver*, 19 March 2009.
[8] Interview with Štefan Füle, Minister for European Affairs, Euractiv.cz, 26 May 2009.

in a number of selected areas (labour-intensive and local services). In the first half of 2009, the EU engaged in the renegotiation of the rules. Initially, France advocated reduced VAT rates (especially in the restaurant sector), while Germany was concerned about reduced state revenues. The Presidency was openly praised for submitting a text that paved the way for a generally acceptable compromise and made possible the resolution of a long-running conflict.[9]

The Presidency was less successful on two other important legislative initiatives – the regulation of telecoms and the working time directive. The Commission together with the European Parliament advocated the establishment of an EU-financed body that would take part in the regulation of telecoms and take binding decisions. By contrast, Member States' governments were in favour of a private body with only advisory powers. Both sides also diverged over the veto power of the Commission over the decisions of national regulation bodies and the distribution of radio frequencies. The Presidency continuously tried to mediate a compromise between the governments and the European Parliament, which seemed to be achieved in April 2009. However, the MEPs watered down the agreement in their final vote in May 2009, primarily due to their concerns about the rights of Internet users.

The Presidency's attempt to reach an agreement on the working time directive turned out to be a similar story. While MEPs pushed for the limitation of the working week to 48 hours, the Member States preferred to keep it between 60 and 65 hours per week. In addition, both sides also differed with regard to how to count on-call time. The Presidency was engaged in a conciliation procedure between the Council and the European Parliament. Even though the Parliament's industry committee adopted the resulting package, the plenary ultimately did not endorse it.

The Presidency also obtained a mixed record on probably its most highlighted aim – the abolition of transition periods for the free movement of labour from the new Member States. In April 2009, Belgium and Denmark announced that they would lift the transitional restrictions. In contrast, Austria and Germany continued to keep the restrictions, informing the Commission that they would maintain them until the last possible date of April 2011. The Presidency, therefore, only partially succeeded in its intention of removing the remaining restrictions in this field, although it strongly disputed the justifications for the maintenance of restrictions put forward by Austria and Germany.

---

[9] *EUobserver*, 10 March 2009.

IV. Financial Crisis

As the global financial crisis intensified, a great deal of the Presidency's attention had to shift from the long-term functioning of the single market to the search for the EU's response to the crisis. Hence, the neo-liberal beliefs of the Czech representatives began to manifest themselves primarily in the Presidency's stance on how the EU should tackle the crisis. The Presidency put the main emphasis on the restoration of the proper working of the financial markets, highlighting the need to restore the supply of bank loans.

The Presidency stood against any attempts at solving the crisis primarily by 'pumping' larger sums of money into the economy. It urged the Member States to reduce their budget deficits and to observe the rules of the Stability Pact. It similarly rejected bank bail-outs and the Eurobonds idea favoured by the French. At the beginning of February, Topolánek openly stated that the attitudes of the euro area members towards the crisis considerably 'deformed' the euro project.[10]

What perhaps became the most visible part of the Presidency's 'anti-crisis' programme were its efforts to block protectionist measures. These efforts intensified as early as January when the French president Nicolas Sarkozy presented a plan to provide €6.5 billion in aid to French car manufacturers. When suggesting to car manufacturers a repatriation of their activities from central and eastern Europe, Sarkozy referred to the branch of the PSA Peugeot Citroen based in the Czech town of Kolín, provoking an open war of words between the Czech and French governments including Topolánek's denunciation of 'the really selective and protectionist steps and statements of, among others, President Sarkozy'.[11] The February European Council, which declared a common rejection of protectionism, was convened partially to end this clash between the two countries of the EU Presidency trio. Tensions between both countries were rooted in French worries about the capability of the Czech Republic as a new Member State to lead the EU as well as in the ideological divergence between both governments. The conflict appeared to become personal when at the end of the Czech Presidency Sarkozy snubbed Topolánek when he praised the caretaker Prime Minister Fischer for being 'calm and intelligent'.

Overall, the Presidency's attempts to make the EU react to the financial crisis had some limited results. Under the Czech chairmanship the EU did adopt a few concrete decisions for dealing with the crisis. The March European Council agreed on a €5 billion programme on energy and Internet

---

[10] *Financial Times*, 11 February 2009.
[11] *New York Times*, 9 February 2009.

infrastructure and also reached a common EU position for the G20 summit. The June European Council accepted a reform of financial rules entailing the establishment of new EU overseeing authorities and the reinforcement of the European Central Bank's authority. However, while centring on the struggle against protectionism and interventionism, the Presidency did not substantially contribute to the debate on longer-term issues (such as financial regulation).

V. Energy and Environment

Right at the beginning of its mandate, the Czech Presidency was confronted with the fallout from the Russian–Ukrainian gas conflict. The Presidency initially described the gas dispute as a bilateral problem and did not step in until gas supplies to the bloc were affected. By 3 January the conflict had escalated, with resultant supply shortages in more than 15 EU Member States. Czech representatives reacted with a frenetic shuttle diplomacy between Moscow and Kiev. After protracted wrangling between Ukraine and Russia over the text of the agreement and technical issues,[12] the gas supply into EU countries resumed.

The Czech government not only paid great attention to the exigent energy crisis, but also tried to shape the long-term goals of EU policies. It placed energy issues high on its agenda, with a focus on the long-term security aspects of energy issues rather than on environmental problems of energy production and consumption. The dependence on external energy supplies (coming from or through Russia) was presented as a threat to long-term economic competitiveness, but also as a threat to the EU's political independence and its geopolitical security.

In line with the Presidency's goal of laying down the foundations of a common European energy policy, the March European Council endorsed the initiatives already set out in the Second Strategic Energy Review. Among other things, it prompted the Commission to table both a new EU Energy Security and Infrastructure Instrument by 2010 and proposals for concrete action on the development of the southern corridor including a mechanism to facilitate access to the Caspian gas.

As a way to diversify external energy suppliers and transit routes (and to reduce the dependence on Russia), the Presidency resuscitated the dying Nabucco project. It won support from the European Commission and reached an agreement on financing the project. On 8 May, the Presidency and the European Commission hosted the 'Southern Corridor' Summit with

[12] *EUobserver*, 19 January 2009.

third countries, i.e. the potential suppliers or transport countries for the project.[13]

Besides the key topic of external energy security, the Presidency concluded the negotiations on the third energy liberalization package. The package received its final approval on 25 June. The final compromise offered companies involved in the electricity market all three options of unbundling, despite the MEPs' initial insistence on full separation of production and transmission assets.

Despite the participation of the Green Party in the Topolánek government, the government was not very enthusiastic when it came to the fight against climate change. Moreover, the credibility of the Presidency as a potential mediator of a common European position for the 2009 Copenhagen conference was undermined by President Klaus, who vocally questions any effort to tackle global environmental problems. It comes as no surprise that the Czech Presidency kept a low profile in the whole climate change agenda (see Král *et al.*, 2009, p. 50). The Presidency made only a limited impact on the agenda, for example when it stressed the need to take into account the development dimension when tackling climate change. Some observers even talked about a 'complete failure', arguing that the Presidency willingly left the field to other actors (like Sweden) who place environmental issues higher on their agenda (Fuksiewicz and Łada, 2009). In sum, the Presidency proved to be effective in the field of energy, in a sharp contrast to environmental issues and climate change in particular.

VI. External Relations

Gaza

Right at the beginning of the mandate, the Czech Presidency was confronted with the armed conflict in Gaza (27 December to 18 January). The Presidency tried to mediate a ceasefire by sending an EU mission headed by Czech foreign minister Karel Schwarzenberg. Yet these brokering efforts were hampered by a parallel mission by French president Sarkozy. A pro-Israeli statement by a Topolánek spokesperson at the very beginning of the crisis, however, did not boost the credibility and neutrality of the EU mission.

The Presidency also refused to drop its priority of upgrading EU–Israel relations and entered into an open split with the Commission which decided to 'pause' the negotiations in the aftermath of the Gaza crisis. In consequence,

---

[13] The final agreement between Turkey, Romania, Bulgaria, Hungary and Austria to construct the long-planned 3,300 km Nabucco natural gas pipeline was signed on 13 July (see Euractiv.com, 14 July 2009).

the Czech Presidency was unable to mediate a common EU position on the Gaza crisis and adequately represent the EU on the global stage.

Eastern Partnership and Relations with Russia

The 2008 Georgian war, the Ukraine–Russia gas dispute (see above) and other events highlighted the fragility of international relations and the domestic situation in eastern Europe, opening the way for the Polish–Swedish initiative called 'Eastern Partnership' to be launched as an official EU project.

Speeding up the preparations for the Eastern Partnership was just one of the three priorities of the Presidency in the field of external relations. But during the mandate itself, the Presidency grasped the opportunity and promoted the project as a way of ensuring stability, security and prosperity not just of all the participants in the Eastern Partnership (Armenia, Azerbaijan, Belarus, Georgia, Moldova and Ukraine), but of the whole of Europe. The Eastern Partnership was approved at the Spring European Council and launched at a dedicated summit in Prague on 7 May, although the leaders of some of the biggest EU Member States were conspicuous by their absence.[14]

In line with what has been said about external energy security and the Eastern Partnership, the Presidency promoted a unified, self-confident and assertive stance towards Russia. These policies were successfully framed as the fulfilment of the old dream of many European leaders: the EU as an independent and economically competitive *global political player*.

Enlargement

As a strong supporter of further EU enlargement, the Czech Republic took over the Presidency at a time of a continuing intra-EU stalemate and entrenched warfare on the fate of EU enlargement policy. After fighting protracted diplomatic battles with France and other opponents of the EU enlargement process, the Czech Presidency was caught by surprise when the enlargement process came under 'friendly fire' from a new Member State, which had hitherto favoured the idea of EU enlargement. In late December 2008, Slovenia blocked the accession process for neighbouring Croatia by emphasizing a long-time maritime border dispute. Initially, Czech representatives expressed their willingness to mediate in the conflict, but stood back to allow the conflict to be dealt with bilaterally.

The suspension of accession talks with Croatia was clearly detrimental to one of the Czech Presidency's key priorities. Elsewhere, the Presidency

[14] *Financial Times*, 8 May 2009.

recorded a rather limited success when it received a membership application from Albania, brought the application of Montenegro before the Commission and opened one chapter (Taxation) in negotiations with Turkey.

Conclusions

The Czech Presidency performed especially well in the sphere of external energy security and in EU relations with eastern Europe. It fulfilled the function of a collective representative through the shuttle diplomacy in the Ukrainian–Russian gas row. As an agenda manager, it reflected on the EU's growing dependence on energy imports and promoted the idea of energy policy with a particular stress on external energy security (greater territorial diversification of suppliers and transit routes). Energy issues were discussed using the new language of geopolitical independence of the EU and the strategic competitiveness of the EU market. Moreover, the Presidency successfully promoted the Polish–Swedish initiative of 'Eastern Partnership' as a response to the growing EU attention to its eastern neighbourhood. The Czech Presidency also managed to handle institutional issues well. Due to a number of successful results, the Presidency was (though with varying success) able to disconfirm the view that it would be marked by a lack of competence and enthusiasm.

However, with regard to several other issues the Presidency could be considered less effective. For example, during the Gaza crisis it acted as an agenda manager (promoting closer EU–Israeli relationship) when there actually was a demand for an intra-EU mediator (forging a common position on who will speak for the EU and what message to convey and in what tone) and a collective representative acting as an impartial mediator in the Gaza conflict. The management of the Gaza crisis, as well as of transatlantic relations, was not free from serious lapses and cumbersome diplomacy. Furthermore, the stress on external energy security came at the expense of progress in environmental issues. Even though the Presidency sought to prevent the EU from interventionism and protectionism in the fight with the global financial crisis, many would probably question whether it exercized enough 'strategic' leadership. The Presidency's performance in the 'standard' single market agenda was equally mixed.

The global financial crisis was arguably the main issue on the EU agenda in the first half of 2009 which provokes a few further observations. First, the clash between the Presidency representatives and their French counterparts revealed the consequences following from the complexity of the Presidency roles. The Czech chairmanship could hardly prioritize certain ways of fighting the crisis and at the same time remain a neutral broker (though a more careful balancing of the political agenda-setting and neutral brokerage roles would certainly have been welcomed).

Second, the way the Czech Presidency handled the financial crisis also showed how the functioning of the Presidency trio and the co-operation between the Presidency and other EU institutions depend on the convergence of preferences. Preferences regarding broader economic strategies largely account for a clash between the Czech and French representatives, but also explain why the Presidency frequently found a 'common voice' with the Commission and Sweden, two actors also generally sympathetic to neo-liberal solutions. An interesting and crucial element of Presidency involvement was the closeness of its positions to that of Germany, which also took a rather modest approach towards anti-crisis interventionism.

Third, the Czech Presidency's actions on the financial crisis also showed that the new Member States as Presidency countries are not very likely to serve on a permanent basis as the defenders of the new Member States' common interests. At least at the rhetorical level, the Presidency centred on arguing that the new Member States did not represent a homogeneous group of countries which would be hit by the crisis to the same extent. This stance confirmed the expectation that the Presidency would closely co-operate with other new Member States only when there was a real overlap of interests and that in several areas an overlap was missing (Karlas *et al.*, 2008).

References

Dinan, D. (2009) 'Institutions and Governance: Saving the Lisbon Treaty – an Irish Solution to a European Problem'. *JCMS AR*, Vol. 47, No. s1, pp. 113–32.

Fuksiewicz, A. and Łada, A. (2009) *The Czech Presidency in the Council of the European Union – the view from Poland* (Warsaw: The Institute of Public Affairs).

Kaczynski, P. (2009) 'How the Czech Presidency Performed up to Now'. *European Voice*, 26 March.

Kajnč, S. (2009) 'The Slovenian Presidency: Meeting Symbolic and Substantive Challenges'. *JCMS AR*, Vol. 47, No. s1, pp. 89–98.

Karlas, J., Kořan, M. and Tulmets, E. (2008) 'Prag, die Visegrád Gruppe und die EU; Tschechiens Ziele in der EU-Ratspräsidentschaft'. *Osteuropa*, No. 7/2008, pp. 153–63.

Král, D., Bartovic, V. and Řiháčková, V. (2009) *The 2009 Czech EU Presidency: Contested Leadership at a Time of Crisis* (Stockholm: Swedish Institute for European Policy Studies).

Lehtonen, T. (2009) 'Czech Point: A Mid-term Evaluation of an On-going
    Small State Presidency'. UPI Briefing Paper 28, Finish Institute of International
    Affairs.
Schout, A. and Vanhoonacker, S. (2006) 'Evaluating Presidencies of the Council of
    the EU: Re-visiting Nice'. *JCMS*, Vol. 44, No. 5, pp. 1051–78.

The Swedish Presidency

LEE MILES
Karlstad University

Introduction

One thing is certain, the experience of the 2009 Swedish Presidency would seem, at first glance, to be somewhat different compared to the 'dull, but successful' Swedish Presidency of 2001 (see Elgström, 2002a,b; Miles 2002a,b, 2005; Tallberg, 2001). Indeed, Sweden's non-socialist Alliance government of Fredrik Reinfeldt intended, at least for the most part, for it to be that way since the Swedish centre-right prime minister was keen not to live in the shadow of Sweden's first experiences of holding the European Council Presidency, which was run by a government of their centre-left, Social Democratic electoral rivals.

The rather workmanlike 2001 Swedish EU Council Presidency had been symbolically important for three reasons. Firstly, the emphasis in 2001 was very much on 'safe but competent' (see Elgström, 2002a; Miles, 2002b) rather than 'ambitious, but costly' and the setting of realistic expectations about what a Swedish Presidency could achieve was one of the reasons for it being regarded by many as successful (Miles, 2005, p. 207). Second, the Swedish government strategy in 2001 was also gauged as being at least partially successful, because of its use of three thematic concepts – the '3 "Es" of Employment, Enlargement and the Environment' in order to translate these realistic expectations into an effective 'results-driven' platform (Miles, 2002b). Third, the 2001 Presidency was perceived to have important domestic spin-offs for the respective Swedish prime minister, Göran Persson, in securing a profile as an international statesmen on the world stage; something that most (if not all) Swedish politicians aspire to as an indirect means of enhancing electoral popularity back home. As Haughton (2010, p. 20) identifies, Presidencies offer a platform for the European 'tweaking' of domestic preferences that will in turn deliver further domestic gains if handled correctly.

Yet, the tone of the Swedish 2009 EU Council Presidency seemed to be slightly different, even if the strategy remained fundamentally pragmatic and result-orientated in practice. For sure, if any analyst scratched below the surface of the veneer of the Alliance government's priorities for Sweden's 2009 Presidency, elements of the '3 "E's" ' (of 2001) were there for all to see with some Swedish recycling in evidence (see Langdal and von Sydow, 2008, p. 4). Nevertheless, the Reinfeldt government seemed to be adopting a somewhat different style in its presentation of the Swedish Presidency.

I. Domestic Stability and International Instability

Unlike its Czech predecessor (see Beneš and Karlas, this volume), there seemed to be no real risk of domestic political instability undermining the Presidency (CER, 2009). To the contrary, the four-party non-socialist coalition government of Fredrik Reinfeldt remained relatively popular, according to opinion polls, and a Swedish general election was not scheduled until September 2010. Moreover, the four-party coalition had established relatively sophisticated political processes to ensure the ironing out of policy positions of the governing partners, with preparations for the Presidency beginning quite soon after Reinfeldt took office in 2006. However, the external circumstances of the 2009 Swedish EU Council Presidency were different from that of 2001 and did in fact change dramatically as governmental preparations, begun quietly back in 2006, gathered pace.

Compared to the 2001 Presidency, which was largely preoccupied with handling concrete accession negotiations and the enlargement portfolio, preparations for the 2009 Swedish Presidency were confronted by an unusual amount of uncertainties as regards the external environment. As Langdal and von Sydow (2009a, p. 1) commented at the time, 'the preconditions for a progressive, efficient, and smooth presidency are adverse'.

First, the Swedes were in the unenviable position of having to plan for their Presidency possibly taking place under two alternative sets of EU rules. Given the constitutional uncertainty surrounding the implementation of the Lisbon Treaty (see Dinan, this volume), the Swedes were forced to plan their

Presidency under Nice Treaty rules (since the Lisbon Treaty rules might not be operational), while simultaneously also considering the possibility of holding their Presidency under the Lisbon Treaty if indeed implementation was achieved.

Second, the general external global environment had changed considerably since initial planning for the Presidency had begun in 2006. The global economy, and indeed, the vast majority of the major Member State economies of the EU were experiencing recession in the aftermath of the 2008 financial crisis. Government accounts had deteriorated, and European industry was having a hard time; illustrated in the Swedish case by the uncertainty over the future of Sweden's flagship car companies – Volvo and Saab – which were both put up for sale by their respective US owners. This 'tricky time' left the Union 'with little, but a co-ordinating role to play' (CER, 2009).

The Presidency term was also confronted by notable institutional changes to the EU institutions including a newly elected European Parliament and freshly appointed Commission, with some expected loss of impetus given that these EU institutions would need time to bed in. Last but not least, the Swedish Presidency – despite being in close contact with the Czechs during their prior Presidency (see Král, 2009, p. 30) – also had to take over from a Czech outfit that had been somewhat disadvantaged by domestic political changes in the Czech Republic during their respective Presidential term (see Beneš and Karlas, this volume). There was a risk that any kind of aspirational list of Swedish Presidential priorities could be seriously undermined by the not ideal, rather unstable and largely external circumstances surrounding the Presidency.

II. The Priorities of the 2009 Swedish EU Council Presidency

As a means of demonstrating its more pro-European outlook in comparison with its Social Democratic government predecessors, Reinfeldt's government expressed in its Presidency priorities a (somewhat rhetorical) commitment to handle the 'big' issues affecting Europe today, including that the EU 'must deal with the economic crisis and unemployment, but also unite the world to tackle climatic change'. The Swedes argued in their Work Programme that the Presidency was 'ready to take on the challenge' (Regeringen, 2009, p. 2) in order to demonstrate to others that, as Reinfeldt admitted, they may have 'woken up late, but we have worked hard to catch up' (Reinfeldt, 2009, p. 4). The Presidency's Work Programme identified six rather wide-ranging political priorities.

'Institutional and Constitutional Questions' – New Parliament, Commission, Referendum and Treaty

The Work Programme specifically acknowledged that the Presidency would 'be affected by special institutional conditions' (Regeringen, 2009, p. 10). In short, the priority of the Presidency was to recognize, that, after fresh elections to the European Parliament in June, and the appointment of the new Commission by October, the Union 'must create good conditions' so that the practical application – if then ratified – of the Treaty of Lisbon would be 'smooth and effective from the very beginning' (Regeringen, 2009, p. 10). This was, of course, a rather coded way of stating that one of the Presidency objectives was to secure the ratification of the new Treaty itself. This was intended to reduce the likelihood of any loss of impetus being caused by the fact that two of the major EU institutions would be renewing their composition during the Swedes' brief six-month Presidency. As Reinfeldt himself noted, the Swedish Presidency 'has no time to wait'.[1]

'Economy and Employment'

Here the Swedish Presidency asserted that the 'EU must emerge from the economic crisis in a stronger position' (Regeringen, 2009, p. 2) and wished to promote 'a common capacity for action in both the financial and economic fields and in the labour market' in order to further stimulate economic recovery. In practice, this translated into a rather more demure commitment to work towards a common joint EU position ahead of the G20 meetings that were to discuss the role and resources of international financial institutions, and rather more vague commitments 'to reach agreement on a new supervisory structure' to promote stability in the international financial system and secure more stringent international financial rules (Regeringen, 2009, p. 4). Similarly, the Presidency intended 'to lay the foundation for the next strategy for sustainable growth and jobs' – in other words, the successor to the EU's rather discredited Lisbon Strategy that was to be agreed during the 2010 Spanish Presidency.

'Climate Change'

Here the Presidency priorities were almost preordained given agreement to hold an international conference under the auspices of the UN Framework Convention on Climate Change in Copenhagen in December. Nevertheless, whilst the Work Programme remained careful to outline the complexity of the issues confronting the Presidency, the Swedes proclaimed that their 'most

---

[1] Taken from a discussion between the author and Prime Minister Fredrik Reinfeldt, Karlstad University, Sweden (7 December 2009).

important objective is to lead the EU, and together with other parties, to agree an international climate agreement at the meeting in Copenhagen' (Regeringen, 2009, p. 6). Yet, the attitude of the Swedish government, and the prime minister himself, went beyond this in consistently stressing that successful agreement at Copenhagen would require major emission reductions embodied in a very serious commitment by international parties to making this work'.[2] As Reinfeldt (2009, p. 5) commented, 'the journey from Kyoto to Copenhagen must go from a coalition of the willing to the responsibility of all'.

The Stockholm Programme

With this priority, the Swedish Presidency sought the EU's adoption of 'a new strategic work programme for the entire policy area' (Regeringen, 2009, p. 7) of EU co-operation in justice and home affairs (JHA) specifying EU measures for 2010–14 in the areas of police, border and customs issues, legal matters and asylum, migration and visa policy (see also Monar's contribution to this volume). In practice, this new Programme was to replace the prior Hague Programme (2004–09), but in many ways, there was only a limited opportunity to put a Swedish mark on it. Such prospects seemed good since the Stockholm Programme was not designed to be legally binding upon Member States, contained political goals that had to be transformed into future specific measures, and the Swedes would steer the final stages of the Programme to agreement (Langdal and von Sydow, 2009b, p. 11).

According to the Work Programme, 'the vision for the work with the Stockholm Programme is a more secure and open Europe where the rights of individuals are safeguarded' (Regeringen, 2009, p. 7). In particular, the Swedish government was a strong proponent of a common asylum system and an enhanced framework for increased burden-sharing, especially since Sweden had been one of the largest recipients of asylum-seekers in the EU over the last decades. Nevertheless, the fact that the primary task for the Presidency was to lead negotiations on common positions relating to a programme that had already undergone public consultation in September 2008 and a Commission Communication in May 2009, offered some potential for the Swedes to have an impact. Yet, in practice, the JHA field incorporates many controversial subject areas in which agreement can be problematic. Indeed, the Swedish government was itself highly sensitive regarding the issue of surveillance and file-monitoring having sparked controversy in Swedish domestic debates in recent years. The reality was that many expected the Stockholm Programme to be agreed during the Presidency, although the

---

[2] Taken from a discussion between the author and Prime Minister Fredrik Reinfeldt, Karlstad University, Sweden (7 December 2009).

real benchmarks for success would come later when and if the degree of consensus behind the Programme that would emerge could facilitate the translation of the Stockholm goals into practical measures.

EU Strategy for the Baltic Sea

In this area – one where Sweden had traditionally been a champion in EU circles (see Miles and Sundelius, 2000; Bengtsson, 2009), the Presidency sought to 'develop the EU's macro-regional co-operation' through the adoption of a specific EU Strategy for the Baltic Sea that 'will contribute to a cleaner sea and make the region more economically dynamic' (Regeringen, 2009, p. 8). In particular, the strategy focused upon addressing a series of issues affecting a region where eight of the principal nine members were also EU Member States, and thus there was deemed potential for handling regional issues such as environmental degradation, enhancing the region's growth potential and negating the impacts of the financial crisis on the region, as well as cross-border crime through increased co-ordination of maritime surveillance. Of course, it was more or less guaranteed that the adoption of this policy area would be successful given that a substantial number of the Member States had a direct stake in the adoption of the Baltic Sea Strategy. Nevertheless, there is more to this than meets the eye. First, by adopting a specific Baltic Sea Strategy, this will have direct implications for other 'more inclusive' EU frameworks, where, more specifically, the Russian Federation enjoys participation rights based on principles of equality, such as the revised EU Northern Dimension, and more northern regional interests such as the Barents-Arctic region have a enhanced profile. For the Presidency, success was formal adoption by the EU during its tenure, yet, for most analysts, the value-added success of the Strategy will lie in the response of the Russians to this initiative (Bengtsson, 2009, p. 8).

The EU, its Neighbourhood and the World

This declared policy priority illustrates, above all, the nebulous aspirations of the declared policy priorities of the 2009 Presidency since the aim was, rather laudably, to 'continue to work to strengthen the EU as a global actor with a clear agenda for peace, development, democracy and human rights' (Regeringen, 2009, p. 9). Although specific reference was made to the European Neighbourhood Policy, the transatlantic partnership and the implementation of the Eastern Partnership, the main practical area where any kind of success could be judged related to the enlargement process: in particular, in making progress with accession negotiations with Croatia and Turkey, as well as making further progress in the EU integration process with the countries of the Western Balkans. However, in this context, the inclusion of such a 'belts and braces' policy priority signifies a departure from the approach taken during the 2001 Swedish Presidency where attempts were made not to include such vague policy priorities (see Miles, 2002c). For some, such as Prime Minister Reinfeldt, the inclusion of such a policy priority would confirm Sweden's reputation as an 'honest broker Presidency';[3] yet, for many analysts, the ambiguities associated with this particular priority also implied a higher political risk that it would be harder for the prime minister to demonstrate practical success with it.

Overall then, the Swedish 2009 Presidency resisted the temptation to adopt a similar conceptual approach to the 2001 Presidency in spite of the Social Democratic opposition's suggestion for a '3 "S's" ' (this time – Sustainability, Security and Solidarity). This time, rather, the Swedish government talked of 'themes' and 'deliverables' and suggested rather broad, if somewhat nebulous, priorities (Langdal and von Sydow, 2009a, p. 1).

To some extent, this was the only viable strategy since the Czech Presidency adopted a '3 "E's" ' approach to highlight the Czech priorities (see Beneš and Karlas, this volume). Nonetheless, it also represented an attempt by the (then) reasonably new non-socialist Alliance government to set this Swedish Presidency apart from the legacy of the prior Social Democratic government-led preparations for the 2001 EU Council Presidency. As the Swedish minister for Europe, Cecilia Malmström commented at the time of the launch of the Swedish Presidency's Work Programme, 'Now it is Sweden's turn to wear the captain's armband. Our ambition is to achieve results on a range of issues with the whole of Europe's best interests in mind' (Regeringen, 2009, p. 11). This was a-not-so-subtle domestic message to all Swedes that the Alliance could prepare and achieve a similarly successful Swedish EU Council Presidency by an, at least officially, different route.

III. Achievements of the Swedish Presidency: Subject To Imbalances?

As Langdal (2009, p. 1) concludes, the Swedish EU Council Presidency 'delivered few surprises, pleasant or otherwise', and views on its success have been somewhat mixed. One leading commentator, Mats Engström, for example, judged Sweden's 'low-profile' Presidency to be 'effective, but not exciting' (Engström, 2009). To some extent, this could be a result of the ambiguous and largely aspirational tone of the Presidency's own outlined policy priorities. Its unbalanced mix of laudable and broad declared

---

[3] Taken from a discussion between the author and Prime Minister Fredrik Reinfeldt, Karlstad University, Sweden (7 December 2009).

aspirations with much more low-key actual policy deliverables gave the impression from the very start that the Swedes might be suffering from a case 'of talking big, but acting little'.

However, if a much more pragmatic attitude prevails – something rather similar to the way that the Swedish political elite approached their Presidency in practice – then a more measured appraisal can be offered. What seems clear is that, for the most part, any memory of success of the Swedish Presidency, when viewed in retrospect, will be derived from the fact that the Presidency was successful in driving several key constitutional and policy packages to final agreement, rather than for more detailed policy initiation and implementation.

First among these is that it can be concluded that – at least regards institutional and constitutional questions – the Swedish Presidency contributed to the successful ratification and entry into force of the Lisbon Treaty during its Presidential term (see Dinan in this volume). Although the Presidency's formal role was of course limited by the fact that it was reliant upon the Treaty's approval in the Irish referendum (which was achieved) on 2 October, and the positive verdicts of both the German (30 June) and Czech Constitutional Courts. Nevertheless, the quiet diplomacy of the Swedish Presidency was very important at critical junctures during the autumn of 2009 (Langdal, 2009). In particular, Reinfeldt was especially effective when steering discussions during and around the European Council meeting in placing pressure on the Czech president, Václav Klaus, to finally give his assent to the Lisbon Treaty, after he had raised consistent concerns about the relationship between the Beneš Decrees and the Charter of Fundamental Rights attached to the Lisbon Treaty (see Král, 2009, pp. 32–3). Equally, the Presidency also deserves credit in its steering of the rapid implementation of the Treaty on 1 December 2009 after the solutions to ratification issues were found. As Langdal (2009, p. 2) notes, 'preparing for a possible implementation of the Lisbon treaty had kept many civil servants and ministers busy since before the inception of the Presidency and most of the necessary spadework was successfully completed by the end of November'.

However, possibly less successful was the handling of the appointment of personalities to the new flagship posts created by the newly ratified Lisbon Treaty. Although the European Parliament delayed the reappointment of Barroso as Commission President for a few months (from July to September), there was never any real doubt surrounding his reappointment, However, the Union came in for widespread criticism regarding the handling and then appointment of the new President for the European Council and the High Representative for Foreign Affairs and Security Policy. Although the Presidency avoided, for the most part, protracted negotiations on the appointees, the

Swedes were criticized, along with other European leaders, for not being more forthright in ensuring agreement involving more higher-profile candidates. In fact, the Presidency let France, Germany and the UK take the lead and 'watched the show' (Kaczyński, 2009, p. 21). The eventual appointees – Herman von Rompuy as the President and Catherine Ashton as the High Representative – neither of which are exactly top-ranking politicians in their own respective countries, let alone across the EU, may have been achieved with unanimity among the EU-27 and, indeed, reflected a fair balance of party affiliations and from small and large Member States, yet were hardly the type of figures that many in the EU would have liked to have seen appointed to these new senior posts created by the new Treaty (see Barber's contribution to this volume).

Overall, the Swedish Presidency seemed unwilling on the institutional and constitutional questions to go the extra mile in seeking more risky but more ambitious solutions and as Langdal (2009, p. 2) neatly puts it, 'did not really capture the imagination of the Swedish government and in all they were probably seen more as an inconvenience than an opportunity'.

Turning to the Economy and Employment brief, the Presidency was responsible for some general progress, most notably agreement in the Council (2 December) on a new structure for financial oversight, aiming to create three new authorities for the supervision of financial services in the EU. There was also some general agreement on the principles underpinning fiscal exit strategies for those Member States using extraordinary measures in the finan-cial markets, with an emphasis on their phasing out. In particular, a loose agreement was brokered by the Presidency which prescribed that subject to self-sustained recovery, fiscal consolidation would begin in 2011, and that consolidation should go beyond a benchmark of 0.5 per cent per year. In addition, progress on the EU 2020 Strategy – to be agreed under the later Spanish Presidency – was made, although the practical impact is hard to quantify (Langdal, 2009, p. 3). Overall, general progress was made on secur-ing broad agreements even if the practical measures were much less distinct or often impressive on closer inspection.

A similar appraisal seems pertinent when considering the Presidency's performance as regards climate change. After the 'big words' of the Work Programme, the Presidency spent most of its time trying to lower expectations as regards achieving a comprehensive, legally binding deal at Copenhagen (Langdal and von Sydow, 2009b, p. 9). A healthy dose of political realism was introduced into Presidency documentation as the Copenhagen summit came ever nearer. There were some notable successes. The Presidency met one of its principal objectives in, for the most part, ensuring that the Union main-tained internal EU co-ordination and common positions on many complex issues in the context of difficult underlying financial conditions.

In addition, the Presidency secured a better than expected financing deal distributing costs for a climatic change deal at the European Council in December 2009, taking account of the positions of less prosperous states (see Král, 2009, p. 34), with the EU pledging €2.4 billion a year. The Swedes set a good example by being the fourth largest contributors to the package.

Nevertheless, the general reaction to the outcome of Copenhagen and thereby the performance of the Presidency was far from optimal. The Swedes came in for criticism for not helping to ensure that no legally binding deal was struck which would commit the countries to meet the 2°C target and the lack of inclusion of a timeline for implementation. The Swedish environmental minister herself labelled it as 'a disaster',[4] others as a 'negotiation failure',[5] while the European Environmental Bureau (EEB) remained 'disappointed' about the overall performance of the Presidency in the environmental sphere (European Environmental Bureau, 2009). As John Hontelez, EEB Secretary-General commented in December 2009, 'Clearly the biggest disappointment was how the EU got itself sidelined in Copenhagen, lacking needed leadership, a combination of poor management of its international relations and an unconvincing internal climate/energy package' (European Environmental Bureau, 2009).

We see a similar profile as regards the Stockholm Programme. Clearly the adoption of the Stockholm Programme, at the JHA Council meeting (30 November–1 December) was a big achievement since a framework is now agreed for this policy area. Perhaps the most notable feature as regards the Swedish Presidency was the agreement to at least attempt to complete a common asylum system by 2012; a major interest of the Swedish government in the face of large waves of recent immigration applications (Langdal and von Sydow, 2009b, p. 11). However, the ambition of the Swedish Presidency to safeguard the rights of individuals and prioritize human rights was not perhaps as fully realized as the Swedes would have hoped (Langdal, 2009, p. 3) in spite of the Council decision highlighting that the Council's 'priority for the coming years will be to focus on the interests and needs of citizens' (European Council, 2009, p. 3). In particular, the Presidency attracted criticism for not addressing the complex relationship between respect for human rights and the demands of the state for surveillance systems (Langdal, 2009, p. 3).

Of course, it was certainly expected that adoption by the EU of a Baltic Sea Strategy would be a 'safe bet' for the Swedish Presidency and so it was in that the Union agreed its first macro-regional strategy under its auspices (Bengtsson, 2009). Yet, again the focus was on the adoption itself rather than

---

[4] *European Voice*, 22 December 2009.
[5] *European Voice*, 22 January 2010.

the limited and somewhat toothless detailed measures of the Strategy. Although the Strategy was widely regarded as relevant and relatively coherent, the usual criticisms of EU Strategies – namely the lack of appreciation of perspectives of external partners, in this case, north-west Russia, and the lack of dedicated additional funding and resources to turn the Strategy into concrete actions – were evident once again (see Bengtsson, 2009).

In the final area – where vagueness and ambiguity were inherent from the Work Programme itself – namely 'the EU, its Neighbourhood and the World', it was very much a case of no news is good news. In one sense, the Swedish Presidency benefited from being a lucky Presidency in that it did not have to handle an unexpected international crisis (see Herz, 2009). Overall, the work of the diplomatic corps of the Swedish Permanent Representation to the EU was regarded as 'exemplary' and, under its auspices, progress was made on the EU Battle Groups (BGs) (see Herz, 2009) and on the External Action Service related to the Lisbon Treaty's adoption.

The enlargement portfolio was actually 'an important success story for the Presidency' (Engström, 2009, p. 2). Steady progress was also made with the Croatian accession negotiations, and the environmental chapter in the Turkish equivalent negotiations was opened (see Whitman and Juncos, this volume). New applications for membership were welcomed from Iceland and Serbia. Yet, in contrast to the 2001 experience, when progress in the enlargement negotiations was presented as a central aspect of the Swedish Presidential notions of success, during the 2009 Presidency these were presented as a much more low-key affair. In the case of the western Balkans, the Presidency also contributed to agreement on 19 December on visa-free access to the EU for Serbs and the citizens of Montenegro and Macedonia (Langdal and von Sydow, 2009b, p. 12). A free trade agreement was also secured with South Korea. However, the failure to make significant progress with the Doha Round, which lay largely outside the control of the Swedes, was an unfortunate blip for the Presidency in terms of its ascribed policy priorities in its Work Programme (Langdal, 2009, p. 4).

Conclusions

The 2009 Swedish Presidency had the potential to be remembered for something. After all, it was, during its six months, the last to be held under the old Nice Treaty rules, and with the coming into force of the Treaty of Lisbon rules in December, the first to be undertaken under the new rules as well.

The reality is that the 'smooth' Presidency (Langdal and von Sydow, 2009b, p. 13) achieved many of its pragmatic aims – yet the original adoption of a broad, ambiguous Work Programme prior to the Presidency meant there was always a risk that there would be a mismatch with the low-key diplomatic style of the Swedes. As the last of the 'old' pre-Lisbon Treaty Presidencies, the Swedish experience illustrates that, in order to be successful in a diplomatically complex EU-27, any Presidency had to be rather low key in order to ensure final agreement. Possibilities for national 'tweaking' (see Haughton, 2010) of EU agendas to reflect the national preferences of the Presidency country had become very limited in an EU of 27 Member States by 2010. The cost for the Swedes was that, beyond the successful preference of securing agreement on key frameworks, most of all, the Lisbon Treaty, the 2009 Swedish Presidency will, rightly or wrongly, be hardly remembered for anything else. Indeed, with the introduction of two new EU political leadership positions via the Lisbon Treaty, the likelihood is that it will be even more the case for respective Presidencies in a post-Lisbon European Union.

References

Bengtsson, R. (2009) 'An EU Strategy for the Baltic Sea Region: Good Intentions Meet Complex Challenges'. European Policy Analysis Report, Issue 9, Swedish Institute for European Policy Studies, Stockholm.

Centre for European Reform (CER) (2009) *The Swedish EU Presidency* (London: Centre for European Reform).

Elgström, O. (2002a) 'Dull but Successful – the Swedish Presidency'. *The European Union: Annual Review of the EU 2001/2002*, pp. 45–8.

Elgström, O. (2002b) 'Evaluating the Swedish Presidency'. *Co-operation and Conflict*, Vol. 37, No. 4, pp. 183–89.

Engström, M. (2009) 'The Swedish Presidency: Effective, but not Exciting'. Available at «http://matsengstrom.wordpress.com/2009/12/14/effective-but-not-exciting».

European Council (2009) 'The Stockholm Programme – an Open and Secure Europe Serving and Protecting the Citizens'. Council of the European Union, Brussels, 2 December.

European Environmental Bureau (EEB) (2009) 'EEB Disappointed about Overall Performance of Swedish Presidency'. Press Release, 23 December, EEB, Brussels. Available at «http://www.eeb.org/index.cfm/news-events/eeb-disapponted».

Haughton, T. (2010) 'Vulnerabilities, Accession Hangovers and the Presidency Role: Explaining New EU Member States' Choices for Europe'. Centre for European Studies Central and Eastern European Working Paper Series 68 (Harvard: Centre for European Studies). Available at «www.ces.fes.harvard.edu/publications».

Herz, J. (2009) 'ESDP and the Swedish Presidency'. *European Security Review*, No. 47, December (Brussels: International Security Information Service [ISIS Europe]). Available at «http://www.isis-europe.org».

Kaczyński, P.M. (2009) 'The Brussels Perspective on the Swedish Presidency'. In Langdal, F. and von Sydow, G. (2009) (eds) *The Swedish Presidency: European Perspectives*, 2009:3op (Stockholm: Swedish Institute for European Policy Studies).

Král, D. (2009) 'Next One in the Relay: A View of the Swedish EU Presidency from Prague'. In Langdal, F. and von Sydow, G. (2009) (eds) *The Swedish Presidency: European Perspectives*, Report 2009: 3op (Stockholm: Swedish Institute for European Policy Studies).

Langdal, F. (2009) 'An Evaluation of the Swedish Presidency: Difficult Setting, Pragmatic Style and Mixed Results' (Madrid: Elcano Royal Institute). Available at «http://www.realinstitutoelcano.org/wps/portal/rielcano_eng».

Langdal, F. and von Sydow, G. (2008) 'The 2009 Swedish EU Presidency – Possible Policy Priorities?' European Policy Analysis Report, Issue 14, Swedish Institute for European Policy Studies, Stockholm.

Langdal, F. and von Sydow, G. (2009a) 'The 2009 Swedish EU Presidency: The Setting, Priorities and Roles'. European Policy Analysis Report, Issue 7, Swedish Institute for European Policy Studies, Stockholm.

Langdal, F. and von Sydow, G. (eds) (2009b) *The Swedish Presidency: European Perspectives*, Report 2009: 3op (Stockholm: Swedish Institute for European Policy Studies).

Miles, L. (2002a) 'Enlargement: From the Perspective of Fusion'. *Co-operation and Conflict*, Vol. 37, No. 4, pp. 190–8.

Miles, L. (2002b) 'Reflections and Perspectives'. *Co-operation and Conflict*, Vol. 37, No. 4, pp. 227–31.

Miles, L. (2002c) 'Are the Swedes "Unofficial Fusionists?" '. *Current Politics and Economics of Europe*, Vol. 11, No. 2, pp. 131–46.

Miles, L. (2005) *Fusing with Europe? Sweden in the European Union* (Aldershot: Ashgate).

Miles, L. and Sundelius, B. (2000) ' "EU Icing on a Baltic Cake": Swedish Policy Towards the Baltic Sea and EU Northern Dimension'. In Miles, L. (ed.) *Sweden and the European Union Evaluated* (London: Continuum).

Regeringen (2009) 'Work Programme for the Swedish Presidency of the EU: 1 July–31 December 2009'. (Stockholm: Regeringen). Available at «http://www.sweden.gov.se/content/1/c6/08/93/60/22265db4.pdf».

Reinfeldt, F. (2009) Speech by the Prime Minister before the European Parliament. Strasbourg, 15 July.

Tallberg, J. (ed.) (2001) *När Europa kom till Sverige. Ordförandeskapet i EU 2001* (Stockholm: SNS Förlag).

Institutions and Governance: A New Treaty, a Newly Elected Parliament and a New Commission

DESMOND DINAN
George Mason University

Introduction

Elections for the European Parliament (EP) and the nomination of a new European Commission made 2009 a particularly important year with regard to European Union institutions and governance. More significant than these five-yearly events, however, was the long-delayed ratification and implementation of the Lisbon Treaty. In June 2009, EU leaders approved a Decision 'on the concerns of the Irish people on the Treaty of Lisbon', which they annexed to the European Council conclusions. They also agreed that 'at the time of the conclusion of the next accession Treaty [. . .] the provisions of the annexed Decision' would be included 'in a Protocol to be attached [. . .] to the Treaty on the European Union and the Treaty on the Functioning of the European Union' (Council, 2009a). The purpose of the promised Protocol was to facilitate a second referendum in Ireland on the Lisbon Treaty and to help ensure a successful outcome. The Irish government soon announced that the referendum would take place on 2 October.

The prospect of a favourable result looked bright, thanks to the global economic crisis, which hit Ireland particularly hard. Although ratifying the Treaty would not make a material difference, it would send a positive signal to international investors and affirm Ireland's good fortune to be in the euro area at a time of global financial turmoil. Armed with legally binding guarantees from the EU to allay the concerns of many who opposed the Treaty in the first referendum, and the decision by the European Council to retain one commissioner per Member State provided that the Lisbon Treaty entered into force, the Irish government conducted a more vigorous campaign the second time around in an effort to increase the turnout and change the minds of as many naysayers as possible. As expected, the Treaty passed by an impressive majority of 67 per cent, with a 59 per cent turnout.

Ireland was not the only country not to have ratified before the end of 2009. President Lech Kaczyński of Poland, who strongly opposed the Treaty, reluctantly signed the instrument of ratification on 10 October. Czech president Václav Klaus, an ardent Eurosceptic, refused to sign the instrument of ratification until the last possible moment. Klaus raised an eleventh-hour concern that the treaty could open the way for property claims by ethnic Germans expelled from Czechoslovakia after World War II. EU leaders appeased Klaus by giving the Czech Republic an opt-out from the Charter of Fundamental Rights. Having milked the ratification procedure for all it was worth, Klaus finally signed on 3 November, allowing the Treaty to come into effect on 1 December 2009.

Germany's parliament had voted in good time to ratify the Treaty, but the president was unable to sign the instrument of ratification pending a ruling by the Constitutional Court on the compatibility of the Treaty with Germany's Basic Law. The Court finally ruled in June 2009 that the Lisbon Treaty was indeed compatible, subject to a change in Germany on the role of parliament in EU decision-making. Although proponents of the Treaty breathed a sigh of relief, a closer look at the lengthy court ruling revealed that it raised several red flags about the direction of European integration (see Dougan, this volume). In particular, the court emphasized the limits of EU competence and the existence of a 'structured democratic deficit' which only national parliaments, not the EP, could possibly close (Federal Constitutional Court, 2009). If anything, the ruling should have reassured Eurosceptics as to the limits of European integration.

This article begins with a comment on the lengthy treaty reform process, the significance of the Lisbon Treaty and the steps taken in 2009 to prepare for its implementation. The article then looks at the conduct and outcome of the EP elections, followed by the nomination of the second Barroso Commission. A final section examines the implications of the financial crisis and economic recession for EU governance and institutions.

I. The Lisbon Treaty

The Lisbon Treaty, the latest and probably the last major revision of the foundational treaties, is highly consequential for the EU. It was also politically costly, having taken eight years to complete, beginning with the Constitutional Convention and ending with the protracted ratification procedure. The saga of the Lisbon Treaty shows how fraught the process of treaty reform has become and the touchiness of European integration for politicians and the public alike. The background to the Treaty was the determination of EU leaders – in national governments and EU institutions – to streamline the EU; revise its institutional arrangements; strengthen its decision-making capacity; make it a more credible international actor; clarify and in some cases extend its scope; and make the EU more accountable, appealing and comprehensible to its citizens. EU leaders were reacting to the organization's manifest inadequacies in the face of growing public disillusionment with European integration; a membership that had more than doubled in less than 15 years; rapid socio-economic change; and a radically altered international environment.

Although a tall order, the rationale for a new round of reform seemed reasonable, even sensible. Yet the process became extraordinarily prolonged and painful, while the outcome – the Treaty itself – was dense and difficult to read. Clearly, the saga and substance of the Lisbon Treaty and the Constitutional Treaty before it reveal much about the nature of the EU more than 60 years after the first, tentative steps toward 'ever closer union'. Treaty reform – changing the rules of what the EU does and how the EU does it – had become exceedingly difficult as governments, keenly aware of the potential losses and gains and of the high domestic political stakes, paid extremely close attention to the form and scope of European integration.

With the intensification of European integration, the EU's impact on policy and politics has become far more conspicuous in everyday life. Referendums on treaty reform give people an opportunity to express their concerns about European integration and dissatisfaction with the EU by either voting against the proposed change or not voting at all. Not that referendums on treaty change always end in defeat (voters in Luxembourg and Spain approved the Constitutional Treaty). Nevertheless fear of defeat has made governments wary of putting painstakingly negotiated treaty changes before the electorate, and fear of challenges before national supreme courts has further curbed governments' appetites for far-reaching treaty reform.

Given the difficulties inherent in the reform process, the Lisbon Treaty is far from ideal. Nevertheless, as noted in the 2007 *JCMS Annual Review*, it represents a definite improvement for the EU. The revised foundational treaties – the Treaty on European Union and the Treaty on the Functioning of the European Union (formerly the Treaty Establishing the European Community) – are long and complex, yet the EU that they describe is more coherent and comprehensible than the pre-Lisbon EU. The treaty unequivocally states that the EU is rooted in democracy, the rule of law and respect for human rights and fundamental freedoms; its organizing principles are conferred powers, subsidiarity, proportionality and co-operation between Member States; and its competences *vis-à-vis* national competences – exclusive, shared or supporting – are clearly spelled out. The pillar structure is gone, but different decision-making procedures remain for foreign and security policy. The confusing distinction between Union and Community is abolished, with the word 'Union' replacing 'Community' throughout the text. The EU finally acquires legal personality.

The Lisbon Treaty strikes a reasonable balance between institutional efficiency and democratic legitimacy. The double majority system for qualified majority voting, due to come into effect in 2014, is more equitable than its predecessor, which was based on a relatively arbitrary allocation of votes per Member State. The EP, the EU's only directly elected body, has additional budgetary authority and a greater legislative role, thanks to the widespread applicability of what is now called the ordinary legislative procedure. Keeping the Commission at one member per Member State – a late revision brought about by Ireland's initial rejection of the Treaty – is arguably good for the EU. Perhaps it is better to have a Commission in which every country is represented than a smaller Commission from which, at any given time, some countries are bound to feel alienated. National parliaments acquire a formal role in the EU legislative process as gatekeepers of the subsidiarity principle, a function that will be interesting to observe in the years ahead.

The institutional innovations in the Treaty portend an improvement in the effectiveness of EU policy, especially in the areas of external relations and justice and home affairs. The treaty recasts the balance among the institutions, with the European Council clearly in the ascendant. Apart from being given responsibility for decision-making in specific, politically sensitive areas other than law-making, the creation of the full-time Presidency is particularly significant for the future of the European Council. Although the Treaty says little about the powers or prerogatives of the new office, experience suggests that it will evolve into an important and influential post. Overall, the Lisbon Treaty reinforces the trend within the EU toward the emergence of a commanding European Council, a confident Council and Parliament sharing legislative responsibility, and a politically constrained Commission.

Implementing the Treaty

EU institutions had begun preparatory work in 2008 on implementing the Lisbon Treaty, but acted discretely pending the outcome of the second Irish referendum. Preparations for the entry into force of the Treaty became a priority of the Swedish Council Presidency in late 2009. At its regularly scheduled meeting soon after the second referendum, the European Council took note of the preparatory work and endorsed the Presidency's report on guidelines for the External Action Service, a particularly important innovation that was already causing friction among Member States as well as between the Council, Commission and EP.

As noted by Tony Barber elsewhere in the *Annual Review*, national leaders reached a political agreement on 19 November 2009 to name Herman van Rompuy as the first full-time President of the European Council and Catherine Ashton as the new High Representative for Foreign Affairs and Security Policy. Two weeks later, on 1 December, the day on which the Treaty entered into force, the European Council formally elected van Rompuy and appointed Ashton, and also appointed Pierre de Boissieu as Secretary-General of the Council for the period from December 2009 until June 2011. De Boissieu, formerly France's Permanent Representative in Brussels, had been Deputy Secretary-General to Javier Solana, who had held the combined positions of Council Secretary-General and High Representative for the Common Foreign and Security Policy since 1999. With the Secretary-Generalship now separated from the High Representative's office, de Boissieu, who under Solana had been the *de facto* Secretary-General, could formally assume that position.

At the end of 8 December 2009 the Council of Ministers took a formal decision, based on a political agreement among national leaders, that Uwe Corsepius, head of the European Policy Division in the German Chancellery and a close adviser to Chancellor Angela Merkel, would take over from de Boissieu (Council, 2009b). This was a good example of a Franco–German deal on top-level EU appointments, which the other leaders had little choice but to accept.

In addition to electing van Rompuy and appointing Ashton, the European Council took formal decisions on 1 December concerning its rules of procedure and the exercise of the Presidency of the Council. At the same time, the Council of Ministers took a raft of decisions relating to Council formations, the rotating Presidency, and the conditions of employment of the European Council President, the High Representative, and the Council Secretary-General. The Lisbon Treaty established two Council configurations, General Affairs (chaired by the rotating Presidency) and Foreign Affairs (chaired by the High Representative), and allowed for additional formations (chaired by the rotating Presidency) to be established along sectoral lines. In effect, EU leaders retained the existing Council formations (see Table 1).

On 10–11 December 2009, the European Council met for the first time following implementation of the Lisbon Treaty. Van Rompuy was present but not in the chair, national leaders having previously decided that Sweden would chair the European Council until the end of its Presidency.

Table 1: Council Configurations

---

1. General affairs*
2. Foreign affairs**
3. Economic and financial affairs (including budget)
4. Justice and home affairs (including civil protection)
5. Employment, social policy, health and consumer affairs
6. Competitiveness (internal market, industry and research) (including tourism)
7. Transport, telecommunications and energy
8. Agriculture and fisheries
9. Environment
10. Education, youth and culture (including audiovisual affairs)

Source: Decision of the Council (General Affairs) of 1 December 2009 establishing the list of Council configurations, *Official Journal*, L 315/46, 1 December 2009.
Notes: * Established by Article 16(6), second subparagraph, of the Treaty on European Union.
** Established by Article 16(6), third subparagraph, of the Treaty on European Union.

Nevertheless van Rompuy spoke at dinner about his plans for the European Council and the entire Council apparatus, suggesting that he would attempt to streamline procedures and greatly improve efficiency. By virtue of convening under the rules of the Lisbon Treaty, which restricts the European Council to the heads of state or government and the Commission President, plus the High Representative, the December summit was the first to which foreign ministers were not automatically invited. This seemed to come as a shock to many of them (European Policy Center, 2009).

On 8 December, the newly configured Foreign Affairs Council met for the first time, although the Swedish foreign minister presided (Ashton delayed presiding over the Foreign Affairs Council until January 2010). Having the High Representative chair the Foreign Affairs Council would deprive foreign ministers of the opportunity to represent the EU internationally with regard to foreign and security policy. Similarly, members of the High Representative's office would assume responsibility for chairing the Political and Security Committee, which prepares meetings of the Foreign Affairs Council, and of the foreign affairs working groups. The transition would not be easy for foreign ministers and their officials, especially for the countries coming into the rotating Presidency in 2010, and would likely affect domestic bureaucratic politics with regard to EU policy formulation and representation. Nevertheless the benefits of the new arrangement, in terms of the operation of the European Council and the Council of Ministers and the continuity and consistency of EU foreign, security and defence policy, were manifest and welcome.

In an effort to improve co-ordination among succeeding Presidencies, each country in the Presidency develops a specific six-month work programme within the framework of an 18-month work programme drawn up by a 'trio' of successive Presidency countries. Spain, the first country to hold the Presidency following implementation of the Lisbon Treaty, formed a Presidency trio with its successors, Belgium and Hungary. The three countries published a draft programme in June 2009 of the 'Spanish-Belgian-Hungarian trio presidency', covering the 18-month period January 2010 to June 2011 (Council, 2009c).

II. The European Parliament

The June 2009 elections to the EP took place under the rules of the Nice Treaty, thereby limiting the EP's size to 736 seats rather than the 751 provided for in the Lisbon Treaty. Implementation of the Lisbon Treaty in December 2009 paved the way for 18 additional seats, distributed among 12 Member States, as well as the loss of three of Germany's seats, thereby bringing the EP to 751 members (see Table 2). Because of a political agreement to allow Germany to retain its extra three seats throughout the mandate of the newly elected Parliament, the arrival of the 18 additional members would push the size of the EP to 754, in violation of the Lisbon Treaty. Accordingly, governments would have to amend Protocol 36 on the transitional provisions of the Treaty to enable the new MEPs to take their seats.

There are two methods of treaty reform under the Lisbon Treaty. Both require an intergovernmental conference (IGC) but only in one case – intended for more far-reaching changes – would a Convention have to precede the IGC. In early December 2009, the Spanish government formally proposed a treaty amendment with regard to the size of the EP, which the European Council endorsed. The European Council then requested consultation with the EP on the suggested treaty change and the consent of the EP not to convene a Convention. The EP was unlikely to hold out for a Convention for such a specific treaty change. Regardless of how the change came about, however, the ratification process would probably revive opposition to the Lisbon Treaty and give Eurosceptics another opportunity to rail against the EU.

In its ruling of June 2009 on the Lisbon Treaty, the German Constitutional Court castigated the appropriation of seats in the EP. 'Measured against requirements placed on democracy in states', the court wrote, elections do 'not take due account of equality, and [the EP] is not competent to take authoritative decisions on political direction in the context of the supranational balancing of interest between the states' (Federal Constitutional Court, 2009). In other words, the fact that the EU is not a federation undermines the EP's claim to democratic legitimacy, and even if the EU were a federation a disparity such as one MEP to 66,000 people in Malta and one MEP to 860,000

Table 2: Seats in the European Parliament, 2009–19*

Member State	Population (in millions)**	% of EU	Seats at end of 2004–09 mandate	Seats at start of 2009–14 mandate (Nice)	Transitional arrangement 2010–14	2014–19 mandate (Lisbon)
Germany	82,438	16.73%	99	99	99	96
France	62,886	12.76%	78	72	74	74
United Kingdom	60,422	12.26%	78	72	73	73
Italy	58,752	11.92%	78	72	73	73
Spain	43,758	8.88%	54	50	54	54
Poland	38,157	7.74%	54	50	51	51
Romania	21,61	4.38%	35	33	33	33
Netherlands	16,334	3.31%	27	25	26	26
Greece	11,125	2.26%	24	22	22	22
Portugal	10,57	2.14%	24	22	22	22
Belgium	10,511	2.13%	24	22	22	22
Czech Rep.	10,251	2.08%	24	22	22	22
Hungary	10,077	2.04%	24	22	22	22
Sweden	9,048	1.84%	19	18	20	20
Austria	8,266	1.68%	18	17	19	19
Bulgaria	7,719	1.57%	18	17	18	18
Denmark	5,428	1.10%	14	13	13	13
Slovakia	5,389	1.09%	14	13	13	13
Finland	5,256	1.07%	14	13	13	13
Ireland	4,209	0.85%	13	12	12	12
Lithuania	3,403	0.69%	13	12	12	12
Latvia	2,295	0.47%	9	8	9	9
Slovenia	2,003	0.41%	7	7	8	8
Estonia	1,344	0.27%	6	6	6	6
Cyprus	0,766	0.16%	6	6	6	6
Luxembourg	0,46	0.09%	6	6	6	6
Malta	0,404	0.08%	5	5	6	6
TOTAL	492,881	100.00%	785	736	754	751

Source: Adapted from European Parliament (2007; 2010).
Notes: * For the EU-27, not taking into account post-2010 enlargement.
** Population figures as officially established on 7 November 2006 by the Commission in Doc. 15124/06 on the basis of Eurostat figures.

people in Germany (following implementation of the Lisbon Treaty) would be democratically unsustainable.

If national governments were to abandon the principle of digressive proportionality and simply divide the number of seats in the EP among the entire population, Germany's delegation would completely dominate the EU and some small Member States would have no representation at all. Based on such an allocation, the possibility of Turkey – a country almost as populous as Germany – joining the EU would be even more worrisome for most Member

States. The current arrangement for the distribution of seats in the EP is far from ideal but is politically sustainable – as long as the EP does not continue to argue that it is the epitome of representative democracy in the EU and that giving it more power is the answer to the EU's democratic deficit. The German Constitutional Court demolished that argument, but the EP is unlikely to cease its political posturing.

The 2009 Elections

Although the EP's profile and power have increased greatly since the first elections in 1979, the experience of direct elections themselves – in terms of national political party behaviour and voter turnout – has been hugely disappointing. The EU-wide turnout has declined consistently over time. Voters seem unaware of or unimpressed by the EP's undoubted importance in the EU system. Much to the dismay of EU leaders, most voters continue to view elections for the EP as second-order or even third-order contests, being less salient than national or regional elections.

The turnout in 2009 was a mere 42.9 per cent. Although high by the standards of mid-term US congressional elections (a point that Europeans like to make), it is low by the standards of national elections in the Member States. The result was especially disappointing because of the Commission's and the EP's efforts to generate voter interest, especially in light of the fate of the Constitutional and Lisbon Treaties. More than anything else, the EP wanted to turn the tide of declining turnout and, if possible, break the 50 per cent threshold. As noted in last year's JCMS Annual Review, the EP launched a public relations campaign in 2008 to apprise voters of the institution's relevance. At the same time, leaders of the two main political groups, the European People's Party (EPP) and the Party of European Socialists (PES), sharpened their attacks against each other in order to heighten interest among the electorate. In a further effort to woo voters, the EP highlighted its major accomplishments since the previous elections, notably the enactment of complex legislation on the control of chemical substances, an issue of great environmental and commercial concern; laws making cell phone calls cheaper by capping roaming charges; and an ambitious energy-climate change package.

Whereas most candidates campaigned to some extent on EU issues and proclaimed their political group affiliation, national political parties and issues predominated during the 2009 elections which, as in EP elections past, were really a set of separate national elections. Just as they dominated the European election campaigns, national political parties also dominated the selection of the approximately 9,000 candidates who stood for election to the EP. The European elections became informal referendums on the performance of national governments, especially in coping with the financial crisis and economic recession. Accordingly, the governing parties in France and Poland did well; those in Britain, Greece, Hungary, Ireland and Spain did not. Germans used the European elections to indicate how they would vote in the forthcoming national elections, due three months later (they favoured the Christian Democratic party of Chancellor Merkel).

The Group of the European People's Party-European Democrats EPP-ED), an alliance of Christian Democrats and conservatives, went into the 2009 elections with the largest number of seats (288). Regardless of the vagaries of electoral politics, they were bound to come out of the election with fewer seats for the simple reason that the British Conservatives, the main party in the European Democrats wing of the EPP-ED, had decided before-hand to pull out of the combined political group. The decision was driven by domestic politics – in an effort to appeal to Eurosceptics during his successful campaign to become Conservative Party leader in 2005, David Cameron promised that he would withdraw the Conservatives from a political group whose largest component, the Christian Democrats, was avowedly Euro-federal. Once elected, Cameron seemed far from enthusiastic about carrying through his promise, but did so nevertheless. The formation by the British and other conservatives of a new group (see below) robbed the EPP-ED of its ED wing. With barely disguised relief, the Christian Democrats reverted simply to the EPP group. Moreover, they emerged from the election with the largest number of seats (265) in the EP (see Table 3). The EPP group fits under the umbrella of the transnational European People's Party which, according to its website, has 74 constituent parties from 38 countries; includes 20 government leaders and a majority of commissioners (including the president); and 'is the leading political force on the continent' (European People's Party, 2009).

The PES fared poorly in the elections, having failed to turn voters' concerns about the dire economic situation into strong electoral support. To be more precise, the PES failed to convince voters that their Christian Democratic rivals, being economically more liberal and mostly in government throughout Europe, were to blame for the financial crisis and should not be trusted to put Europe back on its feet. Instead, the Christian Democrats turned the tables by convincing voters that the socialists lacked the experience and ability to right the economy and by casting themselves as best able to defend the much-cherished European social model. Having gone into the elections with 217 MEPs, the PES came out with only 161, albeit in a Parliament with fewer seats to contest. Nonetheless the PES was buoyed by the decision of Italy's Democratic Party, with 21 MEPs, to join forces with it. As a condition of membership, the Democratic Party pressed the PES to change its name to

Table 3: Results of the 2009 European Parliament Elections

Political Group	Abbreviation	No. of Seats
Group of the European People's Party (Christian Democrats)	EPP	265
Group of the Progressive Alliance of Socialists and Democrats in the European Parliament	S&D	184
Group of the Alliance of Liberals and Democrats for Europe	ALDE	84
Group of the Greens/European Free Alliance	Greens/EFA	55
European Conservatives and Reformists Group	ECR	55
Confederal Group of the European United Left – Nordic Green Left	GUE/ NGL	35
Europe of Freedom and Democracy Group	EFD	32
Non-attached	NA	26
TOTAL		**736**

Source: European Parliament, Results of the 2009 European elections available at «http://www.europarl. europa.eu/parliament/archive/elections2009/en/index_en.html».

Note: The EP's rules of procedure and allocation of resources strongly encourages members to join transnational political groups. The rules governing the formation of political groups have changed over the years, in keeping with the changing size and composition of the EP. After the 2009 elections, the minimum number of MEPs allowed to form a political group was 25, from at least seven Member States.

reflect the combined group's broader political base. After some confusion, PES leader Martin Schulz proposed the 'Group of the Progressive Alliance of Socialists and Democrats', which became known as the Socialists and Democrats or the S&D (Parliament.com, 2009). Following the adhesion of two additional MEPs, the group had 184 seats in the newly elected Parliament.

The Group of the Alliance of Liberals and Democrats for Europe (ALDE) fared better in the elections than they had hoped, given the unpopularity of economic liberals during the economic crisis, winning 84 seats. Once again the liberals emerged as the third-largest group, far behind the Christian Democrats and socialists, with MEPs from 19 Member States. The group's new leader is Guy Verhofstadt, a former prime minister of Belgium and an ardent Euro-federalist.

The Group of the Greens/European Free Alliance, a marriage of convenience between the environmentalist Greens and 'representatives of stateless nations and disadvantaged minorities', won 55 seats (Greens/European Free Alliance, 2009). The Greens, a well-organized transnational party and by far the largest component of the group, fared extremely well, winning 48 seats. The group includes a member of Sweden's Pirate Party, whose sole interest is Internet freedom and which came into existence in 2005 to oppose the proposed EU software patent law.

A new group, the European Conservatives and Reformists (ECR), came into existence after the elections with 55 seats, consisting mostly of disaffected conservatives (the former European Democrats). The British Conservative Party has by far the largest contingent (25 members) in the ECR group, which includes Poland's Law and Justice Party and the Czech Republic's Civic Democrats. The ECR oppose Euro-federalism and want fundamental reform of the EU 'to make it more accountable, transparent and responsive to the needs of the people' (European Conservatives and Reformists, 2009). Being in such an openly Eurosceptical group as the ECR demonstrates how far the British Conservatives have veered from mainstream European political opinion. It was difficult for the Conservatives to have been allied with the Christian Democrats, who openly espouse a federal Europe, but it is striking that they have relegated themselves to a small group that includes parties noted for political intolerance and extreme nationalism (Bale *et al.*, 2009).

The European United Left-Nordic Green Left (GUE-NGL) calls itself a 'confederal group' in order to emphasize the autonomy of its constituent national parties. It is a collection of 35 far-leftists who oppose the way in which mainstream European politics, society and economics are organized. The largest constituent party, with eight members, is Germany's *Die Linke*, which includes the remnants of the Communist party of east Germany. The group also includes some high-profile former German social democrats.

Two parliamentary groups could not sustain themselves after the 2009 elections: the Independence/Democracy Group and the Union for Europe of the Nations Group. Many of the remnants of these groups decided to come together in a new formation, the Europe of Freedom and Democracy (EFD) group, with 32 seats. Despite its innocuous name, the group consists largely of virulent Eurosceptics, who want their countries to leave the EU or want the EU to cease to exist. Its members are in the unusual position of serving in a parliament whose legitimacy they reject. The largest and most striking contingent in the group is the UK Independence Party, which won 13 seats in the elections, beating the governing Labour party into third place in Britain (the Conservatives came first).

The EP after the elections also had 26 non-attached MEPs, mostly individuals or a handful of party members whose far-right, racist views were so objectionable that none of the groups would have them. The independents included MEPs in such notorious parties as Britain's National Party, France's National Front and Hungary's Jobbik. By virtue of being non-attached, however, these MEPs have limited access to parliamentary funds and other resources and could never get into leadership positions.

Although organized into political groups, MEPs remain acutely aware of their national identity and allegiance to national political parties. MEPs caucus in national delegations within their respective groups. Obviously, some national delegations are larger and more influential than others. German MEPs comprise the largest national delegations in five of the EP's political groups; they are especially preponderant in the EPP, S&D and Liberal groups. Britain is not represented at all in the EP's largest group, the EPP, and is poorly represented in the second-largest group, the S&D, having only 13 of the group's 184 seats (this reflects the poor showing of Britain's ruling Labour Party in the elections). Most national delegations are concentrated in the EPP and S&D groups, but some are more diffused than others. Spain's is an example of a highly concentrated delegation: of its 50 members, 23 are in the EPP group and 21 in the S&D group. By contrast, the Dutch delegation (25 members) is spread out in all seven groups, and even includes four independents (this reflects the fragmentation of Dutch politics on EU issues).

One of the most striking results of the elections was the failure of Libertas, the anti-Lisbon Treaty movement led by British-born Irish millionaire Declan Ganley, to win more than one seat. Ganley had become prominent by spear-heading the successful campaign against the Treaty in the first Irish referendum in June 2008. Yet the successful Libertas candidate was not Ganley but Philippe de Villiers, whose *Mouvement pour la France* had joined forces with Ganley during the election campaign. The collapse of Libertas, which hoped to become a large, pan-European political group in the EP, reflected dissatisfaction in Ireland and abroad with Ganley as well as the fractiousness of those anti-Lisbon groups throughout the EU not already part of larger political parties or tendencies. Ganley's poor showing in the election was a harbinger of the outcome of the second Irish referendum on the Lisbon Treaty (*Irish Times*, 2009).

New Leadership

As part of a pre-elections pact, the two biggest groups agreed that a member of the EPP would be elected President of the European Parliament in July 2009, with a socialist to follow in December 2011 until June 2014, when the next elections would take place. It was up to the EPP to decide which of its members to put forward for the post. There were two contenders, an Italian and a Pole, both strongly supported by their national governments. Eventually the Italian withdrew and the Pole, Jerzy Buzek, a former prime minister, was elected president.

Buzek's election, which for the first time placed someone from central Europe in a top EU leadership position, was hailed as a breakthrough. Yet it came about as a result of deal making between the EPP and the PES (as it then was) and backroom bargaining among national leaders. Buzek soon proved himself forceful and energetic, especially in presenting the EP's views at the beginning of meetings of the European Council (being a former prime minister among national leaders undoubtedly enhanced his stature).

The outcome of the Presidential election determines the outcome of the elections for other EP leadership positions (except for political group leaders, who are elected by political group members). Although leadership elections are supposedly open, the political groups decide among themselves who gets what. The leadership's composition following the 2009 elections reflected the distribution of seats by political group and national delegation. For instance, the EPP took ten seats on the powerful Conference of Committee Chairs (three German MEPs, three Italian, two French, one Polish and one Spanish).

III. The Commission

There was growing certainty throughout 2009 that José Manuel Barroso would be nominated by the European Council to serve a second term as Commission President and approved by the EP, unless the socialists won a majority in the June elections and confronted the European Council by opposing Barroso, a centre-right politician. Realizing the unlikelihood that they would beat the EPP in the elections, the socialists did not bother to put forward a candidate for Commission President. Most national leaders were lukewarm about Barroso, but agreed unanimously in the European Council in June 2009 that he was 'the person they intend to nominate as President of the European Commission for the period 2009–14', and asked the current and incoming Presidents of the European Council (the prime ministers of the Czech Republic and Sweden) to 'have discussions with the European Parliament in order to determine whether the Parliament is in a position to approve that nomination at its July plenary session' (Council, 2009a). Having become the accidental Commission President for the period 2004–09, Barroso looked set to become the inevitable Commission President for the period 2009–14.

The Lisbon Treaty was not yet in force when Barroso was being reappointed. Nevertheless the EP pressed the European Council for a political agreement to abide by the Lisbon Treaty rules, which call for the European Council, 'taking into account the elections to the European Parliament and after having held the appropriate consultations', to 'propose to the European Parliament a candidate for President of the Commission [. . .] [who] shall be elected by the European Parliament by a majority of its component members'.[1] Given that the EPP, to which Barroso belonged, won the largest

---

[1] Treaty on European Union, Title III, Article 17.7.

number of seats, and that the Council Presidency was having discussions with the EP on Barroso's nomination, the European Council could fairly claim to be acting in the spirit of the Lisbon Treaty.

That did not satisfy some MEPs, especially the socialists and greens, who reviled Barroso for his neo-liberal economic philosophy and his alleged cosiness with big business. Though the socialists were then in the process of divvying up the Presidency of the EP with the EPP, they claimed that pushing through Barroso's candidacy without due consultation with the EP was a violation of democratic principles. Barroso duly developed a set of guidelines for the next mandate, which he presented at meetings with the political groups in early September (Commission, 2009a). The socialists were split along national lines. For instance, the Portuguese delegation generally supported Barroso. In the event, Barroso convincingly won the vote on 16 September, although by a smaller margin than in 2004 (of the 718 MEPs present, 382 voted in favour, 219 voted against and 117 abstained).

Wolfgang Münchau, the influential *Financial Times* columnist, described Barroso as being 'among the weakest Commission presidents ever, a vain man who lacks political courage' (Münchau, 2009). Other prominent critics of Barroso have been kinder in their choice of words but no less fierce in their disparagement of him. Barroso has been widely but unfairly blamed for not having done enough to prevent voters from rejecting the Constitutional Treaty in 2005 and the Lisbon Treaty in 2008, as if he could have changed the minds of people who, often for irrational reasons, deeply dislike the EU and the Commission. More reasonably, Barroso is blamed for having responded slowly and inadequately to the financial crisis of 2007–09. Barroso may indeed have failed to grasp the enormity of the crisis until late 2008, when he finally rallied the Commission and helped put together the Economic Recovery Plan. However, Barroso's initial underestimation of the extent of the crisis was no different from that of many national leaders, and his ability to respond as Commission President was limited by the nature of the office and the preponderance of national governments.

Barroso has been and should remain a competent Commission President; a safe pair of hands at a difficult time for the institution and the EU. He has tried to restore the institution's prominence and sense of purpose. If not resurgent, arguably the Commission under Barroso is as influential as it could possibly be under extremely difficult circumstances. Barroso is adept at presiding over a fractious Commission of 27 members, partly by introducing procedural changes but largely by adopting a more presidential than collegial style. Under his leadership, the Commission has become more accountable and open and more responsive to the needs of citizens. The Barroso Commission has been pragmatic in highlighting selective policy objectives. Aware of the constraints facing the Commission, Barroso is not inclined to tilt at windmills and challenge the predominance of national capitals. Supranationalists are disappointed with what they see as Barroso's subservience to national leaders and unwillingness to reassert the Commission's authority. A more even-handed assessment is that Barroso is doing as much as he can at a time of resurgent intergovernmentalism, compounded by economic uncertainty and grandstanding by the EP.

Commissioners and Portfolios

Governments began to announce their nominees for the new Commission in mid-2009. Domestic political considerations, rather than ability or merit, usually determine a government's choice of nominee for a lucrative and prestigious Commissionership. This was clearly the case in Germany, where Merkel chose Günther Oettinger, the minister-president of Baden-Württemberg, the third-largest state in Germany, as her country's Commissioner. Until his selection, Oettinger was mostly unknown outside Germany and had little experience of the EU. Given his background, Oettinger would likely be a staunch defender of German interests in Brussels. As France's new Commissioner, Sarkozy chose someone with a prominent international profile and considerable EU experience: Michel Barnier, a former foreign minister and a Commissioner for regional policy in the Prodi Commission (1999–2004).

An unprecedented aspect of the selection process for the second Barroso Commission was that, under the terms of the Lisbon Treaty, one of the Commission Vice-Presidents would also be the High Representative for Foreign Affairs and Security, a position that was allocated on the basis of intensive intergovernmental bargaining.[2] The selection of Catherine Ashton for the position took care of Britain's nomination of a Commissioner-designate.

Fourteen of the new Commissioners-designate were holdovers from the first Barroso Commission. The Commission-designate included nine women (one more than in the preceding Commission). Commissioners may be reappointed any number of times. It is not unusual for them to serve two full terms (now ten years); Viviane Reding had already served in two successive Commissions when the government of Luxembourg renominated her in 2009. Reflecting the composition of most national governments at the time of the Commissioners' nomination, a majority of the new Commission-designate came from the centre-right of the political spectrum, which also corresponded with the make-up of the newly elected EP.

---

[2] See Tony Barber's contribution in this volume.

In principle the Commission President is solely responsible for allocating portfolios; in practice, national governments are constantly interfering. Ever since the first enlargement there have been more Commissioners than substantial portfolios, despite a formidable increase in the EU's policy scope. Responding to criticism that some of the portfolios in his first Commission were too insubstantial, and to shifts in policy priorities over the previous few years, Barroso reconfigured a number of portfolios for his second Commission. For instance, Barroso carved a new portfolio, 'Climate Action', out of the old environment portfolio. Barroso also broke up a single portfolio, 'Justice, Freedom and Security', into two portfolios, 'Home Affairs' and 'Justice, Fundamental Rights and Citizenship', in his second Commission.

Similarly, Barroso divided 'Development and Humanitarian Aid' (from his first Commission) into two portfolios, 'Development' and 'International Co-operation, Humanitarian Aid and Crisis Response'. He also moved 'European Neighbourhood Policy' from 'External Relations' to 'Enlargement', external relations being subsumed into the High Representative/Commission Vice-President's responsibilities. Barroso kept a separate portfolio for trade. In his announcement of portfolios for the Commissioners-designate, Barroso noted that the Commissioners for enlargement and European neighbourhood policy, development and international co-operation would work 'in close co-operation with the High Representative/Vice-President in accordance with the treaties' (Commission, 2009b).

It remained to be seen how Barroso, the High Representative and the European Council President would manage EU external representation among themselves. Barroso was the most eager to be in the limelight, in Europe and beyond. For that reason Barroso must have been pleased that the European Council chose such unassuming people as Ashton and van Rompuy to be the first incumbents of the new positions. All three will, literally, be on the stage together at international meetings. The fact that the EU has three external relations representatives, despite the effort to streamline external relations in the Lisbon Treaty, demonstrates the peculiar nature of the EU itself.

Some national governments competed fiercely for particular portfolios. Thus Sarkozy made no secret in 2009 of his determination that France's next Commissioner be allocated the internal market and services portfolio, thereby ensuring that it did not go to an economic liberal and especially a Briton (for Sarkozy the two are synonymous). Given the dearth of weighty portfolios, Barroso could have split internal market and services into two jobs. Instead, he went along with Sarkozy and handed the portfolio to the new French Commissioner. Germany would appear to have lost out in the second Barroso

Commission, as its Commissioner secured the energy portfolio, an important responsibility but not a high-profile Commission job. Barroso juggled the portfolios in his new Commission so that none of the returning Commissioners kept his or her original portfolio (See Table 4).

The Commission comprises about 40 directorates-general and services, corresponding roughly to its activities, responsibilities and organizational needs. The number and names of the directorates-general and services change constantly, especially with the arrival of a new Commission. For instance, reflecting the growing political salience of energy policy, Barroso established a new energy directorate-general in 2009 (previously energy was part of a combined energy and transport directorate-general).

IV. Implications of the Financial Crisis and Economic Recession

The financial crisis and economic recession continued throughout 2009 and put EU solidarity sorely to the test. Hard-hit countries in central and eastern Europe, with little money to spend on stimulus plans and no prospect in the near future of entering the euro area, felt increasingly resentful. More broadly, the situation demonstrated the fragility of economic integration and monetary union. The tendency on the part of national governments to protect their own banks and industries threatened to pull the single market apart. Similarly, the rapid deterioration of public finances in the euro area undermined the credibility of the Stability and Growth Pact, the fiscal foundation of economic and monetary union (EMU).

Governments' behaviour reflected the political realities in the EU. People look to their national capitals, not to Brussels, for solutions to pressing socio-economic problems. Politicians would have been foolhardy to dismiss calls for national action by claiming that their hands were tied by EU competition policy or the budget deficit threshold of the Stability and Growth Pact. They had to meet urgent national needs within an EU structure that is little liked or understood by citizens, despite the tangible benefits of the single market and the obvious convenience of the single currency. Under the circumstances, most governments managed to strike a reasonable balance between national and European interests, or at least did not blame Brussels unduly for constraining their freedom of manoeuvre. The high and varied number of summits during the crisis demonstrated national leaders' appreciation of the importance of EU co-operation while also giving them an opportunity to let off steam (see Table 5).

The way in which the crisis played out politically underscores the point that national governments are the decisive actors. The EU does not have

Table 4: The Second Barroso Commission-Designate

Commissioner	Country of Origin	Portfolio
José Manuel Barroso	Portugal	President
Catherine Ashton	United Kingdom	High Representative for Foreign Affairs and Security Policy (Vice-President)
Viviane Reding	Luxembourg	Justice, Fundamental Rights and Citizenship (Vice-President)
Joaquín Almunia	Spain	Competition (Vice-President)
Siim Kallas	Estonia	Transport (Vice-President)
Neelie Kroes	The Netherlands	Digital Agenda (Vice-President)
Antonio Tajani	Italy	Industry and Entrepreneurship (Vice-President)
Maroš Šefčovič	Slovakia	Inter-institutional Relations and Administration (Vice-President)
Janez Potočnik	Slovenia	Environment
Olli Rehn	Finland	Economic and Monetary Affairs
Andris Piebalgs	Latvia	Development
Michel Barnier	France	Internal Market and Services
Androulla Vassiliou	Cyprus	Education, Culture, Multilingualism and Youth
Algirdas Šemeta	Lithuania	Taxation and Customs Union, Audit and Anti-Fraud
Karel De Gucht	Belgium	Trade
John Dalli	Malta	Health and Consumer Policy
Máire Geoghegan-Quinn	Ireland	Research, Innovation and Science
Janusz Lewandowski	Poland	Financial Programming and Budget
Maria Damanaki	Greece	Maritime Affairs and Fisheries
Rumiana Jeleva*	Bulgaria	International Co-operation, Humanitarian Aid and Crisis Response
Günther Oettinger	Germany	Energy
Johannes Hahn	Austria	Regional Policy
Connie Hedegaard	Denmark	Climate Action
Štefan Füle	Czech Republic	Enlargement and European Neighbourhood Policy
László Andor	Hungary	Employment, Social Affairs and Inclusion
Cecilia Malmström	Sweden	Home Affairs
Dacian Cioloş	Romania	Agriculture and Rural Development

Source: The Members of the Barroso Commission, available at «http://ec.europa.eu/commission_2010-2014/index_en.htm».

Note: * Rumiana Jeleva stepped down during her confirmation hearings in the European Parliament in January 2010; the Bulgarian government nominated Kristalina Georgieva as her replacement.

responsibility for fiscal policy. Stimulus packages, whether in the form of subsidies or automatic stabilizers, can come only from national budgets. Of course national governments are obliged to co-ordinate such action within the EU and especially in the euro area. But the institutions that manage fiscal

Table 5: EU Summits in 2009

Informal meeting of Heads of State or Government, Brussels, 1 March 2009
Brussels European Council, 19–20 March
(Meeting of Heads of State or Government with the US President, Prague, 5 April)
Brussels European Council, 18–19 June
Informal Meeting of EU Heads of State or Government, Brussels, 17 September
Brussels European Council, 29–30 October
Informal Meeting of Heads of State or Government, Brussels, 19 November
Brussels European Council, 10–11 December

Source: European Council, Presidency Conclusions, 2009, available at «http://www.european-council.
europa.eu/council-meetings/presidency-conclusions.aspx?lang=en».

policy co-ordination – the Economic and Finance Council (of national finance ministers), the Eurogroup (finance ministers of countries in the euro area) and the European Council – influence the direction of national policy without dictating it. When times are tough, governments will not put policy co-ordination ahead of political survival and national recovery.

Apart from the European Central Bank, the EU institutions most directly involved in the crisis were the European Council and the Commission. Once again, the crisis showed that when the political stakes are high, only the European Council is able to hold the EU together and move it forward. The European Council was well served by the French Presidency in the second half of 2008 because Sarkozy appreciated the importance of the EU dimension to the crisis and, as president of a big, resourceful Member State, was able to get things done. The succeeding Czech Presidency was not only hobbled by domestic politics but also lacked the clout necessary to lead the European Council (Beneš and Karlas, this volume). The variable performance of Council Presidencies during the crisis may have strengthened the appeal of the full-time European Council President. But had the Lisbon Treaty been in effect at the time, would Sarkozy – the headstrong leader of a powerful Member State – have allowed himself to be upstaged by Herman van Rompuy, the first elected President of the European Council?

The crisis also showed the difficulty of running the European Council effectively in an EU of 27 Member States. On a number of occasions, a few national leaders got together in smaller summits, notably of the G4 (France, Germany, Italy and the UK), sometimes plus Spain and the Netherlands and always with the Commission President. Having worked out a common position, these leaders were able to foist their views onto the others at the next meeting of the European Council. In theory all countries are equal in the EU; in practice, when it comes to economics and finance, not to mention security and defence, the big countries remain more equal than the others.

Among the big countries, France and Germany predominate. The crisis was another test of their relationship and another opportunity for observers to lament the demise of the Franco–German tandem. Yet once again, despite personal differences (Merkel and Sarkozy could hardly have been less alike) and policy preferences (Germany is deeply averse to deficit spending; France is comfortable with public borrowing), the two countries pulled together and nudged the EU in the direction of their choice. The effectiveness of the Franco–German partnership may have diminished in the enlarged EU, especially in the absence of a project as compelling as the single market or monetary union, but it remains a formidable force.

What more could the Commission have done and what could it have done better? Much of the criticism of the Commission focused on Barroso, who seemed curiously inactive as the crisis unfolded. As noted earlier, he was not the only EU leader to underestimate the severity of the crisis, however. Merkel was similarly detached at the outset. Once roused to action, Barroso led a vigorous response within the constraints that the Commission faced with respect to fiscal and macroeconomic policy. The Commission President's most useful role was to push for concerted national action, using the bully pulpit of the Presidency and participation in the European Council. Barroso could hardly have taken centre stage from Sarkozy or Merkel.

Conclusions

As far as EU institutions and governance are concerned, the year 2009 will be remembered more than anything else for the eventual ratification and entry into force of the Lisbon Treaty, most likely the final round in a bout of major reform that began with the Single European Act (SEA) in 1986. In the intervening quarter-century the European Union came into existence, more than doubled in size and acquired a vastly greater policy scope than the earlier European Community. During the same time, the EU grappled with major institutional and governance issues such as accountability, comitology, subsidiarity and transparency. The Lisbon Treaty may be the last round of major treaty reform not because it has addressed these issues entirely satisfactorily or because the post-Lisbon EU is ideally organized or structured, but because national governments have lost their appetites and European publics have lost their patience for further large-scale reform.

Nevertheless the Lisbon Treaty equips the EU with a robust set of institutional arrangements and policy instruments to address a variety of internal and external challenges. Those arrangements and instruments may be suboptimal in many respects, but they reflect the art of the possible at a particular moment in EU history. Much depends on the ability and willingness of EU actors – at the national and European levels – to make the most of the Lisbon Treaty's potential. That depends to some extent on the strength and impact of Euroscepticism, which the process of treaty reform unintentionally stoked. With the EU no longer engaged in seemingly perpetual treaty change, the post-Lisbon period of consolidation and relative calm should help to reduce Eurosceptical angst.

The EU's obsession with the Lisbon Treaty coincided with the global financial crisis. Joschka Fischer, who launched the debate on the future of Europe at the beginning of the decade, lamented in March 2009 that the crisis 'is relentlessly laying bare the EU's flaws and limitations. Indeed, what Europe lost, first and foremost, with the rejection of the Constitutional Treaty is now obvious: its faith in itself and its common future [. . .] [Europe] threatens to revert to the national egoism and protectionism of the past' (Fischer, 2009). Fischer's alarm may have reflected his frustration with what eventually emerged from the treaty reform process. Undoubtedly European integration has a long way to go – if the destination is a federal Europe. A more realistic appraisal of the Lisbon Treaty and of the EU's response to the financial crisis is that European integration has already come a long way, given the tenacity of national sovereignty in the global system and the immense difficulty of forming and shaping supranational organizations.

Key Reading

Arregui, J. and Thomson, R. (2009) ' "States" Bargaining Success in the European Union'. *Journal of European Public Policy*, Vol. 16, No. 5, pp. 655–76.

Blom-Hansen, J. and Brandsma, G.J. 'The EU Comitology System: Intergovernmental Bargaining *and* Deliberative Supranationalism?' *JCMS*, Vol. 47, No. 4, pp. 719–40.

Fuglsang, N. and Olsen, K.B. (2009) 'Staying in the Loop: The Commission's Role in First Reading Agreements'. EPIN Working Paper, No. 25, September.

König, T. and Junge, D. (2009) 'Why Don't Veto Players Use their Power?' *European Union Politics*, Vol. 10, No. 4, pp. 507–34.

Yordanova, N. (2009) 'The Rationale behind Committee Assignment in the European Parliament: Distributive, Informational and Partisan Perspectives'. *European Union Politics*, Vol. 10, No. 2, pp. 253–80.

References

Bale, T., Hanley, S. and Szczerbiak, A. (2009) ' "May Contain Nuts"? The Reality behind the Rhetoric Surrounding the British Conservatives' New Group in the European Parliament'. *The Political Quarterly*, Vol. 81, No. 1, January–March 2010.

Commission of the European Communities (2009a) 'European Commission President José Manuel Barroso proposes a partnership for progress and ambition to the European Parliament'. Brussels, 3 September. Available at «http://europa.eu/rapid/pressReleasesAction.do?reference=IP/09/1272».

Commission of the European Communities (2009b) 'President Barroso unveils his team'. Brussels, 27 November. Available at «http://europa.eu/rapid/pressReleasesAction.do?reference=IP/09/1837&format=HTML&aged=0&language=EN&guiLanguage=en».

Council of the European Union (2009a) 'Presidency Conclusions'. European Council, 18–19 June, Council, Brussels.

Council of the European Union (2009b) 'Press Release'. 2988th Council meeting, Environment, Brussels, 17764/2/09 REV 2 (Presse 392), 22 December.

Council of the European Union (2009c) 'Spanish-Belgian-Hungarian Trio Presidency of the Council of the European Union, 2010–2011, Operational programme'. 22 June. Available at «http://www.europolitics.info/pdf/gratuit_en/259687-en.pdf».

European Conservatives and Reformists (2009) Website. Available at «http://www.ecrgroup.eu/».

European Parliament (2007) 'Composition of the European Parliament after European Elections in June 2009, Institutions'. 10 December. Available at «http://www.europarl.europa.eu/news/expert/infopress_page/008-11449-283-10-41-901-20071008IPR11353-10-10-2007-2007-false/default_en.htm».

European Parliament (2010) 'Background: Parliament's 18 additional seats'. 23 February. Available at «http://www.europarl.europa.eu/news/expert/background_page/008-69361-053-02-09-901-20100223BKG69359-22-02-2010-2010-false/default_en.htm».

European People's Party (2009) Available at «www.epp.eu/hoofdpagina.php?hoofdmenuID=1».

European Policy Center (2009) *Post-Summit Analysis: The End of the Beginning*, 12 December, p. 2.

Federal Constitutional Court (2009) 'Press release no. 72/2009 of 30 June, Judgment of 30 June'. Press Office. Available at «http://www.bundesverfassungsgericht.de/en/press/bvg09-072en.html».

Fischer, J. (2009) 'Europe in Reverse'. *Project Syndicate*, 9 March. Available at «http://www.project-syndicate.org/commentary/fischer36».

Greens/European Free Alliance (2009) Available at «http://www.greens-efa.org/cms/default/rubrik/6/6270.htm».

Irish Times (2009) 'Late Surge of Reality for Libertas as Truth Dawns', 9 June.

Journal compilation © 2010 Blackwell Publishing Ltd

Münchau, W. (2009) 'Like a Fish, Europe is Rotting from the Head'. *Financial Times*, 11 May.

Parliament.com (2009) 'Mixed Response to PES Name Change'. 17 June. Available at «http://www.theparliament.com/no_cache/latestnews/news-article/ newsarticle/mixed-response-to-pes-name-change/».

Internal Market: Gesture Politics? Explaining the EU's Response to the Financial Crisis*

JAMES BUCKLEY
European Parliament

DAVID HOWARTH
University of Edinburgh

Introduction

The most significant development in internal market legislation in 2009 concerned the regulation and supervision of financial services. This focus is understandable. The worst European financial crisis and economic decline since the Great Depression and unprecedented EU Member State government bail-outs and credit guarantees for a large number of banks created a strong political and populist backlash in many EU Member States against financial institutions, and banks in particular (Quaglia *et al.*, 2009; see also Trichet, this volume). While the future stability of the financial sector is a chimera, particularly in a world of highly complex financial innovation, governments have individually and collectively – at both the EU and international level – looked to the reinforcement and creation of mechanisms that will decrease both the risk of systemic collapse and the future burden of bank failures upon governments and taxpayers. The impact of the financial crisis and recession upon the single European market has also been significant, notably in terms of trade flows, with an estimated 19 per cent drop in intra-EU trade from 2008 and similar declines in EU exports and imports (Eurostat, 2010). Surprisingly though, the application of EU competition policy, in the financial and other economic sectors, has been robust: the EU Commission has warned against the kind of protectionist measures adopted by the Obama administration for

* The authors would like to thank Lucia Quaglia and Iain Hardie for their helpful comments. James Buckley has contributed to this article in a personal capacity.

the US automotive industry and has demanded the sell-off of operations by several banks bailed out by the Member States.

The impressive legislative activity at the EU level on financial sector regulation must be juxtaposed with policy results in 2009 and the likely limited impact of EU legislation upon the activities of financial sector institutions. In October 2008, Member States acted rapidly to adopt bank rescue packages and co-ordinated their activities with some measure of success despite some initial unilateral actions on deposit guarantees (Quaglia *et al.*, 2009; Quaglia, 2009a). However, subsequent EU-level co-ordination is noteworthy for the weakness of its policy results, with a couple of partial exceptions. Our contribution attempts to explain the weakness of the EU's policy response to the financial crisis since October 2008. Our analysis provides a note of caution in relation to accounts (such as Posner's [2010]) which predict the likely development of a more 'managed' approach to financial services at the EU level. The focus will be on three issue areas. First, we analyse the agreement at the June 2009 European Council to create a European Systemic Risk Board (ESRB) and a European System of Financial Supervisors (ESFS). This agreement, designed to provide macro-level oversight and operational consistency to the supervision of financial service providers across the EU, is one of the most significant EU legislative responses to the crisis to date. Second, we examine the push for an EU-level agreement on a new directive covering hedge funds and private equity firms – the Alternative Investment Fund Mangers (AIFM) Directive. Third, we explain the limited progress at the EU level on banking-related regulations, with the partial exception of the so-called Capital Requirement Directive (CRD) 3, the proposal to amend the EU capital requirement directive of 2006.

The Germans and French have a long track record of pushing tighter European and global financial market regulation, while, prior to the financial crisis, the British were in favour of 'light-touch' regulation and supervision at home and hostile to almost all developments abroad, apart from those that opened up international financial markets (Quaglia, forthcoming; Zimmermann, 2010). Even prior to the financial crisis, French and German governments argued in various international and European settings for a fundamental reform of the operation of credit rating agencies (CRA), tighter rules on hedge funds and private equity investors, rules on the pay of chief executive officers (CEOs) and other highly paid executives in the finance industry, stricter reporting requirements covering off-balance sheet activities and more. The French and German push has usually encountered the resistance of the British, and, less vocally, American governments. Not surprisingly, German and French proposals all failed. The current debate in the EU about financial regulation and supervision after the crisis has opened the same cleavage (Quaglia, 2007, forthcoming; Posner, 2010; Tait, 2009). However, we argue that it is important not to exaggerate the importance of this cleavage which fails to apply to a range of possible regulatory responses.

We accept the insights from several distinct analytical approaches to explain national policy-making and EU-level policy. We apply systemic realism and an approach focused upon interest group preferences. We also accept the usefulness of insights drawn from comparative political economy (CPE). We agree with CPE approaches to the extent that they insist that government policies seek to protect national political economies (as in Quaglia, forthcoming). However, we also warn against a CPE approach that relies upon a stagnant understanding of Varieties of Capitalism (VoC) (Hall and Soskice, 2001) because such an approach ignores significant changes that have taken place in European financial systems and capitalisms over the past decade (Hancké et al., 2007). We argue that to understand fully the lack of developments on banking regulation at the EU level and EU-level policy co-ordination on international regulation, it is necessary to incorporate other insights, notably from international policy economy (IPE), into an understanding of how national financial systems and economic interests shape national policy. We cannot divorce this study of EU-level responses to the financial crisis from considerations of the obstacles facing financial market integration in the EU. Clearly, support for integration shaped national policy-making on EU-level developments on financial sector matters. However, we argue that integration considerations were secondary. Our focus upon the Member States with the three largest economies and financial sectors – Germany, France and the UK – and the influence of the positions of the financial interests in these countries corresponds to a Liberal Intergovernmentalist (LI) analysis. However, we do not seek to draw broader conclusions about the applicability of LI to explain developments in this policy area.

I. IPE and CPE Explanations of National Policy Differences and EU Policy Developments in 2009

Systemic realism explains EU-level policy in terms of regulatory competition: states try to upload their model to the EU and international levels to gain and preserve comparative advantages (Zimmerman, 2010). Such initiatives (and resistance to them) originate from strategic efforts to enhance or preserve state power and to promote overarching strategic and economic goals. At the international level, the dominant financial powers, the US and Britain, play the leading role in this game (Helleiner and Pagliari, 2010a,b). Britain's resistance to European regulation can be seen as an attempt to bolster the leading position of London as a financial centre. Similarly, French and German efforts can be seen in terms of efforts to promote Paris and Frankfurt as world financial centres and challenge the position of London.

In France, international competitiveness is a long-standing theme justifying the transformation of the financial sector and political economy (O'Sullivan, 2007). The state-led concentration of the banking sector has been driven explicitly to construct national champions with a global reach (Hardie and Howarth, 2009). Regulatory non-action (as on a bonus tax prior to British action in 2009) has been justified in terms of the competitive disadvantage that unilateral action would impose on the financial sector. In Germany, economic nationalism appears less regularly as an explicit justification of policy in the financial sector. The coalition agreement of the CDU-SDP Grand Coalition government emphasized the necessity of lower regulation to promote the competitiveness of Germany's financial sector (*Koalitionsvertrag*, 2005). However, there was no coherent strategy along these lines (Zimmerman, 2010). Regionalism has had a greater impact than nationalism on the German financial system: a long-standing defence by regional governments of the protected position of semi-public sector banks (notably the *Landesbanken*, LB) until 2005 acted as a drag on transformation. The obstacles to reforming the LB in the context of the current crisis indicates the continued influence of regional governments.

There are obvious limits to realist accounts of EU-level regulatory developments: notably in that they fail to take account of domestic preference formation. Interest group-centred approaches (for example, Frieden, 1991) can partially fill this gap. In line with these approaches, the presence or absence of European financial regulation is seen as a result of successful lobbying by financial interests. There are numerous studies on the pervasive influence of the 'City' on British politics during the last decade, to explain Britain's 'light-touch' regulatory regime and the reluctance of British governments to commit to European and international binding rules (Augar, 2009; Laurence, 2001; Wigley *et al.*, 2008). We test the applicability of an interest group-centred approach to explain the development of EU-level regulation.

We also look to CPE approaches to supplement these perspectives. CPE approaches would claim that the underlying determinant of Member States' preferences on EU-level regulation is the composition of their market economy (Fioretos, 2001). The most prominent of these CPE approaches, the VoC framework (Hall and Soskice, 2001) establishes a distinction between Co-ordinated (CME) and Liberal Market Economies (LME) with Germany and the UK leading European examples of each. France does not sit easily in any categorization of capitalism. The French VoC demonstrates several features of a CME but it has also been described as a unique kind of Mixed

Market Economy (MME) (Hancké *et al.*, 2007), while Schmidt (2002) labels French capitalism as 'managed', pointing to a continued role for the state in directing the economy. CMEs are characterized by the pre-eminence of non-market institutions in co-ordinating the economy. This assures the availability of long-term finance, regulated labour markets, vocational training and extensive co-ordination among firms. The German corporate governance system tied banks, firms and employee representatives into mutual linkages which permitted negotiated consensual solutions to economic conflicts (Cioffi and Höpner, 2006). Analysing the supply of institutionally available resources to firms, VoC claims that LMEs are characterized by the limited role of the state, a low degree of regulation and taxation as well as modest welfare spending. The LME financial system is dominated by equity capital, leading to a short-term, profit-oriented focus for most firms. The system is also geared towards radical innovations and competitive strategies (Hall and Soskice, 2001). The comparative research on capitalisms has concentrated on the consequences of different types of financial systems – LME market-oriented and CME bank-based – for the structure of firms. However, VoC also indicates national resistance to any form of European regulation which would distort the national model of capitalism (Zimmerman, 2010).

Quaglia (2008b, 2009b, forthcoming) presents a variation on this CME/LME theme that demonstrates a more sophisticated understanding of different national financial systems and regulatory and supervisory regimes. She argues that EU-level policies on financial services are shaped by two main competing advocacy coalitions, grouping countries which have different approaches to financial sector regulation and supervision. The 'southern European' group (including France) seeks 'market shaping' regulation. The 'northern European' group (led by the UK) seeks 'market making' (light-touch) regulation. Germany falls in between these two coalitions because of its three-pillar financial system in which financial institutions have very different preferences. For Quaglia, interests, systems and ideas converge with it being impossible to disentangle the explanatory variable for national policy.

II. The Creation of the ESRB and European Supervisory Authorities

The Slow but Steady Progress in EU Regulation and Supervision Prior to 2009

There was progress in EU regulation and supervision prior to 2009 but principally with regard to securities. At the behest of the Commission, Baron Lamfalussy published a report in 2000 on how to improve the speed, quality and evenness of transposition of the EU's output of securities sector legislation (later expanded to banking and insurance legislation). This was in anticipation of the wave of legislation to be generated by the Financial Services Action Plan (FSAP), adopted in 1999 to accelerate the integration of financial services. Lamfalussy's proposals were for a four-level procedure for the creation of securities legislation – known as the Lamfalussy process – with different supervisory and regulatory committees assisting the Commission with different tasks at different levels (Alford, 2006; Lamfalussy, 2001; Quaglia, 2008a).

In 2004, the Committee of European Securities Regulators (CESR), one of the Lamfalussy committees, issued a consultation document to take stock of progress towards FSAP objectives and examine possible supervisory tools to develop over the next five years to ensure fair and transparent securities markets. The document, the Himalaya Report, asked for stakeholder feedback on a range of issues, including the possibility of an enhanced supervisory role for the CESR and the possibility of trans-European supervision (CESR, 2004). Shortly after the Himalaya Report, the Commission published its Green Paper on Financial Services Policy 2005–10. One objective of the consultation was to discuss Commission proposals on enhancing the supervision of financial services through a three-step process, the second step of which included a convergence of supervisory practices between Member States, and the third step the development of new European supervisory structures, if the existing framework proved unsatisfactory.

The de Larosière Committee, Report and Aftermath

Discussions on the development of EU supervision had not progressed by the autumn of 2008. However, the consequences of the banking crisis of September/October of that year, particularly the collapse of several European banks with cross-border operations, led to a renewed focus on the issue. In November 2008, the Commission mandated an advisory group, led by Jacques de Larosière – a former Bank of France governor, International Monetary Fund (IMF) managing director and European Bank for Reconstruction and Development (EBRD) president – to propose a package of reforms that would strengthen the European supervisory framework and increase co-operation on financial stability oversight and crisis resolution. The de Larosière Report, published in February 2009, proposed a two-pronged approach to reform the system of financial services supervision within the EU. This comprised a European Systemic Risk Council (later renamed ESRB), overseen by the ECB and with decision-making by representatives of national central banks, to assess and counter macro-prudential risks posed by and facing all sectors of finance, and a transformation of the Lamfalussy supervisory committees into authorities to allow for the co-ordination and application of high-level supervisory standards and decisions, with national supervisors remaining responsible for micro-prudential supervision of 'home' country institutions. The authorities would comprise representatives of the 27 relevant national supervisors, and would co-ordinate with national supervisors through the ESFS. The report recommended that the transformation of the committees into authorities occur over two stages; the first would see the committees take a more active role in developing and guiding colleges of supervisors, and the second would see the committees become the authorities and the ESFS created (De Larosière, 2009, pp. 47–8). In a March 2009 Communication, the Commission signalled its intention to adopt the recommendations of the report – with the amendment that the two-stage process for creating the ESFS be accelerated into a single action – and called for feedback from stakeholders as part of its impact assessment. The de Larosière proposals and the content of this feedback formed the rump of the Commission's proposals outlined in May for 'European Financial Supervision', the bulk of which were agreed upon by Member States' leaders at the June European Council meeting.

The position of French, British and German financial interests on the ESRB and authorities was mixed. The only point on which nearly all were agreed was that day-to-day supervision should remain a responsibility of national supervisors. French government support for the de Larosière proposals reflected the broadly supportive position of national financial interest groups, which had previously pushed for the reinforcement of EU-level supervision and either supported or accepted the accelerated creation of the authorities and the transfer of arbitration power. They sought economic gains to cut down on the duplication, and hence costs, inherent in dealing with multiple supervisory authorities. French financial interests might also have perceived that they had a competitive advantage if a supervisory approach more focused on stability and consumer protection were adopted given their historic exposure to such practices compared to British and German institutions.[1] There is not, however, any evidence that French financial interests were motivated by the prospect – as Quaglia (forthcoming) suggests – of improving levels of consumer protection per se via EU integration.

UK financial interest groups were supportive of the de Larosière proposals which reflects above all their limited ambition. Most amenable was the UK insurance sector.[2] Prior to 2009, the general consensus among UK financial interests was that existing arrangements following the creation of the Lamfalussy committees should be given the opportunity to 'bed-down' before

---

[1] Interview with AMF official, 28 May 2009.
[2] *Financial Times*, 11 February 2009.

any new initiatives in relation to either supervision or regulation were considered.[3] While there were different priorities on the details, there was a general preference for an 'evolutionary' approach to the convergence of supervisory practices, managed through existing institutions, rather than new bodies, the importance of retaining 'local knowledge' and the need for the EU to retain a 'global focus' whereby any changes would not be at odds with the global direction of financial services supervision. Unofficially, the general consensus among UK financial groups was that their interests were fairly well served under the light-touch supervision of the FSA. During the consultation on the de Larosière report, UK financial interests maintained their long-standing position.

There was a significant divergence of views within the German financial sector on the development of EU-level supervision, as to be expected given the country's bifurcated financial system. Prior to 2009, this divergence explains the ambiguity in German government, *Bundesbank* and BaFin positions. German private sector banks maintained one of the most pro-EU positions in Europe, having long called for a lead supervisor model with the ultimate goal being the creation of a European system of financial services authorities modelled on the European System of Central Banks (ESCB). The large German commercial banks believed that there was no long-term alternative to a European supranational supervisory authority, at least for cross-border institutions. They offered their support to the de Larosière proposals provided that the path taken did not disrupt the ultimate objective of uniform European supervision (BDB, 2009). By contrast the LB, savings banks and co-operatives were more reluctant to accept a single European supervisor, although they softened their previously strong opposition (BVR and DSGV, 2009). They were unconvinced of the need for establishing the new authorities, rather than reinforced co-operation by national authorities. The LB and savings banks representative body outlined its qualified support for the ESRB and put forward new proposals for micro-prudential supervision involving national supervisory authorities co-operating through a transnational network on the basis of intergovernmental co-operation, thereby retaining overall Member State competence (DSGV, 2009, pp. 2–3). Insurance companies appeared to be somewhat more supportive of greater European supervision, calling for the ESRB to be given power over national supervisors in order to

---

[3] See public submissions to the three Commission consultations, published at the following websites: Himalaya Report available at «http://www.cesr-eu.org/index.php?page=responses&id=48», Commission Green Paper available at «http://circa.europa.eu/Public/irc/markt/markt_consultations/library?l=/financial_services/financial_2005-2010&vm=detailed&sb=Title» and Commission consultation on de Larosière report, available at «http://circa.europa.eu/Public/irc/markt/markt_consultations/library?l=/financial_services/supervision&vm=detailed&sb=Title».

respond to risks effectively, and the authorities to be given the power to make binding decisions in disputes between national supervisors (GDV, 2009).

National government positions on the de Larosière proposals were surprisingly similar on the broad lines of the proposals. Although national positions on EU-level supervision have differed markedly over the past decade, governments of all three Member States have consistently opposed the transfer of prudential powers to a single EU-level supervisor but rather supported the lead supervisor concept. All three also opposed the transfer of any matters with fiscal implications. The de Larosière report ruled out from the start any proposition either for a single EU-level supervisor or the pooling of taxpayer funds to a supranational institution, on the basis of the 'political problems' that would be raised (De Larosière, 2009, p. 35). None of the three Member States endorsed the idea of the Lamfalussy committees becoming supervisory authorities. All accepted the de Larosière proposal that the committees be merged into one body responsible for removing national divergences in financial services regulation and the implementation of directives.

French governments have supported the move towards integrated EU supervision of financial services since 2000 if not earlier.[4] The appointment of de Larosière to examine reforms increased *de facto* French influence and the French government positioned itself as the de Larosière report's main cheerleader.[5] However, it is very likely that this ostensible support relied on the knowledge that any radical departure from existing supervisory arrangements would be vetoed by the UK and possibly Germany.[6]

Prior to 2009, British governments consistently opposed the creation of a single European supervisor (HM Treasury, 2000, pp. 25–7, 2005, pp. 6–35; House of Lords, 2009, p. 37) and supported the institutional changes introduced with the Lamfalussy reforms (Lee, 2005). In response to the de Larosière proposals, Chancellor Alistair Darling reaffirmed but somewhat repositioned the UK government's stance. He accepted proposals for a body to provide an early-warning signal for macro-systemic risks along the lines of the ESRB, but stressed the need for non-euro area countries to have equal representation and for the participation of national supervisors (HM Treasury, 2009a, pp. 3–4). The British insisted that the body should be independent of the Commission and national supervisors and with no powers over the latter. As previously, the UK consistently pushed the EU not to move ahead of global developments on supervision.

---

[4] *Financial Times*, 11 July 2000.
[5] Interview with AMF official, 28 May 2009; *Financial Times*, 5 November 2008.
[6] *Financial Times*, 19 March 2009; interviews with senior officials working on regulatory matters in the BBA, 11 June 2009; FSA, 11 June 2009; PwC, 9 June 2009; and Deutsche Bank, 29 May 2009.

This shift in the position of UK financial interests and government appears, on the surface, to contradict the position expected by a VoC approach. The shift can perhaps be explained by a recognition that the LME approach to regulation/supervision had been undermined by the impact of the financial crisis and that a move by the EU to secure greater control over the City was unavoidable and possibly welcome in as much as international co-operation was necessary.[7] However, we argue that the financial crisis did not provoke a significant ideational shift. Rather, the position of the UK financial sector on de Larosière reflects an understanding that the reforms were not going to create any significant new constraints on British financial services. The UK largely got its way in terms of EU supervision.[8] The British were also opposed to a leadership role for the ECB in the ESRB and insisted that operations supervision was to remain in the hands of national supervisors: positions that were upheld at the June European Council and agreed unanimously at the December Ecofin meeting. There is evidence that the UK government accepted the benefits of creating an ESRB from a market efficiency perspective, or 'to bring together understanding of macro-economic and financial market issues' (HM Treasury, 2009a, p. 3), and thus had little trouble agreeing that it should be granted EU-wide monitoring powers. In this sense, the creation of the ESRB conformed to the preferences largely associated with the British LME. Further, the very limited nature of reinforced supervision at the national level in response to the financial crisis – focused principally on dealing with fraud – demonstrates the limited nature of the ideational shift in the UK.

Following the publication of the de Larosière report, the non-committal stance of the German government on EU-level financial supervision was impossible to maintain. Chancellor Angela Merkel endorsed the proposals for the ESRB,[9] but with initially no clarity on the details of the German position. However, in the run-up to and during the June European Council meeting Chancellor Merkel came out strongly in support of the de Larosière proposals.[10] Like the French government, the Germans could voice strong support for the ESRB and the authorities, in the knowledge that the UK would strongly oppose any shift in powers to supranational institutions. The *Bundesbank* was more hostile to the de Larosière proposals on the authorities on the basis of the asymmetries between supranational bodies and Member States which maintained fiscal responsibility.[11]

---

[7] *Financial Times*, 26 March 2009; interview with EBF official, 26 May 2009.
[8] *European Voice*, 9 June 2009.
[9] *European Voice*, 1 March 2009.
[10] *European Voice*, 19 June 2009.
[11] *EuroIntelligence*, 16 April 2009.

The empirical evidence suggests that the LB, savings and co-operative banks played an influential role in shaping German national preference. Their opposition to EU supervision is the result of the economic advantage they perceive in retaining national supervision, which allows them a degree of sectoral self-governance, and has protected them from the drive to greater competition and/or consolidation that would result from adoption of a single European supervisory approach (Story and Walter, 1997, pp. 165–7). The large commercial banks were supportive of a move towards EU supervision because this would cut down on their compliance costs given their international profile. EU supervision would also allow them to compete more effectively with the LB, savings and co-operative banks, since EU supervisors would be less inclined to prevent the acquisition of savings and co-operative banks by larger commercial banks than German *Länder* governments (Hardie and Howarth, 2009). The empirical evidence supports Quaglia's (2008b, forthcoming) argument that Germany is unable to support either the northern or southern European advocacy coalitions given the divergence of ideas between different bank types. However, while the priorities of private banks broadly agree with those of the northern coalition, it can be argued that the LB, savings and co-operative banks views are not always comparable with that of the southern coalition. Specifically, the German banks do not express any particular desire to re-regulate at EU level, be it for consumer protection or 'market-shaping' purposes.

III. Dealing with the 'Vultures' of Global Capitalism

Hedge funds and private equity firms, although frequently criticized by many EU Member States' governments, were not major culprits of the financial crisis. Thus the push to regulate these industries at the EU level is curious. In December 2008, the Commission launched a consultation on the need for EU regulation on these industries which culminated in a Brussels conference in late February 2009 (Commission, 2008). Although most Member States' government and industry respondents to the consultation preferred the development of international guidelines on these industries, a small majority of Member States' governments accepted unilateral EU action if necessary (Quaglia, 2009b). Prior to 2009, Charlie McCreevy, the Internal Market Commissioner, repeatedly expressed hostility to the regulation of these industries. It was thus surprising that in June 2009, the European Commission presented a proposal for the draft directive on Alternative Investment Fund Managers (AIFM) covering managers of hedge funds, private equity firms and real estate funds (Commission, 2009a). The

Commission justified the move in terms of the need for EU regulation given the cross-border dimension of risks posed by these funds and the need to remove obstacles to the cross-border marketing of these funds in the EU.[12] The proposed directive introduces a European passport for AIFM, an EU authorization and supervisory regime for all AIFM above a certain size and capital, governance and transparency requirements. Other controversial features of the Commission's proposal include the introduction of a three-year transition period during which AIFM would not be able to market throughout the EU funds domiciled in third countries (though Member States could continue to allow them to operate via national private placements). Following this period, these funds could be marketed only if their country of domicile complies with the conditions set out in the OECD Model Tax Convention and other requirements.

The VoC approach helps to explain the German and French push on AIFM and British opposition to EU-level regulatory developments (Quaglia, 2009b). German and French governments have regularly presented hedge funds and private equity firms as embodiments of 'vulture capitalism' and fundamentally contradictory to the German system built on 'patient' capital (Engelen, 2005) and France's 'managed' capitalism (Schmidt, 2002). The French and Germans have pushed for the reinforcement of EU-level regulation and international guidelines on these funds for several years on the grounds that only international action could be effective since most of these firms are based abroad. Their action reflects the 'market-shaping' regulatory paradigm (Quaglia, 2009b). The Commission's proposal for the AIFM directive of June 2009 thus stems from the consensus of the biggest EU Member States, apart from the UK, in favour of tighter controls.

British government opposition to the AIFM directive and then demands that its most constraining elements be significantly diluted can be explained through a combination of approaches. From a neo-realist take, the UK opposed EU regulation because this threatened its international 'regulatory arbitrage' which encouraged fund managers to operate in the UK. From an interest group-centred approach, the UK hosts 80 per cent of EU hedge funds managers, who have significant influence in relation to government. In terms of the VoC literature, the British preference for 'market-making' or 'competition-friendly' regulation on hedge funds reflects the British LME.

Quaglia (2009b) argues that it is also necessary to examine the ideas that have driven the EU-level regulatory push on AIFM. The financial crisis reinforced, at least temporarily, the influence of the 'market-shaping' regulatory paradigm, weakening that of the rival 'market-making' approach.

[12] *Financial Times*, 14 July 2009.

However, ideational shift should not be exaggerated: the AIFM has (as of April 2010) yet to be adopted, its most restrictive provisions were watered down in the year following the launch of the regulation[13] and threats of transatlantic tensions over the imposition of regulation on non-EU domiciled funds have encouraged further compromise.[14]

Furthermore, there are reasons to query an approach based on VoC. Zimmerman (2010) argues that the often harsh German rhetoric against AIFM concealed the reality of German government policy. The Schröder SPD-led government was instrumental in opening the German market to hedge funds and private equity firms in 2003 through the investment modernization law and even sold privatized assets to them (Cioffi, 2002; Vitols, 2004). Turning to France, despite government rhetorical hostility, Paris has the largest concentration of hedge funds and private equity firms in the EU after London, although the largest hedge funds are attached to banks (*Euro-Hedge*, 2008). Zimmermann (2010) explains the German push on international regulation on hedge funds and private equity firms in terms of a legitimacy-oriented approach. His claims could apply equally to French efforts in this area. Contrary to the situation in most G20 countries, global finance was a highly politicized issue in both Germany and France already prior to the financial crisis. Effective regulation of global finance had become a benchmark for the legitimacy of German and French governments.

IV. The Limited EU Response on Banking Regulation

The high level of bank financialization[15] was one of the principal causes of the financial crisis that has hit several EU Member States. Various Member States' governments have sought to respond to the increased risk that financialization creates for the stability of individual firms and national banking and financial systems. The development of EU policy will follow on from agreements in late 2010 by the Financial Stability Board (FSB) of the Bank for International Settlements (BIS). On 13 July, the Commission proposed the amendment of the Capital Requirements Directive (CRD3) (Commission, 2009b). CRD3 proposes four main areas of changes that banks need to make in relation to capital: capital requirements for re-securitizations, disclosure of securitization exposures, capital requirements for the trading book, and

---

[13] *Financial Times*, 4 April 2010.
[14] *Financial Times*, 11 March 2010.
[15] Financialization is defined here as the increased trading of, and exposure to, risk, through the increasing importance of 'market' relative to 'credit' portfolios (Aglietta and Breton, 2001, p. 441; see also Froud *et al.*, 2007), the growing importance of the taking of risk in trading activities and the implications for the nature of 'investment banking' activity in universal banks.

remuneration policies and practices. This proposed directive is to delegate to the Commission the adoption of the future FSB guidelines on capital requirements for trading books and re-securitizations into EU law. The existing EU capital requirements directive is, similarly, the legislative response to the Basel II guidelines. Despite CRD3 – the provisions of which are still debated and have yet to be adopted (by April 2010) – and other legislative developments, EU Member States have failed to develop co-ordinated positions on international guidelines and desirable EU policy in a range of areas. We argue that, as with the ESRB and authorities, the differences among the three core Member States on banking regulation should not be exaggerated. All three Member States have been reluctant to impose significant new constraints on the investment activities of their banks.

In none of the three Member States is there much appetite to embrace the kinds of restrictive regulatory and supervisory practices that have protected countries like Spain from the direct impact of the financial crisis. The financialization of banking activities in the three Member States limits the regulatory responses of government despite the severity of the financial crisis, especially in Germany and the UK – where banks counted for an estimated 9 and 12 per cent, respectively, of global write-downs by mid-2009 (IMF, 2009). A range of banks in all three countries – including the German LB and the French mutual banks – are heavily involved in investment banking activities and rely on them for profits and growth. This applies only somewhat less to the large French banks which have a greater retail focus than the large German and British commercial banks (Hardie and Howarth, 2009). The exposure of the French financial system to the crisis was comparatively limited – 3 per cent of global write-downs despite holding 10 per cent of global financial assets, similar to the German share (IMF, 2009). However, the French financial system has liberalized considerably over the past quarter-century and French banks were heavily involved in the trading of securities (Hardie and Howarth, 2009). The VoC approach applies best with regard to the British stance on EU-level banking regulation. It is of less explanatory use regarding German and French positions given the considerable shifts in their national banking systems which have undermined both the German CME and France's 'managed capitalism', especially the German system, where 'patient' bank-provided capital has been a core element (Deeg, 1999; Vitols, 2004; Hardie and Howarth, 2009).

One area where there has been significant progress at the EU level concerns credit rating agencies (CRAs), restrictions on the operations of which are of less sensitivity for national governments. In the early stages of the financial crisis in Europe, in the summer of 2008, the European Commission moved to regulate CRAs operating in the EU and subject them to a single supervisory regime.[16] The Commission's draft regulation of November 2008 targeted, in particular, conflicts of interest issues, rating methodology, transparency and corporate governance. The Commission proposed a more concrete EU version of the international (International Organization of Securities Commission, IOSCO) code of conduct to be backed up by an enforcement system. CRAs would have to register with the Committee of European Securities Regulators (CESR). Supervision would be entrusted to national authorities in the Member States where the CRA is registered, with the possibility of intervention by other Member States. In July 2009, the European Parliament voted overwhelmingly to approve the regulation. EU Member States participating in the G20 also co-ordinated their position on the development of international guidelines. The Commission's draft directive aligned with a long-standing German and French government approach on CRAs and their support for EU-level regulation (Issing *et al.*, 2009). Given that the move here will have limited impact on European bank activities and will affect, above all, US-based agencies, it is not surprising that the British government presented no significant obstacle to the adoption of the new regulation.

On revenue raising regulation, there was no EU-level action in 2009 despite a growing consensus among German, French and British governments on an international tax on short-term financial transactions (such as the Tobin Tax), earnings from which would contribute to a future fund to assist struggling banks or help wind them down without government bail-outs. French governments have long supported the Tobin Tax. With a surprise announcement by Prime Minister Brown in favour of a transactions tax on 21 September, the positions of the three Member States on the matter appear aligned. However, the German government position was more open-minded and 'willing to be directed' by the IMF position which was to be presented in an April 2010 report. Some other EU Member States (for example, Austria) have come out in favour of a backwards-looking levy on the balance sheets of large financial institutions – supported by the Obama administration. Agreement on details remained elusive and there was limited progress at the EU level on a joint position in 2009.[17]

The German Grand Coalition government and the French government saw in the remuneration practices in banks, inspired by Anglo–American practices, one of the principal causes of the crisis. On remuneration, the

---

[16] *Financial Times*, 1 August 2008.

[17] During the first months of 2010, German, French and British governments shifted their position to support, in principle, a global bank levy, which has been advocated by the Obama administration (*Financial Times*, 1 April 2010). The three EU Member States differ on their ambition for a levy: Germany wants an insurance fund to pay for a future banking crisis; the UK wants a future 'pollution tax' on banks; and France wants something similar applied to the entire financial services sector.

distinction between populist rhetoric and real policy preference is frequently far from certain. EU-level policy on the issue was initially limited to co-ordinated positions on appropriate international recommendations and then turned to incorporating these recommendations into EU law. The preference to wait for international recommendations reflected the concern that unilateral EU action would have a detrimental effect on the competitiveness of EU-based financial services. There were repeated public disagreements between Member States' positions on appropriate international recommendations. In the weeks leading up to the London G20 summit in September, the French supported the deferral of 60 per cent of bonuses over a three-year period and the establishment of a maximum ratio of gross operating income to be distributed in variable pay. The British challenged a cap and recommended greater flexibility on deferred bonuses.[18] However, following the adoption of G20 standards in September, all three Member States moved rapidly to adopt them. At the EU level, the G20 standards were incorporated into the proposed CRD3. Based on FSB recommendations, these aims at aligning compensation with long-term value creation, not excessive risk-taking and, more specifically, a ban on multi-year guaranteed bonuses and that 50 per cent of large bonuses should be deferred over three years with the possibility of claw-backs if profits sink. None of the three Member States introduced or recommended the restrictive practices adopted unilaterally in the Netherlands where bonuses were capped at 100 per cent of salary and none were likely to accept the amendment tabled in March 2010 by the European Parliament's Committee on Economic and Monetary Affairs which pushed to adopt Dutch policy at the EU level (European Parliament, 2010).

There have been no unilateral Member State or EU moves to strengthen the quality of capital of European banks. BIS rules will dictate EU and national policies here. None of the three EU Member States has pushed actively for a new Basel agreement on capital adequacy. All have focused on the improved, faster and more universal enforcement of Basel II by national regulators, and the reinforcement of existing requirements. The Obama administration has taken the lead internationally in this regard by calling for the strengthening of the capital banks are required to keep (a ban on 'hybrid' capital), and an increase in the amount of this capital through leverage rules. The Financial Stability Forum has embraced a similar but vaguer position on capital quality and quantity (a commitment to an agreement by the end of 2010) with support for the introduction of a leverage ratio as a supplementary measure to the Basel II risk-based framework. In December 2009, the Basel Committee on Banking Supervision took a surprisingly hard-line approach on capital requirements,

---

[18] *Financial Times*, 2 September 2009.

pushing for a higher adequacy threshold and a restriction on hybrids with minimum capital to be composed of predominantly equity capital.

The governments of the three EU Member States have been aligned in their opposition to the exclusion of hybrid capital given that European banks have tended to make greater use of hybrids to meet capital requirements and they would be disadvantaged – both in their ability to lend and in their competitiveness with US banks – if hybrid rules were enacted. European central bankers have favoured the adoption of a leverage ratio to determine the quantity of capital to be held by banks as a simple mechanism to curb excessive risk-taking. However, the governments of the three Member States have been opposed because most of their large banks are highly leveraged. Given the growth and competition effects of capital strengthening it is not surprising that Member States' governments have not opted to tighten national rules unilaterally and have failed to develop EU positions.

German government policy on capital adequacy has directly contradicted its otherwise strong push for tighter EU and international regulation. In early July 2009, just prior to the adoption of its own ostensibly restrictive national legislation, the German government lobbied for a temporary loosening of existing EU capital and accounting rules. Officially, this was motivated by the German government's push to give banks more leeway to make additional loans. Observers however have noted that the move appeared to be driven by a desire to avoid too much transparency on bad loans.[19] The German government request was rebuffed by the other EU Member States but the debate on the matter has reinforced a growing impression that Germany remains intent on pursuing a policy of forbearance towards its troubled banks – on capital rules, accounting and much else.

National regulators and governments have moved more quickly to clarify national regulation on bank liquidity. The moves are similar in the three Member States and are in response to recommendations made by a number of international bodies, including the Basel Committee on Banking Supervision, the G7 and the G20 (15 November 2008 recommendations). However, Member States reform would have taken place without the financial crisis given the need to transpose the liquidity provisions outlined in the 2006 Capital Requirement Directive's Pillar 2. Moreover, the three Member States have proceeded each in their own way on liquidity and there is resistance to the development of tighter EU-level legislation in this area. Interestingly, the VoC approach is not supported by national regulatory developments on liquidity provisions: adopted British regulation is set to be more constraining on banks than either French or German regulation (Financial Services

---

[19] *Financial Times*, 8 July 2009.

Authority, 2009, p. 6; Commission Bancaire, 2009, p. 148; BaFin, 2009). All three Member States remained opposed to Basel Committee proposals to increase liquidity cushions and require the 'too big to fail banks' (20 in the EU) to match lending more closely with deposits.[20]

Despite EU-level moves to reinforce the internal governance and transparency of CRAs, there have been no similar efforts in internal bank governance and transparency at the EU level. Proposed and adopted modifications in the UK, France and Germany have been surprisingly limited. The Walker Report on bank governance of November 2009 (Walker, 2009) and the Lagarde report of February 2008 (Lagarde, 2008) were limited to 'tweaking'.[21] The increased push at the EU level by French authorities in favour of transparency is also unlikely to have a significant effect. The French have pushed most actively for rigorous and preferably EU-wide co-ordinated stress tests, which focus on the quantity and quality of capital needed, as well as on the co-ordinated publication of stress-test results. Given the perilous state of many of their banks, the Germans opposed both the transparency and co-ordination of stress tests, although they accepted a future role for the authorities in co-ordinated stress tests.

Conclusions

2009 was a year of considerable debate and legislative activity on EU-level financial regulation and supervision. The financial crisis was the catalyst for EU-level developments – on cross-border supervision and the regulation of AIFM and CRAs. This activity can be explained in large part by an ideational shift which strengthened the hand of Member States' governments which have long sought reinforced EU-level regulation and supervision. The importance of this shift should not, however, be exaggerated, as demonstrated by the surprisingly modest push for the reinforcement of regulation and supervision of banks at both the national and EU levels. A realist-inspired approach, emphasizing competitiveness, improves our understanding, albeit rather superficially, of UK and French policy on EU-level regulation. It applies less usefully to Germany. An interest group-centred understanding of national policy is more helpful and applies to a broad range of EU-level developments and non-developments.

The evidence supporting the claim that the push by German and French governments for EU-level regulatory and supervisory changes in order to defend a national variety of capitalism defined in the VoC literature is mixed. On cross-border supervision, the French and Germans have shared some of the reticence of the British, notably on a single supervisor and national fiscal

---

[20] *Financial Times*, 5 January 2010.
[21] *The Guardian*, 26 November 2009.

responsibility. On AIFM, VoC-inspired claims are somewhat more supported by the evidence but it is also important to consider the domestic politicization of hedge funds and private equity firms and questions of government legitimacy. In practice, German and French governments have facilitated the domestic operation of hedge funds and private equity firms in recent years. On CRAs, the rapid push for EU-level regulation was acceptable to all Member State governments, including the British, which have become wary as to the impact of these institutions. A VoC-inspired approach applies poorly to banking regulation and ignores important developments in the British, German and French systems of capitalism, and in particular the operation of banks in the three countries. Likewise, we argue that, despite its insights, the explanatory merits of Quaglia's 'market-shaping' versus 'market-making' are similarly mixed, especially in the context of an explanation focused upon German, French and British policy on banking regulation and supervision.

An analysis of government responses to the financial crisis demonstrates that the British, French and German governments do not want EU-level regulatory change that will have a significant impact on domestic regulatory and supervisory frameworks, domestic financial sectors and the activities of financial institutions. The largest CRAs are American: new EU rules will not have asymmetric affects on Member States' financial systems that have been exposed to the inappropriate rating of complex financial products. On banking, EU liquidity rules will almost certainly have a significant impact upon banks but these rules were adopted prior to the financial crisis. They reflect a long-standing concern for bank stability in the event of financial crisis and the freezing up of wholesale markets. The remuneration guidelines to be adopted in the CRD3 are unlikely to be constraining. The capital requirement rules adopted by the Basel Committee will almost certainly constrain the activities of European banks. However, these rules will be adopted despite EU Member States' reticence. An EU or internationally agreed bank levy remains a distinct possibility but, while this will raise funds to help dismantle failing banks in the future without government intervention and bolster systemic stability, it will not act as a significant constraint on banking activities. The proposal for a new directive on over-the-counter derivatives trading will also, in all likelihood, be watered down considerably prior to its adoption. The policies of the three largest EU Member States on EU financial regulation and EU-level supervision demonstrate the limited nature of the ideational shift since the start of the financial crisis in 2008. Clearly, Member State governments are keen to bolster the stability of the financial system. However, they do not wish to constrain significantly the activities of their banks in order to achieve this stability. EU-level regulatory developments in 2009 reflected the demands of many Member State governments, the European Commission and European Parliament for action to tackle some of the destabilizing features of European financial systems. It would be difficult to argue that most EU-level efforts – the AIFM directive excluded – were driven by gesture politics. However, in the context of compromises amongst the governments of Member States, notably the largest three, EU legislation was watered down and the significance of its likely effect on EU financial markets uncertain.

References

Aglietta, M. and Breton, R. (2001) 'Financial Systems, Corporate Control and Capital Accumulation'. *Economy and Society*, Vol. 30, No. 4, pp. 433–66.

Alford, D. (2006) 'The Lamfalussy Process and EU Bank Regulation: Preliminary Assessment and Future Prospects'. *Journal of International Banking Law and Regulation*, Vol. 21, No. 2, pp. 59–68.

Augar, P. (2009) *Chasing Alpha: How Reckless Growth and Unchecked Ambition Ruined the City's Golden Decade* (London: Bodley Head).

BaFin (2009) 'Minderstanforde rungen an das Risikomanagement – Me Risk, Rund-schreiben 15/2009 (BA)', 14 August.

BDB (2009) 'Comments of the Association of German Banks: European Commis-sion's consultation on the recommendations of the de Larosiere Group of 25 February 2009'. Berlin, April. Available at «http://circa.europa.eu/Public/irc/markt/markt_consultations/library?l=/financial_services/supervision/individual_contributions/bdb_enpdf/_EN_1.0_&a=d».

BVR and DSGV (2009) 'Comments on the Commission's Document "Driving Euro-pean Recovery" and on the de Larosière Report entitled "Future of Financial Supervision in Europe" '. Berlin, April. Available at «http://circa.europa.eu/Public/irc/markt/markt_consultations/library?l=/financial_services/supervision/individual_contributions/bvr-dsg-vb-vdp_enpdf/_EN_1.0_&a=d».

CESR (Committee for European Securities Regulators) (2004) 'Which Supervisory Tools for the EU Securities Markets? Preliminary Progress Report (Himalaya Report)'. CESR, Paris, October.

Cioffi J. (2002) 'Restructuring "Germany, Inc.": The Corporate Governance Debate and the Politics of Company Law Reform'. *Law & Policy*, Vol. 24, No. 4, pp. 355–402.

Cioffi, J.W. and Höpner, M. (2006) 'The Political Paradox of Finance Capitalism: Interests, Preferences and Centre-Left Party Politics'. *Politics & Society*, Vol. 34, No. 4, pp. 463–502.

Commission of the European Communities (CEC) (2008) Consultation paper on hedge funds, 18 December.

Commission of the European Communities (2009a) 'Proposal for a Directive of the European Parliament and of the Council on Alternative Investment Fund Managers'. *COM*(2009)0207.

Commission of the European Communities (2009b) 'Proposal for a Directive of the European Parliament and of the Council amending Directives 2006/48/EC and 2006/49/EC as Regards Capital Requirements for the Trading Book and for Re-securitizations and the supervisory review of remuneration policies'. *COM*(2009)0362.

Commission of the European Communities (2009c) 'Macro-Prudential Oversight of Financial System and Establishment of European Systemic Risk Board (ESRB)'. *COM*(2009)0499.

Commission of the European Communities (2009d) 'Omnibus Directive on Financial Supervisory Architecture (Banking-UCITS)'. *COM*(2009)0576.

Commission Bancaire (2009) 'Annual Report 2008'. Paris.

Deeg, R. (1999) *Finance Capital Unveiled* (Ann Arbor, MI: University of Michigan Press).

De Larosière Group (2009) 'The High Level Group on Financial Supervision in the EU'. Brussels, 25 February.

DSGV (2009) 'Proposal for the Intensification of Pan-European Co-operation in the Field of Micro-Prudential Supervision'. DSGV, Berlin, April.

Engelen, K.C. (2005) 'Blinking Left, Driving Right: Germany's Flirtation with Anti-capitalist Populism'. *The International Economy*, 22 March.

EuroHedge (2008) 'Hedge Funds in France: A New Esprit de Corps'. HedgeFund Intelligence. Available at «http://www.hedgefundintelligence.com/eh/Article. aspx?Task=Report&IssueID=66649&ArticleID=1904086».

European Parliament (2010) 'Draft Report on the Proposal for a Directive of the European Parliament and of the Council Amending Directives 2006/48/EC and 2006/49/EC as Regards Capital Requirements for the Trading Book and for Re-securitizations, and the Supervisory Review of Remuneration Policies'. Committee on Economic and Monetary Affairs, 2009/0099 (COD), 2 March.

Eurostat (2010) 'First Estimate for 2009 Euro Area External Trade Surplus €22.3 billion, €105.5 billion deficit for EU-27'. STAT/10/23, 17 February. Available at «http://europa.eu/rapid/pressReleasesAction.do?reference=STAT/10/23&type= HTML».

Financial Services Authority (2009) 'Strengthening Liquidity Standards'. Available at «www.fsa.gov.uk/pubs/policy/ps09_16.pdf».

Fioretos, O. (2001) 'The Domestic Sources of Multilateral Preferences: Varieties of Capitalism in the European Community'. In Hall, P. A. and Soskice, D. (eds) *Varieties of Capitalism. The Institutional Foundations of Comparative Advantage* (Oxford: Oxford University Press).

Frieden, J. (1991) 'Invested Interests: The Politics of National Economic Policies in a World of Global Finance'. *International Organization*, Vol. 45, pp. 425–51.

Froud, J., Leaver, A. and Williams, K. (2007) 'New Actors in a Financialised Economy and the Remaking of Capitalism'. *New Political Economy*, Vol. 12, No. 3, pp. 339–47.

GDV (2009) 'Comments of the German Insurance Association (ID: 6437280268-55) on the consultation of the European Commission on supervision of the financial

services sector in the EU (Communication 2009/114 and de Larosière Report)',
Berlin, April. Available at «http://circa.europa.eu/public/irc/markt/markt_
consultations/library?1=/financial_services/supervision/registered_organisation/
gdv_enpdf/_EN_1.0_&a=d».

Hall, P.A. and Soskice D.W. (eds) (2001) *Varieties of Capitalism: The Institutional Foundations of Comparative Advantage* (Oxford: Oxford University
Press).

Hancké, B., Rhodes, M. and Thatcher, M. (eds) (2007) *Beyond Varieties of
Capitalism* (Oxford: Oxford University Press).

Hardie, I. and Howarth, D. (2009) '*Die Krise* but not *La Crise*? The Financial Crisis
and the Transformation of German and French Banking Systems'. *JCMS*, Vol. 47,
No. 5, pp. 1015–36.

Helleiner, E. and Pagliari, S. (2010a) 'Crisis and the Reform International Financial
Regulation'. In Helleiner, E. Pagliari, S. and Zimmermann, H. (eds) *Global
Finance in Crisis* (Abingdon: Routledge).

Helleiner, E. and Pagliari, S. (2010b) 'The End of Self-Regulation?' In Helleiner, E.
Pagliari, S. and Zimmermann, H. (eds) *Global Finance in Crisis* (Abingdon:
Routledge).

House of Lords (2009) 'Select Committee on Economic Affairs: Banking Supervision and Regulation'. (London: The Stationery Office).

HM Treasury (2000) 'Completing a Dynamic Single European Financial Service
Market: A Catalyst for Economic Prosperity for Citizens and Business across the
EU'. HM Treasury, London, July.

HM Treasury (2005) 'Supervising Financial Services in an Integrated European
Single Market: A Discussion Paper'. HM Treasury, London, January.

HM Treasury (2009a) 'European Financial Regulation and Supervision – Letter to the
Czech Presidency of the EU Council'. HM Treasury, London, March.

HM Treasury (2009b) 'Reforming Financial Markets'. Government White Paper, 8
July.

IMF (2009) 'France: Selected Issues'. Country Report, 09/233, July.

Issing, O., Asmussen, J., Krahnen, J.P., Regling, K., Weidmann, J. and White, W.
(2009) 'New Financial Order. Recommendations by the Issing Committee. Preparing G-20 – London'. Frankfurt Center for Financial Studies, White Paper No.
II, February. Available at «http://www.ifk-cfs.de/index.php?id=1571».

Koalitionsvertrag (2005) 'Gemeinsam für Deutschland mit Mut und Menschlichkeit:
Koalitionsvertrag von CDU, CSU und SPD'. Available at «http://www.cducsu.
de/upload/koavertrag0509.pdf».

Lagarde, C. (2008) 'Rapport au Premier Ministre'. Ministère de l'économie et
des finances, Paris. Available at «http://www.minefe.gouv.fr/directions_services/
sircom/secteur_bancaire_financier/rap_societe_generale080204.pdf».

Lamfalussy, A. (2001) 'Final Report of the Committee of Wise Men on the Regulation
of European Securities Markets'. European Commission, Brussels, February.

Laurence, H. (2001) *Money Rules: The New Politics of Finance in Britain and Japan*
(Ithaca, NY: Cornell University Press).

Lee, R. (2005) 'Politics and the Creation of a European SEC'. Sciences Po, Paris, July. Available at «http://aei-brookings.org/admin/authorpdfs/redirect-safely. php?fname=../pdffiles/phpTg.pdf».

O'Sullivan, M. (2007) 'Acting Out Institutional Change: Understanding the Recent Transformation of the French Financial System'. *Socio-Economic Review*, Vol. 5, No. 3, pp. 389–436.

Posner, E. (2010) 'Is a European Approach to Financial Regulation Emerging from the Crisis'. In Helleiner, E. Pagliari, S. and Zimmermann, H. (eds) *Global Finance in Crisis* (Abingdon: Routledge).

Quaglia, L. (2007) 'The Politics of Financial Service Regulation and Supervision Reform in the European Union'. *European Journal of Political Research*, Vol. 46, No. 2, pp. 269–90.

Quaglia, L. (2008a) 'Financial Sector Committee Governance in the European Union'. *Journal of European Integration*, Vol. 30, No. 4, pp. 563–78.

Quaglia, L. (2008b) 'Explaining the Reform of Banking Supervision in Europe: An Integrative Approach'. *Governance*, Vol. 21, No. 3, pp. 439–63.

Quaglia, L. (2009a) 'The "British Plan" as a Pace-Setter: The Europeanization of Banking Rescue Plans in the EU?' *JCMS*, Vol. 47, No. 5, pp. 1059–79.

Quaglia, L. (2009b) 'The "Old" and "New" Political Economy of Hedge Funds Regulation in the European Union'. Paper presented at 'The European Union and the Financial Crisis Conference', University of Edinburgh, 4 December.

Quaglia, L. (forthcoming) 'Completing the Single Market in Financial Services: The Politics of Competing Advocacy Coalitions'. *Journal of European Public Policy*, Vol. 17, No. 7.

Quaglia, L., Eastwood, R. and Holmes, P. (2009) 'The Financial Turmoil and EU Policy co-operation in 2008'. *JCMS*, Vol. 47, No. s1, pp. 63–87.

Schmidt V.A. (2002) *The Futures of European Capitalism* (Oxford: Oxford University Press).

Story, J. and Walter, I. (1997) *Political Economy of Financial Integration in Europe: The Battle of the System* (Manchester: Manchester University Press).

Tait, G. (2009) *Fool's Gold* (London: Little Brown).

Vitols, S. (2004) 'Changes in Germany's Bank-Based Financial System: A Varieties of Capitalism Perspective'. WZB Working Paper SP II 2004 – 03.

Walker, D. (2009) 'A Review of Corporate Governance in UK Banks and Other Financial Industry Entities: Final Recommendations'. HM Treasury, 29 November. Available at «http://www.hm-treasury.gov.uk/d/walker_review_261109.pdf».

Wigley, R. (chair) (2008) 'London: Winning in a Changing World. A Review of the Competitiveness of London's Financial Centre'. London. Available at «http://www.thecityuk.com/media/153763/London%20winning%20in%20a%20 changing%20world.pdf».

Zimmermann, H. (2010) 'Varieties of Global Financial Governance? British and German Approaches to Financial Market Regulation'. In Helleiner, E. Pagliari, S. and Zimmermann, H. (eds) *Global Finance in Crisis* (Abingdon: Routledge).

JCMS 2010 Volume 48 Annual Review pp. 143–162

Justice and Home Affairs

JÖRG MONAR
College of Europe

Introduction

2009 was a year of transition for the justice and home affairs (JHA) domain: The Hague Programme which had governed much of the development of the Union's 'area of freedom, security and justice' (AFSJ) since 2004 came to an end and new perspectives were opened up by the entry into force of the Lisbon Treaty and the adoption of the new 2010 to 2014 Stockholm Programme. While the intense negotiations on the Stockholm Programme were overshadowed until October by the uncertain fate of the Lisbon Treaty, the institutions focused mainly on a range of leftovers from the Hague Programme. Whereas several significant legislative texts were adopted on immigration and criminal justice co-operation issues, other fields were marked primarily by continuing negotiations and new Commission proposals (asylum), the strengthening of external action capacity (civil law), efforts to improve the implementation of adopted measures (border controls, the fight against organized crime and terrorism) and institutional consolidation (Europol). The total annual output of the JHA Council dropped from 144 adopted texts the year before to 121 texts,[1] perhaps a sort of end of programming period fatigue which could also be observed at the end of the preceding Tampere period.

---

[1] Lists of texts provided by the General Secretariat of the Council and own calculations.

Journal compilation © 2010 Blackwell Publishing Ltd, 9600 Garsington Road, Oxford OX4 2DQ, UK and 350 Main Street, Malden, MA 02148, USA

I. Developments in Individual Policy Areas

Refugee Policy

During the whole year negotiations continued on the first package of Commission legislative proposals for completing the Common European Asylum System (CEAS) which the Commission had submitted the year before (see Monar, 2009). Progress on recasting of the 2003 Reception Conditions Directive, the 2003 Dublin and the 2000 Eurodac Regulations was only modest. Not without some reason several Member States took the view that the proposals could not be properly considered without a full evaluation of the application of the existing texts, but for this the ambitious original deadline for the CEAS had left too little time to the Commission. Issues concerning a more effective burden-sharing under the Dublin system, possibilities and conditions of detention and the rights of children emerged as the most controversial on the agenda.

While these negotiations went on, the Commission added three further proposals to the already charged agenda.

On 18 February it presented a proposal for the establishment of a European Asylum Support Office (EASO) as an EU-funded agency for supporting and strengthening practical co-operation between the Member States in the context of the CEAS (Commission, 2009a). According to the proposal the supporting functions should extend to exchanges of good practice, information on countries of origin, support for co-operation between Member States under the Dublin Regulation, support for relocation, translation and interpreting, training, technical support and support in external matters. In addition the Commission wants the EASO to be able to support Member States under particular pressure through an early warning system, help with the initial assessment of asylum requests and the speedy establishment of appropriate reception facilities by Member States subject to pressure as well as the co-ordination of asylum support teams. Finally the Office should also be responsible for certain reporting functions, such as an annual report on the asylum situation in the EU and an evaluation of implementation, as well as – at the request of the Commission – the drawing up of guidelines and operating manuals. The EASO proposal was partly clearly modelled on other existing AFSJ agencies, such as Europol as regards its reporting functions and Frontex regarding its operational co-ordination and support functions. While a broad majority of the Member States support the establishment of the EASO – which could become an important burden-sharing and analysis instrument – it became rapidly clear that the Council is divided about the extent of the agency's functions and their financial implications as well as about the possibilities of the EASO to evaluate national implementation practices and issuing guidelines on those.

Wanting to have at least all key proposals for the CEAS on the table before the end of the Hague Programme, the Commission then presented on 21 October another proposal package consisting of the recasting of the 2004 Qualification and 2005 Asylum Procedures Directives.

Regarding the former, the Commission took on board some of the criticisms of NGOs and the UNHCR that the existing minimum standards for the qualification and status of refugees as beneficiaries of international protection had not achieved a sufficient level of harmonization and had impacted negatively on the quality of decision-making of national authorities. It also stressed the need for the further harmonization of protection standards in order to reduce secondary movements of refugees between Member States resulting from the diversity of national legal frameworks and decision-making practices and different levels of rights provided (which account for much of the different 'attractiveness' of Member States to asylum seekers). The Commission's proposal therefore aims at the clarification of key legal concepts such as 'actors of protection' or 'internal protection' used to define the grounds for protection, thus enabling decision-makers throughout the EU to apply the criteria consistently and to identify correctly who is really in need of protection. According to the Commission this could ensure both a more rapid access of genuine refugees to their rights – a key UNHCR concern – and allow for a more rapid removal of persons not qualifying – a key concern for Member States. The Commission proposal also provides for the elimination of the differences between the rights of refugees and beneficiaries of subsidiary protection, for instance regarding the duration of residence permits or access to social welfare, health care and to the labour market, and the facilitation of the recognition of qualifications, access to vocational training and employment as well as to integration facilities (Commission, 2009b).

The Commission's proposal for the recasting of the Procedures Directive is intended to streamline the examination process of applications by setting out a general time limit of six months for completing procedures at first instance and by simplifying and clarifying procedural notions and devices such as the concept of 'safe country of origin' or the accelerated procedures. It also aims at improving the quality of asylum decisions, by 'frontloading' services, advice and expertise and encouraging Member States to deliver 'robust' determinations at first instance with an improved defendability of negative decisions. The Commission, finally, also wants to enhance access of refugees to effective procedures by including territorial waters in the scope of the Directive – a reaction to the high number of refugee incidents at sea in the Mediterranean – and by specifying the obligations of border guards, police and personnel of detention facilities (Commission, 2009c). While NGOs generally welcomed the increased level of procedural safeguards in the

Commission's proposal, the maintenance of the controversial 'European safe third-country' concept, which would allow Member States according to Article 38 of the revised Directive to deny applicants from, for instance, Belarus, Moldova and the Russian Federation, a full or even any examination of an asylum application, was met with widespread concern.

The strong links between the different CEAS proposals – the important role the EASO could play for ensuring the effective implementation of the (recast) Procedures Directive is one of the most obvious – as well as the financial implications of the CEAS make this one of the biggest legislative and political 'packages' on the AFSJ agenda so far. Agreeing on it will require a massive compromise-building effort between the Member States in the Council on the one hand and between Council and Parliament on the other, and at the end of the year it seemed perfectly clear that this would not be achieved by the original Hague Programme deadline of 2010. While negotiations were going on the discrepancies in first instance recognition decision rates – from 0.2 per cent in Greece to 65.3 per cent in Poland in the previous year (Eurostat, 2009) – and the disproportionally high number of Iraqi asylum applications in Germany and of Serbian applications in France (UNHCR, 2009) showed again the major imbalances in the current EU system.

Migration Policy

With the Union's migration policy often being criticized because of its stronger focus on the fight against illegal immigration rather than facilitating legal immigration, a slight step towards a better balance between the two was taken on 25 May with the adoption of the Directive 2009/50/EC on the conditions of entry and residence of third-country nationals for the purposes of highly qualified employment – better known as the 'Blue Card Directive' (Council, 2009a). It introduces a fast-track procedure for issuing a special combined residence and work permit – the 'Blue Card' – to highly qualified third-country workers who have been offered a job in the EU. Aimed at reducing the 'skills gap' between the Union and major international competitors, such as the USA, which have so far been much more successful in attracting highly qualified third-country nationals to their job markets, the Blue Card Directive constitutes the so far most significant legislative EU measure in the domain of legal immigration for work purposes. However, an already not overly ambitious initial Commission proposal and the subsequent watering down of the initiative during more than a year of negotiations in the Council made this instrument in the end subject to so many restrictions that it is unlikely to compete effectively with major international rivals such as the US 'Green Card'.

A first major restriction is that the Commission failed in its attempt to make the Blue Card the only such scheme for facilitating access of highly qualified third-country nationals. Member States, apart from remaining in control of overall volumes of admission, remain free to maintain or introduce similar 'skill selective' national immigration schemes which can be more attractive to third-country nationals and hence undercut the value of the common EU scheme. Even this does not go far enough for Denmark, Ireland and the United Kingdom, which all have schemes (such as the 'Danish Green Card') already in place. They made use of their 'opt-out' rights under the Treaty of Amsterdam to stay out of the Directive altogether, which hardly strengthens the international image of the EU as a 'single' market as regards highly qualified jobs. The conditions for obtaining the Blue Card, while not unreasonable for an instrument aimed at highly qualified workers, clearly limit the range of potential applicants and include a valid work contract or binding job offer, the possession of documents attesting to equivalent professional qualifications and a salary of at least 1.5 times the average gross annual salary in the Member State concerned (Article 5 of the Directive). The period of validity – between one and four years (renewable) depending on the Member State concerned (Article 7) – also compares poorly with its 'green' US rival.

Yet, having regard to the rather rudimentary state of the EU's common approach to legal immigration for work purposes the Blue Card Directive can nevertheless be regarded as ground-breaking. This is not only because of the single fast-track procedure combining work and residence permit, but also because of the provisions on a progressive access to the labour market of the Member State concerned (Article 12), the allowance made for temporary unemployment (Article 13), the extensive rights to equal treatment with nationals of the respective Member State (Article 14), the right to family reunification (Article 15), the possibility to cumulate Blue Card residence periods for qualifying for long-term resident status (Article 16) and the possibility – subject to certain conditions – to move to another Member State after 18 months (Article 18) with family reunification rights (Article 19).

Whether the Blue Card Directive will increase significantly the integration of highly skilled third-country nationals in the EU job markets will to a considerable extent depend on the implementation of the Directive by the Member States – for which they have much margin to manoeuvre and two years' time. This might give the EU time also to give further consideration to mechanisms of 'circular migration' to counter the accusation that the Blue Card might contribute to a 'brain drain' in countries of origin. As Caritas Europa has rightly noted, Article 16(3) of the Directive according to which Blue Card holders can only return to their country for up to 12 consecutive months without putting their long-term resident status at risk can hardly be regarded as an encouragement for circular migration (Caritas Europa, 2009).

The adoption of the Blue Card Directive did not weaken in any way the Member States' resolve to strengthen their armoury for combating illegal immigration. This was shown by the adoption on 18 June of the Directive 2009/52/EC providing for minimum standards and sanctions against illegal employment of third-country nationals (European Parliament/Council, 2009a). Such illegal employment – which is particularly common in agriculture, catering, cleaning and construction – is not only a major 'pull' factor for illegal immigration, but also exposes the respective third-country nationals to exploitation and abuse by illegal employers and has become a major source of revenue for organized crime. According to 2007 Commission estimates the phenomenon might extend to between 4.5 and 8 million third-country nationals staying illegally in the EU (Commission, 2007). The Directive of 18 June obliges employers – which include both companies and individuals – to require from a third-country national as a condition of employment his or her holding of a valid residence permit or other authorization for his or her stay, to keep a copy or record of these available for possible inspection and to notify the competent authorities of the Member States of the start of employment (Article 4). Financial sanctions for non-compliance will increase in amount according to the number of illegally employed third-country nationals and the employer will also have to bear the costs of the return of illegally employed third-country nationals in those cases where return procedures are carried out. Yet Member States may provide for reduced financial sanctions where the employer is a natural person who employs an illegally staying third-country national for his or her private purposes and where no particularly exploitative working conditions are involved (Article 5). The main objective of the measure to target illegal employers and not illegal migrants is highlighted by Article 6 which obliges employers to pay to the illegally employed third-country national any outstanding remuneration at least at the level of the legal minimum wage in the respective Member State. In addition employers can be excluded from entitlement to public funding (including EU funding), disqualified from public contracts and obliged to reimburse public subsidies (Article 7). Member States are also required to provide for criminal penalties in the five most serious cases: continuation or repetition of an infringement, simultaneous employment of a significant number of persons, particularly exploitative working conditions, the knowing use of work or services exacted by a person who is a victim of human trafficking and the illegal employment of a minor (Articles 9 and 10).

The Directive against illegal employment of third-country nationals can be regarded as being almost as important for the fight against organized crime and trafficking in human beings as it is for the combating of illegal immigration. As regards its effectiveness much will – again – depend on its implementation by the Member States. National authorities have tended to not always cast too sharp an eye on illegal employment of third-country nationals as some economic sectors and a lot of private households are known to be heavily dependent on such 'cheap' labour. The continuous checks necessary for an effective implementation will in many cases require a significant additional administrative effort, and both the Commission and Member States will have to watch mutually over adequate enforcement standards and mechanisms.

Border and Visa Policy

During the reporting period Frontex was again at the forefront of EU external border policy by co-ordinating a range of joint operations. An example was the operation 'Saturn 2009', carried out in four operational phases of one month each and with over €1.4 million of EU funding, whose general objective was to tackle illegal immigration via and from Turkey and Albania towards the EU by enhancing the efficiency of the overall border control in the operational areas at the Greek–Albanian, Greek–Turkish and Bulgarian–Turkish borders, including checks at crossing points and the detection of illegal crossings by intensifying the green border surveillance activities (Frontex, 2009a). Frontex fulfilled its risk analysis function, *inter alia*, by a highly differentiated report on the impact of the global economic crisis on illegal migration to the EU. It concluded, because of the reduced labour demand and increased entry restrictions, on a likely decrease of illegal immigration pressure on the EU as well as on a higher return migration potential at least until 2010 (Frontex, 2009b) – which may be among the very few positive consequences of the financial crisis for the Union.

As foreseen by the Frontex Regulation in 2009, the agency went through an external evaluation process which resulted in a detailed external report and a reaction of the Frontex Management Board to its recommendations. The evaluation report was broadly positive about the progress the agency had made with mastering its rapidly expanding tasks but also identified a number of weaknesses (Frontex, 2009c). As regards the planning and co-ordination of joint operations at external borders, arguably the most important of the agency's tasks – the report pointed to deficits in terms of practical planning, uniform modalities for participating officers, slow reimbursement of costs, limited availability of equipment as well as language problems and lack of secure communication lines. The report acknowledged that some of the problems of Frontex – such as its very limited control of technical equipment which remains in the hands of the Member States – are outside of the agency's control, and pointed to some of the paradoxes of EU external border action, such as increased surveillance measures at sea borders actually resulting in an increase in illegal immigration as the vessels intercepting illegal immigrants are unable to turn them back. Naturally, not all of these and other conclusions were welcomed by the Management Board, but as a result of the evaluation process the Board agreed on no less than 16 recommendations for changes to the Frontex Regulation (Frontex, 2009d).

As regards the future evolution of Frontex its management board had also commissioned a report evaluating the feasibility of establishing specialized branches of Frontex in several Member States to enhance its reach and effectiveness. The report, submitted in December, came out in favour of such a partial decentralization which could include an improved understanding of local conditions, enhanced effectiveness in the use of risk information through more direct support of Member States regarding intelligence gathering and increased communication between Member States and Frontex fostered by offices located closer to national border management authorities (Frontex, 2009e).

While the fundamental utility and progress of Frontex was at no stage questioned, the putting into place of the second generation Schengen Information System (SIS II), with its advanced biometric functionalities, continued to be affected and delayed by technical problems regarding data consistency (needed for the equivalence of data between the national systems and the central system) as well as performance, robustness and security of the system (Council, 2009b; Commission, 2009d). These led the Council in June to decide formally on giving up the existing SIS II project altogether in case of further test failures and replacing it by an enhanced version of the existing SIS I system (Council, 2009c). Such a move could entail more limited new functionalities than originally planned for this biggest EU data-exchange instrument for border control and general law enforcement purposes and the loss of millions of euro already invested into the SIS II system architecture.

The EU's visa policy – which can be regarded as a major component of the Union's external border shield – took a step forward with the adoption on 13 July of the new Community Code on Visas (European Parliament/ Council, 2009b). The 'Visa Code', which replaces the former 'Common Consular Instructions' (CCI), clarifies which Member State is responsible for processing a visa application, defines the different phases for examination and decision-taking, harmonizes the fees that can be charged and sets common standards for the service provided which include rules on non-discrimination (Article 39) and on deciding on applications within 15 calendar days (Article 23). The position of visa applicants is strengthened by newly defined obligations for the Member States to give refused applicants the reasons for their decision and to inform them about their rights of appeal (Article 32(3) and Annex VI). Yet the Schengen visa regime overall is toughened by the new Code as biometric identifiers (including the ten fingerprints of the applicants) have now to be collected (Article 13), new defined conditions (including 'integrity and reliability') apply to the issuing of multiple entry visas (Article 24(2)) and former CCI provisions on group visas have not been retained.

The visa liberalization dialogue with the western Balkans, which is conducted by the EU on the basis of benchmarks regarding border controls, passport security, the fight against organized crime and corruption as well as external relations and fundamental rights, led to a first breakthrough: on 30 November the Council decided to grant visa-free travel to and throughout the Schengen area – with effect from 19 December – for citizens of the former Yugoslav Republic of Macedonia, Montenegro and Serbia by amending Regulation (EC) 539/2001 (Council, 2009d). Yet this liberalization measure applies only to holders of biometric passports, and Albania and Bosnia and Herzegovina were considered as having failed so far to meet all benchmarks so that further efforts on their side and monitoring by the EU will be necessary. The conditionality of visa liberalization has been an important instrument for the Union to induce the western Balkan countries to adjust their legislation, structures and practices to EU objectives and standards in the fight against illegal immigration and crime.

Judicial Co-operation in Civil Matters

While there were no major new internal developments in judicial co-operation in civil matters the year saw a strengthening of its external side: on 7 July the Council adopted EC Regulation 664/2009 establishing a procedure for the negotiation and conclusion of agreements between Member States and third countries concerning jurisdiction, recognition and enforcement of judgments on a range of family law matters (Council, 2009e). It covers agreements concerning matters falling, entirely or partly, within the scope of EC Regulation 2201/2003 of 27 November 2003 concerning jurisdiction and the recognition and enforcement of judgments in matrimonial matters and the matters of parental responsibility and 4/2009 of 18 December 2008 on jurisdiction, applicable law, recognition and enforcement of decisions and co-operation in matters relating to maintenance obligations, to the extent that those matters fall within the exclusive competence of the Community. The adoption of this Regulation was largely motivated by the fact that the Court of Justice had confirmed – in its Opinion 1/03 of 7 February 2006 relating to the conclusion of the new Lugano Convention – that the Community has acquired exclusive

competence to conclude an international agreement like the Lugano Convention with third countries on matters affecting rules adopted internally in the
domain of civil law matters. As a result it had to be ensured that bilateral
agreements of Member States with third countries in matters covered by
internal EU legislation do not interfere with Community competences. The
Regulation provides that when a Member State intends to enter into negotiations in order to amend an existing agreement or to conclude a new agreement
falling within the scope of the Regulation it has to notify the Commission in
writing of its intention at the earliest possible moment before the opening of
formal negotiations, providing a copy of the existing agreement, the draft
agreement or the draft proposal, and any other relevant documentation. The
Commission then has to give a reasoned decision on the application of the
Member State within 90 days. It has to determine whether there is sufficient
Community interest in concluding a Community agreement instead and can
either authorize the Member State to open formal negotiations on the proposed
bilateral agreement or refuse to do so. In the first case the Commission may
propose negotiating guidelines and may request the inclusion of particular
clauses in the envisaged agreement. In the second, 'discussions' between the
Commission and the respective Member State can follow. The Commission
can also take part as an observer in the Member State's negotiations which also
has to seek an authorization from the Commission prior to the conclusion of
the agreement. This the Commission can again refuse in which case 'discussions' in order to find a solution can take place. A Regulation (EC 662/2009)
providing for an identical procedure for the negotiation and conclusion of
agreements between Member States and third countries on particular matters
concerning the law applicable to contractual and non-contractual obligations
was adopted on 13 July (European Parliament/Council, 2009c).

The Regulations 662/2009 and 664/2009 are a reflection of the growing
external action capacity of the Union in the civil law domain – with corresponding restrictions on Member States' bilateral international action possibilities – which follows from the progressive expansion of its internal
legislation in this field. A further indication of this in the field of family law
was the Council Decision of 30 November on the conclusion by the Community of the Hague Protocol of 23 November 2007 on the Law Applicable
to Maintenance Obligations (Council, 2009f).

Judicial Co-operation in Criminal Matters

Partially driven by the intention to get certain texts adopted before the Lisbon
Treaty reforms could subject them to co-decision by the European Parliament, the Council's decision-making accelerated during the year on a number

of criminal justice matters. On 26 February the Council adopted Framework Decision 2009/315/JHA on the organization and content of the exchange of information extracted from the criminal record between Member States (Council, 2009g). This Framework Decision, which supplements provisions of the 2000 EU Convention on Mutual Legal Assistance in Criminal Matters which were not any longer considered adequate, went partly back to an initiative by Belgium. Under the impact of the 2004 child abuse and murder case of Michel Fourniret, Belgium had sought, in particular, to make sure that persons subject to convictions and disqualifications relating to child abuse cases would no longer be able to conceal such convictions or disqualifications with a view to performing professional activity related to supervision of children in other Member States. In addition to the obligations of a convicting Member State to transmit information to the Member State of the convicted person's nationality about the convictions handed down against their national – which the Framework Decision incorporates and further defines – it also provides for an obligation of the Member States of the person's nationality to store information transmitted in order to ensure that they are able to reply fully to requests for information from other Member States. The competent national authorities have to reply to requests for information about convictions within ten working days.

The exchange of criminal record data was further strengthened by the adoption on 6 April of the Council Decision on the establishment of the European Criminal Records Information System (ECRIS) (Council, 2009h). It partially implements the Framework Decision of 26 February by providing for the development of a computerised information exchange system on convictions between Member States for communicating information on convictions in a uniform, electronic and easily computer-translatable way. ECRIS has been designed as a decentralized information technology system. The criminal records data will be stored solely in databases operated by Member States, and there will be no direct online access to criminal records databases of other Member States. The Decision includes reference tables of categories of offences and categories of penalties and measures provided to facilitate automatic translation and the mutual understanding of the information transmitted by using a system of codes. Yet these tables are not intended to set up legal equivalences between offences and penalties and measures existing at national level and cover categories of offences – such as 'insults of the state, nation or symbols' – which (perhaps fortunately) fall well outside the scope of EU minimum harmonization acts and the European Arrest Warrant.

The prevention and settlement of conflicts of jurisdiction is a crucial element of the construction of a European criminal justice area. On 30 November, the Council adopted a Framework Decision (2009/948/JHA) on this important matter whose primary objective is to prevent situations where the same person is subject to parallel criminal proceedings in different Member States in respect of the same facts, which might lead to different final judicial outcomes in two or more Member States (Council, 2009i). The adoption of this measure was in part a reaction to the case law of the Court of Justice which had given a broad interpretation of the applicability of the double jeopardy ('*ne bis in idem*') principle since its 2003 landmark judgment in *Gözütok and Brügge* (joined cases C-187/01 and C-385/01). The Framework Decision provides for a competent judicial authority in a Member State to contact the competent authority of another Member State if it has 'reasonable grounds' to believe that parallel criminal proceedings are being conducted in that other Member State in respect of the same facts involving the same person. The contacted authority then has a deadline-linked obligation to reply with a defined minimum of information to be provided. When it is established that parallel proceedings exist, the competent authorities of the Member States concerned have to enter into direct consultations in order to reach consensus on any effective solution aimed at avoiding the adverse consequences arising from such parallel proceedings, which can lead to the concentration of the criminal proceedings in one Member State. If no consensus can be reached the case should be referred to Eurojust for possible arbitration if the case falls within the scope of its competences.

EU legislation regarding the recognition and/or execution of judicial decisions in one Member State (the executing Member State) issued by another Member State (the issuing Member State) has occasionally been rendered ineffective by different applicable national rules as regards procedural guarantees in case of the absence of the person at the trial. In response to this problem the Council passed on 26 February a Framework Decision (2009/299/JHA) aimed at helping authorities in the executing Member State prior to execution to ascertain whether certain minimum procedural rights of the person subject to the judicial decision but absent during the trial – such as adequate information and legal representation – have been respected (Council, 2009j). By formulating certain minimum procedural rights the Framework Decision slightly extends, *inter alia*, the number of grounds for refusal of the execution of the European Arrest Warrant, highlighting again the difficulties of ensuring an effective application of EU mutual recognition instruments in the context of still widely differing national criminal procedural law provisions.

A more comprehensive EU instrument on the strengthening of procedural rights of suspected or accused persons in criminal proceedings is still missing. The Council was able to agree on 30 November on a 'road map' for strengthening these rights which identified six major fields of action, but the road map remained vague about the level of the rights and did not set a deadline for legislative action for which the Commission was invited to submit proposals (Council, 2009k). However, the rights of persons awaiting trial were slightly strengthened by the adoption on 23 October of a Framework Decision (2009/829/JHA) on the application of mutual recognition to decisions on supervision measures as an alternative to provisional detention (Council, 2009l). By providing rules for the execution of supervision orders issued in another Member State this measure fulfils a non-discrimination objective as it allows reduction of the risk of a non-resident being remanded in custody pending trial even where, in similar circumstances, a resident would not.

Police Co-operation and the Fight against Organized Crime and Terrorism

On 6 April the Council adopted the new Europol Decision (2009/371/JHA) which replaces the 1995 Europol Convention and will transform the police organization into an EU entity funded from the general budget of the EU (instead of from national budgets) with effect from 1 January 2010 (Council, 2009m). While not transferring any executive law enforcement powers to Europol, the Decision extends the agency's possibilities to assist national authorities, *inter alia*, by no longer being bound by the current precondition of factual indications of involvement of organized crime structures, the facilitation of its participation – in a supportive function – in Joint Investigation Teams (JITs) and simplifying the direct access of national authorities to the Europol Information System. The changes made to the governance structure of Europol are very limited and unlikely to resolve fully some of the existing problems such as the often detailed interference of the powerful management board with the running of the institution by the Director of Europol. However, the passage to an 18 rather than six-month period for the Chairmanship of the Management Board could provide both greater continuity and a framework for a more effective working relationship with the Director.

The co-operation between Europol and its counterpart in the cross-border prosecution domain, Eurojust, made further progress during the year with the elaboration by both agencies of a common 'Joint Investigation Teams Manual' (Council, 2009n). It provides practitioners with guidelines and recommendations for setting up and increasing the effectiveness of JITs. Although one of the few cross-border operational law enforcement means established by the EU, JITs remain a legally and operationally cumbersome and still sparsely used instrument whose use Europol and Eurojust wish to encourage.

Based on Europol's 2009 Organized Crime Threat Assessment (OCTA) and Russian Organised Crime Threat Assessment (ROCTA) reports the

Council adopted at its meeting of 4–5 June new Conclusions on the EU's priorities for the fight against organized crime (Council, 2009o). In terms of trends the Council noted, in particular, the increasing share of non-EU based organized crime within the EU, the role of the EU as a long-term investment area for external organized crime as investments in western Europe provide more stability and increase in value, the threat posed by criminal hubs in west Africa (in particular for drug trafficking and trafficking in human beings) and the increasing number of crimes against persons (in particular the use of systematic violence in order to intimidate local communities). In the light of the OCTA and ROCTA reports the Council then defined the following criminal markets as EU priority fields in the fight against organised crime for 2009–10: drug trafficking with a focus on the use of the west and central African route (including drugs from Latin America and the Caribbean) for storage and transit, but also processing, trading and/or production; trafficking in human beings (including from Africa), especially for the purpose of sexual exploitation; fraud, corruption and money laundering, as well as other activities related to organized crime involvement in the economy, especially if they seriously distort legal competition or lead to an increase of criminals' influence in the political, economic and judicial sphere (as this is especially the case in connection with Russian-speaking organized crime groups). These priorities were fewer in number than in the past as the Council had come to realize that the proliferation of priorities of recent years had reduced the overall efficiency of EU action and made it more difficult for Member States to adequately reflect those in their national action plans. The Conclusions defined a number of specific tasks for Commission, Council, Eurojust, Europol, the Police Chiefs Task Force, customs authorities and the European Police College, this with a clear emphasis on greater inter-institutional synergy.

The fight against terrorism remained a priority for the AFSJ throughout the year: on the internal side the Council approved at its 4–5 June meeting a detailed implementation plan for the revised EU counter-terrorism 'Radicalization and Recruitment Plan', which the Swedish Presidency was prevented from making a public document because of internal security considerations of a minority of Member States (Council, 2009p). An Action Plan on strengthening chemical, biological, radiological and nuclear (CBRN) security adopted at the 30 November–1 December meeting of the Council was extended to a wide range of measures regarding prevention, detection and response regarding terrorist risks in the CBRN domain (Council, 2009q). On the external side a report on the co-operation with the western Balkan countries on the fight against organised crime and terrorism adopted in May emphasised the need for more EU action to strengthen counter-terrorism capabilities in those countries, to establish specialised counter-terrorism contact points and to enhance the role of Europol and Eurojust in the co-operation (Council, 2009r). Co-operation with the US in the counter-terrorism field made some progress with the Council's decision of 30 November to sign a provisional Agreement with the US on the exchange of financial messaging data which would give US authorities access to European financial transaction data handled by the Society for Worldwide Interbank Financial Telecommunication (SWIFT) for the purposes of the US Terrorist Finance Tracking Programme (Council, 2009s). Yet the Council went ahead with this decision in spite of the fact that under the new Lisbon Treaty rules the agreement would need to get the consent of the European Parliament, and by the end of the year it seemed increasingly likely that the Parliament might reject the agreement both because of concerns about inadequate protection of personal data and anger about the Council's disregard of its new prerogatives.

The most thoughtful evaluation of the progress and limitations of EU counter-terrorism measures came – once more – from the EU's Counter-terrorism Co-ordinator, Gilles de Kerchove. In a discussion paper on counter-terrorism strategy he warned about the concentration on terrorism simply as a criminal phenomenon tending to downplay the factors that motivate terrorism and encouraging a straightforward repressive approach, and also about 'counter-terrorism fatigue' resulting from taking rapid and massive action after terrorist attacks only to fall up behind once the immediate pressure has decreased. The paper suggested giving more priority to measures regarding the prevention and response to terrorist attacks, including the promotion of good relations and practices in terms of community engagement and cross-cultural dialogue as part of the strategy against radicalization and recruitment, making effective counter-terrorism measures and the promotion of human rights mutually reinforcing goals, measures to support the victims of terrorism and developing security in failed and failing states, which provide safe havens for terrorists, through CFSP/ESDP tools (Council, 2009t). While some of these issues are already recognized in EU strategy and action plan documents, it has so far been far easier for the Council and the Member States to agree rapidly on 'visible' repressive action rather than on such wider and often more complex prevention and response measures.

New Perspectives: The Treaty of Lisbon and the Stockholm Programme

The end of the year saw both constitutional and programmatic change for the AFSJ which will influence its development over years to come.

The entry into force of the Treaty of Lisbon on 1 December underlined the political importance which the AFSJ has acquired for the Member States as masters of the Treaties. Of all the EU policy-making domains the AFSJ has been the object of the greatest number of treaty changes, and it was also moved up in the list of the fundamental treaty objectives (new Article 3(2) TEU) ranging now before the EMU, the internal market and the CFSP. The main constitutional reforms include the absorption of the former 'third pillar' (police and judicial co-operation in criminal matters) in a new Title V of Part III of the TFEU, which for the first time creates a unified legal framework for both internal and external JHA action; enhanced EU competences (especially in the field of criminal justice co-operation, Article 82–83), the extension of the Parliament's co-decision powers and qualified majority voting to most former 'third pillar' matters and the lifting of most of the existing limitations of judicial control by the Court of Justice. The TFEU even opens up the possibility of establishing a European Public Prosecutor's Office (Article 86), but this remains subject to unanimity in the Council as this is also the case for the newly provided definition of the conditions and limitations under which police authorities may operate in the territory of another Member State (Article 89). All this progress, however, had to be bought at the price of both extending the opt-out of the United Kingdom and Ireland to the former 'third pillar' matters and facilitating the access of potential pioneer groups of at least nine Member States to enhanced co-operation on certain criminal justice and police co-operation matters, thereby enhancing the risks of further differentiation within the AFSJ. The Lisbon Treaty reforms also do not remove the tension between common objectives on the one hand and the protection of national competences on the other as this is exemplified by the maintenance of national control of volumes of admission under the new 'common migration policy' (Article 79(5) TFEU) and a new provision according to which the Union has to 'respect essential state functions including [. . .] maintaining law and order and safe-guarding national security' (Article 4(2) TEU).

Formally launched by a (late) Commission Communication of 10 June (Commission 2009e) the negotiations on the new 2010–14 Stockholm Pro-gramme – the successor to the 2005–09 Hague Programme – led to a longer and longer text as the Swedish Presidency bravely tried to accommodate all the different priorities and reservations of the Member States. The result, formally adopted by the European Council on 10–11 December, is an 82-page-long programming framework for the further development of the AFSJ of uneven substance (Council, 2009u): while a stronger emphasis is placed on the protection of individual rights, the envisaged implemen-tation action is – as, for instance, in the case of the rights of the indivi-dual in criminal proceedings (2.4.) – often vague in substance and not deadline-linked. More forceful priority settings in some fields – such as information exchange (4.2.2.), trafficking in human beings (4.4.2.), economic crime (4.4.5.), terrorism (4.5.) and integrated management of external borders (5.1.) contrast with much more vaguely defined objectives in others – such as mutual trust building (1.2.1.), the introduction of the European Public Prosecutor's Office (3.1.1.), approximation of national criminal laws (3.3.1.), the fight against drugs (4.4.6) and action on labour immigration (6.1.3.). The Programme includes some innovative elements, such as the provision made for the adoption of a comprehensive EU internal security strategy (4.1.) and the possibility to establish an EU Anti-Trafficking Co-ordinator (4.4.2.), which could both contribute to more coherence of EU action. It also clearly identifies some strategic challenges – such as the need to improve the effective implementation of JHA measures by more extensive evaluations (12.2./ 5.), to ensure high data protection standards (2.5.) and to strengthen coherent external action (7.1.). While in no way guaranteeing the necessary political will, the Lisbon Treaty provides the EU at least with an improved constitutional framework to deliver on the Stockholm Programme objectives.

Key Readings

Laviero, B. (2009) 'From Tampere to The Hague and Beyond: Towards the Stockholm Programme in the Area of Freedom, Security and Justice'. *ERA-Forum: scripta iuris europaei'*, 10, No. 3, pp. 333–42.

Mitsilegas, V. (2009) *EU Criminal Law* (Oxford: Hart).

Wolff, S., Wichmann, N. and Mounier, G. (eds) (2009) 'The External Dimension of Justice and Home Affairs: A Different Security Agenda for the EU?'. *Journal of European Integration*, Vol. 31, No. 1.

References

Caritas Europa (2009) 'Caritas Europa Comments on the new EU "Blue Card System" '. Brussels, June.

Commission of the European Communities (2007) 'Proposal for a Directive [. . .] Providing for Sanctions Against Employers of Illegally Staying Third-Country Nationals'. *COM*(2007)249, 16 May.

Commission of the European Communities (2009a) 'Proposal for a Regulation [. . .] Establishing a European Asylum Support Office'. *COM*(2009)66, 18 February.

Commission of the European Communities (2009b) 'Proposal for a Directive [. . .] on Minimum Standards for the Qualification and Status of Third Country Nationals or Stateless Persons as Beneficiaries of International Protection and the Content of the Protection Granted'. *COM*(2009)551, 21 October.

Commission of the European Communities (2009c) 'Proposal for a Directive [. . .] on Minimum Standards on Procedures in Member States for Granting and Withdrawing International Protection'. *COM*(2009)554, 21 October.

Commission of the European Communities (2009d) 'Report [. . .] on the Development of the Second Generation Schengen Information System (SIS II). Progress Report July 2008–December 2008. *COM*(2009)133, 24 March.

Commission of the European Communities (2009e) 'Communication [. . .] An Area of Freedom, Security and Justice Serving the Citizen'. *COM*(2009)262, 10 June.

Council of the European Union (2009a) 'Council Directive 2009/50/EC of 25 May 2009 on the Conditions of Entry and Residence of Third-Country Nationals for the Purposes of Highly Qualified Employment'. OJ L155, 18 June.

Council of the European Union (2009b) 'Report of the SIS II Task Force'. 7789/09, Brussels, 19 March.

Council of the European Union (2009c) 'Council Conclusions on the further direction of SIS II'. 10708/09, Brussels, 5 June.

Council of the European Union (2009d) 'Council Regulation (EC) No 1244/2009 of 30 November 2009 Amending Regulation (EC) No 539/2001 Listing the Third Countries Whose Nationals Must be in Possession of Visas When Crossing the External Borders and those whose Nationals are Exempt from that Requirement'. OJ 336, 18 December.

Council of the European Union (2009e) 'Council Regulation (EC) No 664/2009 of 7 July 2009 Establishing a Procedure for the Negotiation and Conclusion of Agreements between Member States and Third Countries Concerning Jurisdiction, Recognition and Enforcement of Judgments and Decisions in Matrimonial Matters, Matters of Parental Responsibility and Matters Relating to Maintenance Obligations, and the Law Applicable to Matters Relating to Maintenance Obligation'. OJ L 200, 31 July.

Council of the European Union (2009f) 'Council Decision of 30 November 2009 on the Conclusion by the European Community of the Hague Protocol of 23 November 2007 on the Law Applicable to Maintenance Obligations'. OJ L 331, 16 December.

Council of the European Union (2009g) 'Council Framework Decision 2009/315/JHA of 26 February 2009 on the Organization and Content of the Exchange of Information Extracted from the Criminal Record between Member States'. L 93, 7 April.

Council of the European Union (2009h) 'Council Decision 2009/316/JHA of 6 April 2009 on the Establishment of the European Criminal Records Information System (ECRIS) in Application of Article 11 of Framework Decision 2009/315/JHA'. OJ L 93, 7 April.

Council of the European Union (2009i) 'Council Framework Decision 2009/948/JHA of 30 November 2009 on Prevention and Settlement of Conflicts of Exercise of Jurisdiction in Criminal Proceedings'. OJ L 328, 15 December.

Council of the European Union (2009j) 'Council Framework Decision 2009/299/JHA of 26 February 2009 Amending Framework Decisions 2002/584/JHA, 2005/

214/JHA, 2006/783/JHA, 2008/909/JHA and 2008/947/JHA, thereby Enhancing the Procedural Rights of Persons and Fostering the Application of the Principle of Mutual Recognition to Decisions Rendered in the Absence of the Person Concerned at the Trial'. L 81, 27 March.

Council of the European Union (2009k) 'Resolution of the Council of 30 November 2009 on a Roadmap for Strengthening Procedural Rights of Suspected or Accused Persons in Criminal Proceedings'. OJ C 295, 4 December.

Council of the European Union (2009l) 'Council Framework Decision 2009/829/ JHA of 23 October 2009 on the Application, between Member States of the European Union, of the Principle of Mutual Recognition to Decisions on Supervision Measures as an Alternative to Provisional Detention'. L 294, 11 November.

Council of the European Union (2009m) 'Council Decision of 6 April 2009 establishing the European Police Office (Europol)'. L 121, 15 May.

Council of the European Union (2009n) 'Joint Investigation Teams Manual'. 13598/ 09, Brussels, 23 September.

Council of the European Union (2009o) 'Draft Council Conclusions Setting the EU's Priorities for the Fight Against Organised Crime Based on the OCTA 2009 and the ROCTA'. 8301/3/09 REV 3, Brussels, 20 May.

Council of the European Union (2009p) 'Revised EU Radicalization and Recruitment Action Plan'. 15374/09, Brussels, 5 November.

Council of the European Union (2009q) 'Council Conclusions on Strengthening Chemical, Biological, Radiological and Nuclear (CBRN) Security in the European Union – an EU CBRN Action Plan'. 11513/3/09 REV 3, Brussels, 12 November.

Council of the European Union (2009r) 'Implementation of the Council Conclusions on the Co-operation with Western Balkan Countries on the Fight Against Organised Crime and Terrorism'. 10232/09, Brussels, 26 May.

Council of the European Union (2009s) Council Decision 2010/16/CFSP/JHA of 30 November 2009 on the signing, on behalf of the European Union, of the Agreement between the European Union and the United States of America on the Processing and Transfer of Financial Messaging Data from the European Union to the United States for Purposes of the Terrorist Finance Tracking Program'. L 8, 13 January 2010.

Council of the European Union (2009t) 'EU Counter-Terrorism Strategy – Discussion paper'. 15359/1/09 REV 1, Brussels, 26 November.

Council of the European Union (2009u) 'The Stockholm Programme – An Open and Secure Europe Serving and Protecting the Citizens'. 17024/09, Brussels, 2 December.

European Parliament/Council of the European Union (2009a) 'Directive 2009/52/EC [. . .] of 18 June 2009 Providing for Minimum Standards on Sanctions and Measures against Employers of Illegally Staying Third-Country Nationals'. OJ L 168, 30 June.

European Parliament/Council of the European Union (2009b) 'Regulation (EC) No. 810/2009 [. . .] of 13 July 2009 establishing a Community Code on Visas (Visa Code)'. OJ 243, 15 September.

European Parliament/Council of the European Union (2009c) 'Regulation (EC) No. 662/2009 [. . .] of 13 July 2009 Establishing a Procedure for the Negotiation and Conclusion of Agreements between Member States and Third Countries on Particular Matters Concerning the Law Applicable to Contractual and Non-Contractual Obligations'. OJ L 200, 31 July.

Eurostat (2009) 'Statistics in Focus 92/2009: 75,000 Asylum Seekers Granted Protection Status in the EU in 2008'. 10 December.

Frontex (2009a) 'Parliamentary Seminar on Visa and Border Management with Members of the EP and Western Balkans' Parliaments. Speech of Mr Gil Arias, Deputy Executive Director of Frontex'. Warsaw, 31 March.

Frontex (2009b) 'The Impact of the Global Economic Crisis on Illegal Migration to the EU'. Warsaw, August.

Frontex (2009c) 'External Evaluation of the European Agency for the Management of Operational Co-operation at the External Borders of the Member States of the European Union. Final Report (COWI)'. Warsaw, January.

Frontex (2009d) 'Recommendations Issued Following the Evaluation of the European Agency for the Management of Operational Co-operation at the External Borders of the Member States of the European Union. Warsaw, July.

Frontex (2009e) 'Study on the Feasibility of Establishing Specialized Branches of Frontex Final Report (Deloitte)'. Warsaw, 11 December.

Monar, J. (2009) 'Justice and Home Affairs'. *JCMS*, Vol. 47, s1, pp. 151–70.

UNHCR (2009) 'Asylum Levels and Trends in Industrialized Countries. First Half of 2009'. 21 October.

Legal Developments

MICHAEL DOUGAN
Liverpool Law School, University of Liverpool

Introduction

2009 will be remembered, first and foremost, as the year when the Treaty of Lisbon entered into force, thoroughly recasting the Union's constitutional fabric. But this is not the place for summarizing, let alone exploring, the myriad reforms introduced by Lisbon.[1] We will retain our usual focus on the case law of the Union courts, in which regard 2009 actually proved a relatively quiet year. Not that we lacked a multitude of new rulings, a great many of which can be considered significant within their own particular doctrinal and policy spheres. Far from it. Consider judgments such as *Elgafaji* on the definition under Union law of third-country nationals or stateless persons as refugees or persons who otherwise need international protection,[2] or *Apostolides* concerning the politically sensitive issue of how far Union law suspends application of the *acquis communautaire* in disputes concerning areas falling outside the effective control of the Cypriot government.[3] A group of Commission enforcement proceedings tested the compatibility with Article 351 of the Treaty on the Functioning of the European Union (TFEU) (previously Article 307 EC) of provisions affecting the free movement of capital contained in bilateral investment treaties concluded between various Member

---

[1] Last year's 'Legal Developments' article contained several suggestions for further reading on/analysis of the Lisbon Treaty.
[2] Case C-465/07 (17 February 2009).
[3] Case C-420/07 (28 April 2009).

States and third countries.[4] Another series of rulings explored the principle of non-discrimination on grounds of nationality as regards domestic measures implementing the European Arrest Warrant,[5] the rights of migrant work-seekers[6] and the Euratom Treaty.[7] Several judgments were delivered considering the implications of the freedom of establishment for national rules regulating the organization and provision of public welfare services within the domestic territory.[8] As the year drew to a close, the Court decided a set of cases clarifying the extent to which Member States may invoke the 'essential security interests' clause contained in Article 346 TFEU (ex-Article 296 EC) as a means of derogating from their obligations under Union law.[9]

But overall, 2009 delivered few rulings that can be described as truly path-breaking for the Union legal order viewed from a broader perspective. For that reason, this review of legal developments can exercise an even greater freedom than usual in its choice of titbits from Luxembourg. In particular, we will focus on two *prima facie* quite distinct rulings – *Commission v. Italy (Motorcycle Trailers)*[10] addressing the definition of measures having equivalent effect to a quantitative restriction on imports for the purposes of Article 34 TFEU (ex-Article 28 EC), and *Ireland v. Parliament and Council (Data Retention Directive)*[11] concerning the scope of the Union legislature's power to adopt harmonizing measures pursuant to Article 114 TFEU (ex-Article 95 EC) – which were nevertheless delivered on the same day and are in fact united by a common theme: the apparently inexhaustible controversy of how to delimit the proper scope of Union internal market law and its relationship to the Member States' own regulatory competences. Our conclusions will then attempt to link those two rulings with another legal development, this time not in the case law of the Union courts but rather in the jurisprudence of the German Federal Constitutional Court, which is nevertheless likely to prove of great importance to the Union legal order: the ruling on the compatibility of the Lisbon Treaty with the German Basic Law.[12]

---

[4] Case C-249/06 *Commission v. Sweden* (3 March 2009); Case C-205/06 *Commission v. Austria* (3 March 2009); Case C-118/07 *Commission v. Finland* (19 November 2009).
[5] Case C-123/08 *Wolzenburg* (6 October 2009).
[6] Cases C-22 & 23/08 *Vatsouras* (4 June 2009).
[7] Case C-115/08 *ČEZ* (27 October 2009).
[8] Including: Case C-169/07 *Hartlauer* (10 March 2009); Case C-531/06 *Commission v. Italy* (19 May 2009); Cases C-171 & 172/07 *Apothekerkammer des Saarlandes* (19 May 2009).
[9] Case C-461/05 *Commission v. Denmark* (15 December 2009); Case C-409/05 *Commission v. Greece* (15 December 2009); Case C-387/05 *Commission v. Italy* (15 December 2009); Case C-372/05 *Commission v. Germany* (15 December 2009); Case C-294/05 *Commission v. Sweden* (15 December 2009); Case C-284/05 *Commission v. Finland* (15 December 2009); Case C-239/06 *Commission v. Italy* (15 December 2009).
[10] Case C-110/05 (10 February 2009).
[11] Case C-301/06 (10 February 2009).
[12] BVerfG Judgment of 30 June 2009.

I. Defining the Boundaries of the Free Movement of Goods under Article 34 TFEU: The Triumph of 'Market Access'?

In *Commission v. Italy*, the ECJ delivered an important ruling concerning the concept of measures having equivalent effect to a quantitative restriction on imported goods as defined in the foundational *Dassonville* case.[13]

EU lawyers might be accused of fetishizing the case law on the scope of the Treaty rules on the free movement of goods. But some fetishes are there to be wallowed in. The scope of application of Article 34 TFEU is not only a central issue for the substantive law of the internal market, but also a crucial element in determining the constitutional relationship between the Union and its Member States. The broader the scope of the free movement provisions, the greater the range of national policy choices that are brought under the scrutiny of the Court of Justice, and become more readily amenable to the regulatory competence of the Union legislature under provisions such as Article 114 TFEU. In particular, choices about the interpretation of Article 34 TFEU are decisive for defining both the fundamental ambitions and the institutional dynamics of the internal market bargain. If the Court adopts a restrictive understanding of Article 34 TFEU, it signals that the judicial role is limited to scrutinizing national measures that have a direct and specific impact on cross-border trade; the pursuit of any deeper form of economic integration lies (if at all) with the political institutions. By contrast, when the Court expands the potential reach of Article 34 TFEU, it risks beginning to ensnare domestic rules which tend simply to restrict the market freedom of economic undertakings, even in the absence of any distinctly cross-border obstacle to trade. In the latter situation, Article 34 TFEU morphs from a guarantee of *cross-border* trade into an instrument for promoting *free* trade: the deregulatory power of the primary Treaty provisions is certainly enhanced; the harmonizing competence of the Union institutions is potentially expanded.

By the beginning of 2009, the 'state of play' on the scope of application of Article 34 TFEU might have been summarized (i.e. highly simplified) as follows. On the face of it, the Court seemed to pursue a 'categorization' approach to defining the reach of the free movement of goods: different types of national rule were subject to distinct presumptions concerning their potential to fall within or outside the scope of the Treaty. According to the case law delivered under *Cassis de Dijon*,[14] product requirements – affecting the physical integrity of goods as regards matters such as their composition, packaging

---

[13] Case 8/74 *Dassonville* [1974] ECR 837.
[14] Case 120/78 *Cassis de Dijon* [1979] ECR 649.

or labelling – would always fall within the scope of Article 34 TFEU. According to the jurisprudence following *Keck and Mithouard*,[15] selling arrangements – governing the place, time or manner in which goods are sold – should fall outside the scope of the Treaty unless (in particular) they either discriminate against imported goods or prevent the latter's access to the domestic market. Other types of rule which could not be classified as either product requirements or selling arrangements in their strict sense had to be scrutinized on an ad hoc basis: some might indeed create barriers to cross-border trade within the meaning of *Dassonville*;[16] others had effects too uncertain and indirect to warrant the application of Article 34 TFEU.[17]

However, many scholars argued that such different categories and distinct presumptions could and/or should in fact be rationalized into some more unified theory of free movement law.[18] At one extreme, some supported a relatively narrow discrimination-based approach to Article 34 TFEU: the Court should scrutinize only those national rules that treat imported goods less favourably than domestic ones. At the other extreme, some argued for a very wide conception of the free movement provisions: the Court should use the fact of importation as an opportunity to investigate every restriction on economic activity. In between those extremes lay two more popular interpretations. The first held that Article 34 TFEU should embody the principle not only of non-discrimination but also of mutual recognition: if French cheese is good enough for the French, and has already been regulated once for that purpose by the French authorities, then there is no reason why it should not also be eaten by the British or the Poles, who must positively justify any attempt to regulate the imported products a second time. The second interpretation argued for Article 34 TFEU to be based rather upon a principle of market access: the Court should scrutinize any national measure that prevents or hinders the access of imported goods to the domestic market, even in the absence of discrimination or a double regulatory burden. Precisely what kind or degree of hindrance to market access proved rather difficult even for its supporters to define – but the implication of this interpretation was that the Treaty could indeed serve to prise open previously closed national markets, or even to create new markets in Member States where they did not previously exist, yet without going so far as to catch every possible constraint upon absolute commercial freedom and amount in practice to a charter for unabashed free trade.

[15] Cases C-267 & 268/91 *Keck and Mithouard* [1993] ECR I-6097.
[16] E.g. Case C-105/94 *Celestini* [1997] ECR I-2971; Case C-434/04 *Leppik* [2006] ECR I-9171.
[17] E.g. Case C-69/88 *Krantz* [1990] ECR I-583; Case C-44/98 *BASF* [1999] ECR I-6269.
[18] Consider, e.g. C. Barnard, 'Fitting the Remaining Pieces into the Goods and Persons Jigsaw' (2001) 26 *European Law Review* 35.

Commission v. Italy presented the Court with an opportunity to clarify the case law and express its view on which – if any – 'grand theory' of free movement law stood reflected in Article 34 TFEU. The dispute concerned an Italian prohibition on any motorcycle towing a trailer on the national road network. Believing that this constituted a measure having equivalent effect to a quantitative restriction on imported trailers, the Commission brought enforcement proceedings against Italy under Article 258 TFEU (ex-Article 226 EC).

The Court's analysis began with some rather important 'preliminary observations' on the scope of Article 34 TFEU as interpreted in *Dassonville*.[19] That provision 'reflects the obligation to respect the principles of non-discrimination and of mutual recognition of products lawfully manufactured and marketed in other Member States, as well as the principle of ensuring free access of [Union] products to national markets'. The Court then recalled the *Cassis de Dijon* case law whereby product requirements are always presumed to fall within the scope of Article 34 TFEU; and the *Keck and Mithouard* jurisprudence to the effect that selling arrangements will fall outside the Treaty unless (in particular) they discriminate against imported goods or prevent the latter's access to the host market. The Court continued to observe that, '[c]onsequently, measures adopted by a Member State the object or effect of which is to treat products coming from other Member States less favourably are to be treated as measures having equivalent effect to quantitative restrictions on imports [. . .] as are [product requirements as dealt with under *Cassis de Dijon*]. Any other measure which hinders access of products originating in other Member States to the market of a Member State is also covered by that concept'.

Applying those principles to the disputed Italian rules, the Court held that it was necessary to distinguish between trailers specially designed to be used with motorcycles and other types of trailers capable of being towed also by other types of vehicle. In the latter case, the Commission had failed to demonstrate that the Italian rules hindered access to the Italian market. But in the former case, it was accepted that the possibilities for using such trailers other than with motorcycles were very limited. A prohibition on the use of a product in the territory of a Member State has a considerable influence on the behaviour of consumers which, in turn, affects that product's access to the national market. Consumers, knowing that they are not permitted to use their motorcycle with a specially designed trailer have practically no interest in buying those goods. The Italian rules prevented a demand for such trailers from existing in the national market and therefore hindered their importation

[19] See paras. 33–37.

– and constituted a measure having equivalent effect to a quantitative restriction on imports, within the meaning of Article 34 TFEU, unless they could be objectively justified. In that regard, the Italian rules served the legitimate objective of ensuring road safety; analysis of whether those rules were appropriate and necessary for achieving that purpose revealed no factor to suggest they were disproportionate and hence unlawful. The Commission's action was thus dismissed.

The Court could have dealt with *Commission v. Italy* in accordance with its previous case law based on categories and presumptions: a restriction on use is neither a product requirement nor a selling arrangement; its effects were therefore to be analysed on an ad hoc basis directly under *Dassonville*, for which purpose, it was obvious that a total ban on the use of trailers specifically designed for use with motorcycles had a certain and direct effect on cross-border trade and runs contrary to the spirit of the principle of mutual recognition. The Court instead chose to go further – explicitly clarifying that the conceptual foundations of Article 34 TFEU are cumulatively based upon the requirement of non-discrimination, *and* a presumption of mutual recognition, *plus* a principle of free market access. The question is: how much further did the Court intend to go with those preliminary musings upon the conceptual foundations of the free movement of goods? Two main questions arise in that regard. First, to what extent does *Commission v. Italy* signal the end of the previous categories-and-presumptions approach to defining the boundaries of Article 34 TFEU, in favour of a unified test indeed based upon the concept of 'market access'? Secondly, to the degree that 'market access' is to play a more explicit role in the Court's reasoning, does *Commission v. Italy* shed any greater light upon the kind or degree of hindrance required to trigger the application of the Treaty?

As for the first question, it seems rather unlikely that the Court intended to abandon altogether its well-established division of the case law between *Cassis*-style product requirements, *Keck*-style selling arrangements and those residual rules dealt with directly under *Dassonville*. Perhaps the real issue is how far the 'market access' approach propounded in *Commission v. Italy* might come to inform the Court's legal assessment of whether those different categories of national measures fall within the scope of Article 34 TFEU. For those purposes, it is difficult to see how the 'market access' concept can add anything useful to the case law derived from *Cassis de Dijon*: product requirements are already irrefutably presumed to fall within the scope of the Treaty and thus require objective justification. But it is perfectly possible and indeed probable that the 'market access' test developed in *Commission v. Italy* will come to govern more explicitly the Court's assessment of whether national measures falling within the residual category of rules are deemed compatible with the *Dassonville* formula. Certainly, the *Commission v. Italy* 'market access' test was employed by the Court in its subsequent ruling in *Mickelsson and Roos*, to determine whether Swedish restrictions on the use of personal watercraft fell within the scope of Article 34 TFEU.[20]

The most difficult questions relate to how far *Commission v. Italy* will impact upon the approach to selling arrangements laid down in *Keck and Mithouard*. In one scenario, it could be that *Keck* continues to play a distinctive role under Article 34 TFEU, albeit subtly modified by the Court's new conceptual vision in *Commission v. Italy*. Thus, selling arrangements would still be presumed to fall outside the scope of Article 34 TFEU unless (in particular) they either discriminate against imported goods or hinder (as opposed to prevent) the latter's access to the domestic market. In another scenario, however, it could be that *Keck* and its selling arrangements are being quietly retired from active service as a distinct category-plus-presumption under free movement law. To the extent that selling arrangements discriminate against foreign goods, they will be caught immediately by the principle of equal treatment embodied in Article 34 TFEU. Otherwise, insofar as selling arrangements might hinder market access for imported products, they will be treated like any other type of (residual, non-product requirement) national measure (such as restrictions on use) in accordance with *Commission v. Italy*.

The ruling in *Commission v. Italy* itself is rather ambiguous about the role and future of *Keck*. On the one hand, the Court's 'preliminary observations' unfold by identifying the case law on selling arrangements as a distinct legal category. On the other hand, those 'preliminary observations' conclude by dividing the scope of Article 34 TFEU into three: discriminatory rules; product requirements; and 'any other measure' hindering market access – the latter presumably conflating selling arrangements with all other residual rules. Nevertheless, the traditional *Keck* approach has since been relied upon by the Court in *Fachverband der Buch- und Medienwirtschaft,* to settle a dispute about the compatibility with Article 34 TFEU of Austrian rules governing the minimum retail price of imported books.[21] It might thus appear that *Keck* is indeed to be modified, not overturned: a selling arrangement will breach Article 34 TFEU (in particular) if it either discriminates against imports or hinders their access to the host market.

This brings us to our second main issue: precisely what constitutes a 'hindrance to market access' for the purposes of triggering the application of

---

[20] Case C-142/05 *Mickelsson and Roos* (4 June 2009).
[21] Case C-531/07 *Fachverband der Buch- und Medienwirtschaft* (30 April 2009).

Article 34 TFEU; surely as regards residual categories of national measure such as restrictions on use, possibly also when it comes to selling arrangements as dealt with under a now-modified *Keck* formula. In this respect, it might again feel as if *Commission v. Italy* raises as many questions as it solves. On its face, the Court's 'preliminary observations' might suggest that a very low threshold will be required to trigger the application of the Treaty: the ruling refers merely to a hindrance, without expressly specifying any additional quantitative or qualitative criteria by which to separate tolerable hindrances from objectionable ones, such as a requirement that the barrier to market access be 'total' or 'substantial' or even 'appreciable'. Taken literally, such a liberal understanding of the market access test could create serious definitional problems – and tip the constitutional balance once again away from Article 34 TFEU as an instrument for guaranteeing cross-border trade into a tool for promoting free trade.

But it is worth recalling, in this regard, that the disputed rules in *Commission v. Italy* included a complete restriction on the use of trailers specifically designed for motorcycles, creating a relatively high barrier, tantamount to a total prevention of market access for imported goods. Moreover, there is no reason to believe that such a the Court will abandon its existing case law casting outside the scope of Article 34 TFEU domestic measures whose effects on cross-border trade are considered too uncertain and indirect. In other words: one can safely assume the Court will apply some qualifying threshold for triggering the application of the Treaty – it just needs to be clarified in future case law. That such a threshold may even prove to be pitched at a relatively high standard is supported by the ruling in *Mickelsson and Roos*: the Court observed that the disputed Swedish rules would hinder access to the domestic market where they prevented or greatly restricted the use of personal watercraft – suggesting the need to demonstrate a considerable impact on consumer demand for the relevant goods, perhaps even of practical equivalence to a total prohibition on use of the sort at issue in *Commission v. Italy* itself.

Nevertheless, until the case law develops further, *Commission v. Italy* will undoubtedly be the cause of considerable legal uncertainty, with speculation not only about what threshold might apply but also which criteria should be taken into account to calculate it: for example, whether the test should be purely abstract/intuitive; or also incorporate elements of economic/empirical analysis. In the meantime, what does seem clear from *Commission v. Italy* is that Article 34 TFEU can serve as an instrument not only by which imported goods might access, or access more easily, an existing national market, but also to create new markets in Member States where such markets do not already exist and (due to the pre-existing regulatory framework) could not exist in the first place.

Finally, it is worth noting that *Commission v. Italy* should be seen not only in its particular doctrinal context of Article 34 TFEU on the free movement of goods, but also against the background of a broader academic debate about convergence and divergence in the Court's approach to defining the scope of application of the Treaty, right across the fundamental freedoms. It is certainly true that *Commission v. Italy* brings the rules on imported goods closer to the position which already governs the free movement of workers, freedom of establishment, free movement of services and free movement of capital (and indeed, one might add, the free movement of Union citizens also for non-economic purposes). In each of those fields, it is clearly established that the relevant Treaty provisions prohibit not only discrimination, but also double regulatory burdens, as well as mere restrictions on market access. Indeed, if greater convergence is one of the Court's objectives, then we might find that the threshold for triggering Article 34 TFEU on the basis of a hindrance to market access will indeed be pitched at a relatively low level, just above the basic exclusion of measures whose effects are too uncertain and indirect. After all, the Court's understanding of restrictions on free movement that require objective justification, in the context of the other free movement provisions, has been marked by a liberalness bordering on the all-encompassing (Spaventa, 2009b). But in one crucial respect, the free movement of goods remains (for now at least) distinct from the other Treaty provisions: Article 35 TFEU (ex-Article 29 EC) prohibits only discrimination against exported products;[22] it has not yet been interpreted as subject to a 'market access' test of the sort applied to imported goods in *Commission v. Italy* or familiar to all the other fundamental freedoms contained in the Treaty.

II. Union Competence to Regulate the Internal Market under Article 114 TFEU: Another Nail in the *Tobacco Advertising Directive* Coffin?

If *Commission v. Italy* illustrates the ongoing difficulties of negative integration under the primary Treaty provisions for the purposes of the internal market, then *Ireland v. Parliament and Council* highlights the continuing controversies surrounding positive integration by the Union legislature through the harmonization of national laws.

Article 114(1) TFEU (ex-Article 95(1) EC) provides that the European Parliament and the Council shall (acting in accordance with the ordinary legislative procedure) adopt the measures for the approximation of the provisions laid down by law, regulation or administrative action in Member States which have as their object the establishment and functioning of the internal

---

[22] In particular: Case 15/79 *Groenveld* [1979] ECR 3409; Case C-205/07 *Gysbrechts* [2008] ECR I-9947.

market. As is well known, the manner in which that provision was interpreted and applied by the Union institutions attracted considerable criticism over the years, in particular, on the grounds that the harmonization powers conferred under ex-Article 95 EC were allegedly being put to use for purposes only remotely connected with the functioning of the internal market, merely because the Member States considered it politically expedient to achieve certain extraneous objectives through common action but regardless of the constitutional niceties associated with the principle of attributed powers. Such criticism about improper 'competence creep' was particularly acute in those situations where the policy objectives effectively being smuggled into ex-Article 95 EC related to fields where Union competence, as provided for under the remainder of the Treaties, was either non-existent, severely circumscribed or subject to very different institutional arrangements.

The Court of Justice responded to such concerns in its famous ruling in the *Tobacco Advertising Directive* case.[23] The latter judgment clarified that ex-Article 95 EC cannot be construed so as to confer upon the Union legislature a general power to regulate the internal market in the public interest. Measures adopted under ex-Article 95 EC must therefore *genuinely* have as their object the improvement of conditions for the establishment and/or functioning of the internal market. For those purposes, if a mere finding of disparities between national rules, or an abstract risk of obstacles to the exercise of the fundamental freedoms or of distortions of competition, were sufficient to justify reliance upon ex-Article 95 EC, judicial review of compliance with the conditions underpinning that legal basis might be rendered nugatory. To avoid that risk, measures adopted under ex-Article 95 EC must *actually* contribute to the elimination of obstacles to free movement, or remove *appreciable* distortions of competition within the internal market. Nevertheless, provided those criteria are fulfilled, the Union legislature cannot be prevented from exercising its competences on the grounds that (for instance) considerations of environmental, consumer or public health protection are a decisive factor in the regulatory choices to be made.

The *Tobacco Advertising Directive* ruling generated considerable scholarly comment, with a broad consensus emerging around the proposition that the Court seemed determined to put an end to the political institutions' abuse of ex-Article 95 EC and to enforce more rigorously the principle that the Union enjoys only those competences conferred upon it under the Treaties.[24] In particular, the *Tobacco Advertising Directive* ruling seemed to offer a

---

[23] Case C-376/98 *Germany v. Parliament and Council* [2000] ECR I-8419.
[24] See further, e.g. *The ECJ's Tobacco Advertising Judgment*, CELS Occasional Paper Number 5 (CUP, Cambridge, 2001).

balanced *quid pro quo* in the operation of ex-Article 95 EC: on the one hand, the threshold for relying upon that provision would be pitched at a level designed to guarantee that proposed measures should have a meaningful and demonstrable connection to the internal market; on the other hand, provided that threshold was crossed, the fact that other policy objectives were being pursued by the Union legislature, and indeed might play a crucial role in its decision to regulate in this way or even at all, would not in itself preclude the valid exercise of Union power under ex-Article 95 EC.

However, as time went on, certain commentators began to query whether the Court's initial bark was proving far worse than its actual bite. In subsequent cases, the criteria in the *Tobacco Advertising Directive* seemed to be interpreted and/or applied in a manner which only ever justified, and rarely constrained, the exercise of harmonizing competences by the Union legislature under ex-Article 95 EC: consider, for example, the ruling in the *Biotechnology Directive* case to the effect that potential future as well as actual current barriers to trade were amenable to regulation under ex-Article 95 EC;[25] the finding in *Österreichischer Rundfunk* that internal market harmonization measures could govern also wholly internal situations with no relevant cross-border implications;[26] and the judgment in *Swedish Match* affirming the Union's competence to enact a total ban on any given product or activity, even though this seemed only to eliminate markets rather than to integrate them.[27] According to Wyatt (2009), the promise made in the *Tobacco Advertising Directive* case to stamp out 'competence creep' had not been fulfilled; the Court was prepared precisely to recognize for the Union a general power to regulate the internal market in the public interest.

It is against that background that we should consider the dispute in *Ireland v. Parliament and Council*. In 2004, several Member States (including Ireland) presented a joint proposal for a framework decision concerning the retention of data by providers of electronic communications services for the purposes of combating crime, based upon ex-Title VI TEU governing cross-border police and judicial co-operation in criminal matters. However, the Commission considered that aspects of the proposed framework decision could and therefore (under ex-Article 47 TEU) should be adopted using Community (first pillar) rather than Union (third pillar) competence. The Commission's alternative proposal for a directive based on ex-Article 95 EC was subsequently adopted by the Union legislature as Directive 2006/24,[28] though with Ireland and the Slovak Republic voting against the measure in

---

[25] Case C-377/98 [2001] ECR I-7079.
[26] Cases C-465/00, C-138/01 & C-139/01 [2003] ECR I-4989.
[27] Case C-210/03 [2004] ECR I-11893.
[28] [2006] OJ L 105/54.

Council. The Directive's preamble observed that several Member States had already adopted legislation providing for the retention of data by service providers with a view to the prevention, detection and prosecution of criminal offences; the legal and technical differences between those national rules presented obstacles to the proper functioning of the internal market in electronic communications, since service providers were faced with different requirements concerning the types of traffic and location data to be retained as well as the conditions and periods of retention. The Directive itself therefore harmonized the data retention obligations of service providers, as regards both the nature of the data to be retained and the actual period of such retention; as well as certain ancillary matters such as data protection and security, and the conditions for data storage. Ireland, supported by the Slovak Republic, sought annulment of the Directive on the grounds that it had been adopted under an improper legal basis: the measure was not primarily concerned with the functioning of the internal market but with combating crime; if such provisions were to be adopted by the Union at all, they should have been enacted pursuant to ex-Title IV TEU.

The Court began its judgment by clarifying that this was not a dispute about whether the Union had competence to regulate the relevant field at all, only whether that competence should be exercised in accordance with ex-Title VI TEU or instead pursuant to ex-Article 95 EC. For those purposes, it was necessary to determine whether Directive 2006/24 satisfied the conditions for relying on the competences conferred under ex-Article 95 EC. In particular, it was necessary to demonstrate that disparities between national rules are such as to obstruct the fundamental freedoms or create distortions of competition and thus have a direct effect on the functioning of the internal market. That may include preventing the emergence of future obstacles to trade resulting from the divergent development of national laws, provided such emergence is likely and the relevant measures are designed to prevent them.

The evidence submitted to the Court demonstrated that various Member States had indeed enacted measures concerning the imposition of data retention obligations upon service providers; that such obligations have significant economic implications for service providers insofar as they may involve substantial investment and operating costs; that the relevant national measures differed considerably as regards the nature of the data to be retained and the applicable period of retention; and that it was entirely foreseeable other Member States would follow suit in due course, thus accentuating even further the differences between national law. Viewed in that light, the current situation was liable to have a direct impact on the functioning of the internal market and that impact was likely to become more serious with the passage of time – justifying the adoption of harmonizing measures by the Parliament and Council.

That conclusion was reinforced by an analysis of the content of Directive 2006/24, whose provisions were essentially limited to the commercial activities of service providers in the relevant sector of the internal market. By contrast, Directive 2006/24 did not govern those activities of public authorities which properly fell within the scope of ex-Title IV TEU, such as access to data by, and the use and exchange of data between, national law enforcement agencies. Overall, the disputed measure related predominantly to the functioning of the internal market and had been properly adopted under ex-Article 95 EC. Ireland's action was therefore dismissed.

The ruling in *Ireland v. Parliament and Council* raises two main sets of issues. The first concerns the relationship between the Union's internal market competences and other legal bases under the Treaties. In the dispute itself, the relevant relationship was between ex-Article 95 EC and ex-Title IV TEU, as governed by the 'Community preference clause' in ex-Article 47 TEU. If the Treaty of Lisbon had not entered into force, *Ireland v. Parliament and Council* would therefore have been worth discussing as another important chapter in the controversial *Environmental Crimes* line of jurisprudence concerning cross-pillar competence disputes.[29] However, as the law now stands under the revised Treaties, this particular aspect of *Ireland v. Parliament and Council* has since become rather of limited interest: after all, the third pillar has been effectively dismantled and the 'Community preference clause' has (in this context) been deleted.

Of course, that is not to deny the continued potential for legal basis disputes to arise over the relationship between Article 114 TFEU (on the one hand) and the new provisions of Chapters 4 and 5, Title V, Part Three TFEU concerning judicial and police co-operation in criminal matters (on the other hand). In that regard, *Ireland v. Parliament and Council* will indeed remain relevant for its guidance on the distinction between commercial activities falling within the scope of the Union's single market powers versus the law enforcement activities of public authorities belonging to the Union's competence over criminal co-operation. And of course, nor is it to deny the continued potential for legal basis disputes to arise over the borderline separating Article 114 TFEU from a wide range of other Treaty legal bases on potentially overlapping policy competences (for example) in fields such as agriculture,

---

[29] Case C-176/03 *Commission v. Council* [2005] ECR I-7879. Note especially the ECJ's discussion in *Ireland v. Parliament and Council* of the significance of the fact that Directive 2006/24 itself amended various existing Community directives on data protection; and also the ECJ's reasoning to distinguish *Ireland v. Parliament and Council* from the previous dispute over passenger name records in Cases C-317 & 318/04 *Parliament v. Council and Commission* [2006] ECR I-4721.

transport, environmental protection and public health. In this regard, even though *Ireland v. Parliament and Council* may not tell us very much new, it does illustrate well a rather serious issue: *if* the Court applies a relatively low threshold for connecting a given measure with the establishment or functioning of the internal market, and that suffices to justify treating the measure as predominantly connected with Article 114 TFEU – even though such a legal fiction cannot disguise the reality that the Union legislature was in fact primarily concerned with regulating for some other public interest – then Article 114 TFEU will occupy a position of unusual strength *vis-à-vis* the other legal bases contained in the Treaties, and could threaten to undermine the principle of attributed powers as regards those policy fields where dedicated Union competences are either weak or non-existent.

That *if* brings us directly to our second main issue: identifying the conditions for validly relying upon Union competence under Article 114 TFEU in the first place, and in particular, the question of whether the Court has indeed lowered the threshold for internal market harmonization so much that the *Tobacco Advertising Directive* case is now more rhetoric than reality. In that regard, *Ireland v. Parliament and Council* does seem to continue the trend evident from previous case law such as *Biotechnology Directive*, *Österreichischer Rundfunk* and *Swedish Match*. It is not that the *Tobacco Advertising Directive* judgment has been formally overruled in law; it seems rather that its spirit has been steadily undermined by a series of small yet significant steps.

We saw in our discussion of *Commission v. Italy* that a test based on 'hindrances to market access', for the purposes of triggering scrutiny under Article 34 TFEU, might be pitched at a relatively low and abstract level (which will tend to expand the reach of Union law into issues which are more about pure economic liberty than cross-border economic integration); or instead defined through the use of more demanding qualitative and/or quantitative criteria (which should limit the application of the Treaty to those national rules capable of having a direct and specific impact upon free movement). A similar choice applies with the *Tobacco Advertising Directive* test for the existence of harmonizing powers by the Union legislature pursuant to Article 114 TFEU: if the concepts of barriers to movement and/or distortions of competition are conceived in a relatively broad way, it becomes easier to employ Article 114 TFEU as a means of achieving public interest objectives in reality far removed from the functioning of the internal market; whereas a more stringent interpretation of barriers/distortions, supported by relatively detailed legal and perhaps also empirical analysis, will tie the Union's harmonizing competence more strongly to the particular goal of closer economic integration.

The Court's approach in *Ireland v. Parliament and Council* leans towards a broad rather than a strict reading of ex-Article 95 EC. In particular, the abstract legal test applied so as to trigger the Union's internal market competence in the first place was phrased in undemanding terms. The criterion of appreciability laid down in the *Tobacco Advertising Directive* case was not even expressly mentioned in *Ireland v. Parliament and Council*.[30] Perhaps the Court assumed the crossing of such a threshold to have been obvious from the facts, in particular, because present and future differences between national laws on data retention did have certain economic implications for service providers as regards matters like investment and running costs. But in a politically and constitutionally important dispute, whose outcome centred almost entirely on the contested issue of 'distortions of competition', such silent assumptions should have been no substitute for a more clearly articulated legal test. As it stands, the Court seemed content to investigate only the bare existence of a distortion of competition, based on the inevitable costs of complying with the relevant national measures.

A threshold so apparently low and potentially subjective as to no longer guarantee that a given proposal manifests any meaningful and demonstrable connection to the internal market would indeed threaten to unravel the *quid pro quo* established in *Tobacco Advertising Directive*. The Union legislature becomes effectively free to base both its desire to regulate, and the actual content of that regulation, upon the pursuit of policy objectives extraneous to the establishment or functioning of the internal market per se. In *Ireland v. Parliament and Council* itself, the Court's apparent search for any distortion of competition between service providers as regards their data retention obligations was bound to justify the Union legislature's reliance upon ex-Article 95 EC; yet the functioning of the internal market in electronic communications was undeniably a distant relation to the real purpose of Directive 2006/24, i.e. enhancing public security by facilitating co-operation between the competent national police and judicial authorities in combating serious crime. In the context of a cross-pillar competence dispute such as *Ireland v. Parliament and Council*, the dice were thus loaded in favour of ex-Article 95 EC by the 'Community preference clause' in ex-Article 47 TEU. But even in the context of other legal basis disputes, the dice were and remain similarly loaded in favour of the internal market by what remains of the *Tobacco Advertising Directive* ruling. Following that path, there is almost no limit to the circumstances in which some disparity between how different Member States chose to intervene in the marketplace can act as a trigger for the Union's internal market competences – a trigger which in practice gives

---

[30] Cp. Case C-380/03 *Germany v. Parliament and Council* [2006] ECR I-11573.

the green light to fulfil other policy goals without having to worry about the competence straitjackets otherwise imposed in such spheres by their dedicated Treaty provisions.

To that extent, Article 114 TFEU really does risk morphing into a general power for the Union to regulate in the public interest. Moreover, the problems associated with a low threshold for triggering the power of the Union legislature to enact harmonizing measures under Article 114 TFEU are arguably more troubling than the parallel application of an often equally low threshold for triggering the judicial scrutiny of national measures creating barriers to free movement under the various primary Treaty provisions. After all, under the primary Treaty provisions, the Member States at least retain the initiative of public regulation; the Court's role is to ensure that their choices meet certain – admittedly often very intrusive – administrative law standards as expected under Union law (such as proportionality and respect for fundamental rights). But in the case of Article 114 TFEU, the consequences of the Court's lax approach to identifying the all-important barriers/distortions go much further and deeper. One need only recall that the power to harmonize involves an effective transfer of regulatory initiative to the Union legislature in a manner which can ultimately not merely *dis*place but *re*place individual national political choices. An approach to Article 114 TFEU which greatly facilitates such transfers of competence is of especial constitutional significance not only because such transfers imply in every case fundamental reconfigurations in the exercise and accountability of public power, but also because such an approach poses specific legitimacy problems for the Union – problems arguably aggravated since the entry into force of the Lisbon Treaty, since the Union's primary law now places renewed emphasis on the principle of the Union as an organization of only limited powers,[31] and contains a more formalized system of differentiated competences explicitly attached to different policy spheres.[32]

The question therefore arises whether the Court's current approach to judicial review over the exercise of Article 114 TFEU is sufficient to safeguard the spirit as well as the letter of the principle of attributed powers. Should the test for engaging Union regulatory competence as regards the internal market be based on more demanding criteria, for example, the requirement of a 'substantial' (not merely an 'appreciable', let alone simply 'any') distortion of competition? Should that test incorporate also a requirement for more detailed evidence to substantiate the relevant barriers and/or distortions, for example, including quantitative data which (even if it would

---

[31] In particular: Arts 4 and 5 TEU.
[32] In particular: Arts 2–6 TFEU.

not be realistic to expect national courts to procure when interpreting the primary Treaty provisions) might reasonably be demanded from the Union institutions when they propose regulating under Article 114 TFEU? In any event, should the relationship between Article 114 TFEU and other legal bases for Union action be reconsidered, so that the internal market does not exert such an irresistible gravitational pull whenever the basic threshold for its particular competences has been crossed?

It might be recalled that such questions were in fact placed on the agenda of the Convention on the Future of Europe by the European Council in its 2001 Laeken Declaration.[33] In the end, neither the Convention nor any of the subsequent IGCs proposed making relevant substantive amendments to Article 114 TFEU.[34] It is also worth observing that the 'yellow card' system for monitoring compliance with the principle of subsidiarity was not extended so as expressly to offer national parliaments the opportunity to query not only whether Union legislative competence should actually be exercised in any given situation, but also whether the constitutional preconditions for the very existence of such competence have been satisfied in the first place.[35] Perhaps it was assumed (however superficially) that the *Tobacco Advertising Directive* ruling had curtailed the potential for undesirable 'competence creep' via the Union's internal market competences. Or perhaps this is a problem which bothers academics on paper more than it really upsets the Member States in practice.

Conclusions

But on which side of that fence sit the national judges? Although the Lisbon Treaty itself may not have engaged very closely with the particular issues surrounding the interaction between Union and national competences as highlighted in *Commission v. Italy* and *Ireland v. Parliament and Council*, the process of ratifying Lisbon did produce another major legal development in 2009 which may well prove of far greater significance, not only for the specific issue of delimiting the scope of the Union's internal market powers, but more broadly, for the fundamental parameters which define the interaction between the Union and national legal orders. We refer, of course, to the German Federal Constitutional Court's ruling on the compatibility of the Lisbon Treaty with the German Basic Law.[36]

[33] Presidency Conclusions of 14 December 2001.
[34] Contrast with the amendments to that other *bête noire* of the 'competence creep' literature: Art. 352 TFEU (ex Art. 308 EC).
[35] In particular: Art. 5(3) TEU and Protocol No. 2.
[36] BVerfG Judgment of 30 June 2009.

This is not the place for a detailed treatment of such a lengthy, complex and important text: the suggestions for further reading (below) include several much more expert and considered analyses. Suffice for now to observe how the FCC stresses that, even after Lisbon, the EU remains an association of sovereign states founded upon international law. The Member States continue to provide the primary focus of democratic expression for their own citizens, on whose behalf the domestic authorities retain primary responsibility for the European integration process. The FCC also sends a clear warning that this 'union of nation states' must be taken seriously in practice as well as on paper. Ultimately, the FCC reserves to itself the right to ensure that the Union neither abuses the limits of its own competences in an *ultra vires* sense, nor exercises those powers in a manner that compromises the fundamental constitutional identity of the German state, which must retain sufficient room for the political formation of the economic, social and cultural destiny of its own population. In particular, the FCC signalled that it expects a strict interpretation to be given to Union powers which touch upon fields such as the administration of criminal law; the civil and military monopoly over the use of force; fundamental fiscal decisions over revenue and expenditure; shaping the circumstances of life by social policy; and important decisions on cultural issues such as education, the media and religion.

This idea of national judicial supervision over EU competences, not only so as to enforce the limits of the Treaties, but also and more generally so as to safeguard the continued vibrancy of national democratic life through an 'identity review', has potentially far-reaching implications for the exercise of Union power after Lisbon – though those implications remain sufficiently contingent as to be capable of leading the Union in various different future directions. It might be that the Union's political institutions will collectively heed the warnings of the FCC and show greater self-restraint in their interpretation and exercise of Union competences. Or that the dampened ambitions of only certain Member States – including but not limited to Germany – will imply the growth of further differentiation within the Union based (for example) upon greater use of the enhanced co-operation provisions. It is possible that the FCC's ruling will spur the Court of Justice to more critical reflection upon its own possible excesses when interpreting the Treaties, so as not to risk an outright and highly damaging confrontation with the national supreme courts. Or perhaps some serious challenge to European stability and solidarity – such as the euro crisis prompted by the woes of the Greek economy, or a major security threat from within or outside the Union – will provide a momentum for further integration sufficiently potent as to numb judicial misgivings of the sort voiced by the senior German bench.

Key Reading

For further analysis of the rulings in *Commission v. Italy* and *Ireland v. Parliament and Council*:

Horsley, T. (2009) 'Annotation of *Commission v. Italy et al.*'. *Common Market Law Review*, Vol. 46, pp. 2001–19.

Herlin-Karnell, E. (2009) 'Annotation of *Ireland v. Parliament and Council*'. *Common Market Law Review*, Vol. 46, pp. 1667–84.

Konstadinides, T. (2010) 'Wavering between Centres of Gravity: Comment on *Ireland v. Parliament and Council*'. *European Law Review*, Vol. 35, pp. 88–102.

Spaventa, E. (2009a) 'Leaving *Keck* Behind? The Free Movement of Goods after the Rulings in *Commission v. Italy* and *Mickelsson and Roos*'. *European Law Review*, Vol. 34, pp. 914–32.

See also, for background discussion:

Spaventa, E. (2009b) 'The Outer Limit of the Treaty Free Movement Provisions'. In Barnard, C. and Odudu, O. (eds) *The Outer Limits of European Union Law* (Oxford: Hart Publishing).

Wyatt, D. (2009) 'Community Competence to Regulate the Internal Market'. In Dougan, M. and Currie, S. (eds) *50 Years of the European Treaties: Looking Back and Thinking Forward* (Oxford: Hart Publishing).

For more detailed scholarly consideration of the FCC's ruling on the Lisbon Treaty:

Doukas, D. (2009) 'The Verdict of the German Federal Constitutional Court on the Lisbon Treaty: Not Guilty, But Don't Do It Again!'. *European Law Review*, Vol. 34, pp. 866–88.

Thym, D. (2009) 'In the Name of Sovereign Statehood: A Critical Introduction to the *Lisbon* Judgment of the German Constitutional Court'. *Common Market Law Review*, Vol. 46, pp. 1795–822.

JCMS 2010 Volume 48 Annual Review pp. 183–204

Relations with the Wider Europe

RICHARD G. WHITMAN
University of Bath
ANA E. JUNCOS
University of Bristol

Introduction

After the dramatic events in the EU's neighbourhood in the previous year the last 12 months were a period of relative stability. However, the crises that marked 2008 were stabilized rather than resolved. The conflict between Georgia and Russia over Abkhazia and South Ossetia remained in stalemate, and although Israeli troops ended their military intervention in Gaza in January 2009, the conflict between Hamas and Israel persisted. The year commenced with issues of energy security again, with a recurrence of disputes between Russia and Ukraine which interrupted gas supplies to EU Member States. Furthermore, the global financial and economic crisis placed governments and political systems in the neighbourhood under severe pressure.

The EU's policies for the wider Europe in 2009 were marked by the development of existent policies rather than new policy departures or innovations. The EU gained new candidates for future membership of the Union but also made only modest progress towards the accession of its enlargement front-runners. The new directions for policy for the neighbourhood adopted in the previous year (the Eastern Partnership and the Union for the Mediterranean) were given substance in 2009 but it is too early to assess whether they represent successful innovations. A new departure is the creation of a Commissioner for Enlargement and Neighbourhood Policy within the 2010–14 Commission which brings together two key strands of the EU's policy towards its neighbours. However, the extent to which the new High Representatives for Foreign and Security Policy will also involve themselves in defining and implementing the EU's policy in the wider neighbourhood is still to be determined (see Dinan's contribution to this volume).

I. Enlargement

General Developments

The number of applications for EU membership soared, which is testimony that membership continues to be a very attractive incentive for countries in the EU's neighbourhood. However, the effectiveness of EU conditionality remained low in countries where the legacies of ethnic conflict made compliance with EU criteria very costly, especially in Bosnia and Herzegovina. Here domestic political elites felt threatened by EU reforms and even short-term incentives, such as visa liberalization, were not enough to promote rule adoption. Bilateral issues also undermined the credibility and effectiveness of EU conditionality and constituted an additional obstacle to integration for many of the candidate and potential candidate countries. Moreover, five years after the 'big bang' enlargement to central and eastern Europe, enlargement fatigue was still evident in many EU Member States despite the fact that the last hurdle of institutional reform was lifted with the ratification of the Lisbon Treaty in November 2009. Lastly, it became clear that the economic crisis had not only had a negative effect on candidate and potential candidate countries, but it had also increased concerns among EU Member States about the financial burdens associated with enlargement.

On the plus side, some progress was recorded in the adoption and implementation of EU-related reforms, in particular in Croatia, Serbia and Macedonia (Commission, 2009c). The EU continued to provide financial assistance to the western Balkans and Turkey through the Instrument for Pre-Accession Assistance (IPA) which amounted to €1.5 billion in 2009. Citizens from Serbia, Montenegro and Macedonia were granted visa-free travel to the EU in December 2009 following the implementation of the road maps adopted in 2008. However, progress in meeting the conditions was not deemed satisfactory in the cases of Bosnia, Kosovo and Albania, creating new dividing lines in the region. Indeed, the EU has been criticized for excluding the majority of the Muslim populations in the Balkans. After years of protracted internal discussions about institutional issues, the year ended with the ratification of the Lisbon Treaty which should facilitate the integration of new Member States. One might expect that any future EU institutional reforms will be built into accession agreements rather than take the form of a new treaty – an option which was also considered when the Lisbon Treaty looked in danger of not being ratified.

In 2009, the EU celebrated the fifth anniversary of the enlargement to ten new Member States, which also coincided with the 20th anniversary of the fall of the Berlin Wall. To celebrate this anniversary, the European Commission presented a study which heralded the 2004 enlargement as a success, bringing economic prosperity to the new Member States and increasing the role of the EU as a global player in the world economy (Commission, 2009a). However, the financial and economic crisis slowed down the process of economic convergence between the new and old Member States and had a particularly negative effect on some central and eastern states like Hungary and the Baltics. Public perceptions of enlargement were also relatively positive according to the Eurobarometer survey published in February 2009, especially among citizens from new Member States. However, respondents from old Member States were more sceptical about its impact on the stability and security of the Union and pointed to its negative impact in terms of job losses, insecurity and making the EU more difficult to manage (Eurobarometer, 2009).

As far as future enlargements were concerned, 2009 was a frantic year for DG Enlargement. The EU received four new applications for membership from Montenegro (December 2008), Albania (April 2009), Iceland (July 2009) and Serbia (December 2009). Accession negotiations continued with Croatia and Turkey, with the former entering the final stages. In its October Enlargement Strategy, the Commission also recommended the opening of accession nego-tiations with Macedonia. Given the number of applications filed during this period, the Commission and the Council reminded applicant countries of the meritocratic nature of the process: '[e]ach country's progress towards the European Union must be based on individual merits and rigorous condition-ality, guiding the necessary political and economic reforms' (Presidency of the EU, 2009a; see also Council of the EU, 2009d). However, some candidate and potential candidate countries expressed their disappointment with what seemed like privileged treatment for Iceland. While it took the Council a mat-ter of days to refer Iceland's membership application to the Commission, Montenegro's application was only referred after five months and Albania's application took even longer.

Bilateral disputes continued to jeopardize progress towards integration. A case in point was Croatia's accession which was halted because of a border dispute with Slovenia. Bilateral disputes also held up progress in the cases of Macedonia and Turkey. For its part, the Netherlands maintained a veto over the implementation of the EU's Interim Agreement with Serbia until Decem-ber. To this long list of bilateral issues, another emerged between Iceland, the UK and the Netherlands over the repayment of billions of deposits lost as a result of the collapse of the Icesave bank in 2008. Bilateral issues also contributed to the politicization of the process and undermined its credibility. As Schimmelfennig and Sedelmeier (2004, p. 664) put it, the effectiveness of EU conditionality depends on the 'credibility of the threats and rewards'. Thus, the politicization of enlargement sends the wrong message to the applicant countries and weakens the Commission's emphasis on a transparent and a merit-based process whereby 'the pace of a country's progress towards the EU is determined by the pace of its reforms' (Commission, 2009c, p. 6; see also Commission, 2006).

Progress in the implementation of reforms was slow in the period under review. Problems in the candidate and potential candidate countries plagued the implementation of the rule of law, in particular in relation to the independence of the judiciary, the fight against organized crime and corruption (Commission, 2009c, p. 5). In addition, administrative capacity was still considered weak in Turkey and the western Balkans, affecting the record of implementation of reforms. Problems with freedom of the media and freedom of expression were noted, especially during the elections that took place in some of the western Balkan countries. Although the work of several regional organizations such as the Regional Co-operation Council or the Central European Free Trade Agreement was encouraging, bilateral disputes, and in particular the Kosovo issue, remained a significant obstacle to regional co-operation.

The economic crisis did not spare the candidate and potential candidate countries, although it affected some countries (Bosnia and Herzegovina, Serbia) more than others. In the first stages of the financial crisis, its impact was more limited than in some EU Member States because of the resilience of a stable banking sector. However, the effects of the economic crisis became more noticeable by mid-2009 because of the reduction in foreign direct investment and exports. The economic crisis resulted in an increase of unemployment, which was already very high in some countries (for example, Bosnia) and worsened the fiscal position of many of these countries. Serbia and Bosnia had to turn to the IMF for financial assistance. The EU also created an IPA crisis package of €200 million to support the economies of the western Balkans.

Candidate Countries

Croatia

Croatia's accession was brought to a standstill in 2009 as a result of a border dispute with Slovenia. From the end of 2008, the dispute over the bay of Piran had prevented the opening and closure of negotiation chapters. The

Commission expressed its disappointment with this state of affairs on several occasions declaring that 'bilateral issues should not hold back the accession negotiations' (Commission, 2009c, p. 11). In July, the prime minister and leader of the centre-right HDZ party, Ivo Sanader, resigned and was replaced by Jadranka Kosor. This smoothed negotiations as Ms Kosor was more inclined to refer the dispute to international arbitration as requested by Slovenia. In September, the prime ministers of Slovenia and Croatia agreed that bilateral issues should not hold up accession negotiations and days later the two countries agreed to submit the dispute to international arbitration. An arbitration agreement was signed in Stockholm in November.

Despite the political impasse, considerable progress was achieved in completing the road map set by the Commission in its 2008 Enlargement Strategy. In particular, Croatia made significant progress in the area of rule of law. But the Commission repeatedly identified problems regarding compliance with the International Criminal Tribunal for the Former Yugoslavia (ICTY) and the implementation of minority rights and the return of refugees, the independence of the judiciary, the fight against organized crime and corruption (Commission, 2009c). Corruption was also a key issue during the presidential election campaign in December. The social democrat Ivor Josipović won the second ballot in January 2010 after running with an anti-corruption and pro-EU campaign.[1] Croatia also needs to strengthen the capacity of its public administration to ensure the effective implementation of EU legislation and to be able to manage the EU's financial assistance.

By the end of 2009, 17 out of the 35 negotiation chapters had been closed; 11 remained open and another seven had yet to be opened. Despite progress over the border dispute, Slovenia blocked the opening of three chapters at the December's Accession Conference. The opening of another chapter, on the judiciary and fundamental rights, was vetoed by the Netherlands, the UK, Belgium, Finland and Denmark due to concerns about non-compliance with the ICTY.[2] The chief prosecutor of the ICTY had on several occasions requested military documents relating to the case against the Croatian general Ante Gotovina, a case which had also been at the heart of the delay in opening accession negotiations with Croatia in 2005. Despite these problems, the Croatian government expects to complete accession negotiations in 2010 and enter the EU in 2012. In line with this schedule, a working group was set up at the end of 2009 to draft the Accession Treaty of Croatia and a communication on a financial package for the accession negotiations with Croatia was presented by the Commission to the General Affairs Council in December.

---

[1] *European Voice*, 10 January 2010.
[2] *European Voice*, 17 December 2009.

Turkey

Turkey's negotiations with the EU made little progress in 2009. Two more chapters on taxation and the environment were opened during this period, taking the number of open chapters to 12. Turkey also adopted a National Programme for the Adoption of the Acquis and appointed a full-time chief negotiator and state minister, Egemen Bağış. However, the Cyprus issue continued to slow down integration – only one chapter has been closed since the start of accession negotiations in 2005 and eight chapters remain officially blocked since 2006. For another year, Turkey refused to normalize relations with Cyprus and implement the Additional Protocol regarding the access of Greek Cypriot vessels into Turkish harbours.

In its October report, the Commission noted some improvements in the reform of the judiciary, civil–military relations and the Kurdish issue. Regarding the latter, a new Kurdish-language channel was established on the public television network. In addition, a government consultation process, the Democratic Initiative, was launched in 2009 aimed at addressing the Kurdish and other minority issues. Nevertheless, some concerns were raised by the decision of the Constitutional Court to ban the Democratic Society Party, a Kurdish political party allegedly linked to the PKK.

Although the ratification of the Lisbon Treaty was welcomed in Turkey, it did not decrease fears of exclusion as the newly appointed President of the European Council, Herman van Rompuy, had reportedly stated his opposition to Turkish membership in the past. Repeated statements made by Sarkozy and Merkel favouring a privileged partnership with Turkey instead of full membership also caused anger in Istanbul.[3]

EU leaders have nonetheless repeatedly acknowledged the role of Turkey in the area of energy security and its key role in the Middle East and the southern Caucasus (Council of the EU, 2009f). As far as energy is concerned, Turkey signed the agreement on the Nabucco gas pipeline in July, a vital project aimed at reducing energy dependence from Russia. Its mediation during the war in Gaza was crucial in the achievement of the final ceasefire. It also mediated between Iraq and Syria, and between the US and Iran in 2009 (Düzgit and Tocci, 2009, p. 1). In a historic move, Armenia and Turkey signed protocols for the normalization of relations in October 2009,[4] although disagreements over the Armenian genocide and the 'frozen conflict' in the Azeri region of Nagorno-Karabakh continue to cause tensions. The new phase of negotiations between the leaders of the Turkish Cypriot and Greek Cypriot

---

[3] *EUobserver*, 18 May 2009.
[4] *BBC News*, 10 October 2009.

communities that was launched in 2008 and sponsored by the UN continued in 2009, albeit that no agreement had been reached by the end of the year.

Macedonia

Macedonia stepped up its efforts to implement EU-related reforms in 2009. Progress was made in the implementation of the Ohrid Framework Agreement and the priorities of the SAA. In particular, progress was noted in the implementation of the police and judicial reforms, the fight against organized crime, and improving the capacity of its public administration. As a 'reward' for the implementation of EU benchmarks, visa liberalization was agreed for Macedonia at the end of the year. The presidential and local elections in spring 2009 were considered to have met most international standards and violent incidents, which had marred the parliamentary elections of June 2008, were not recorded this time. Last but not least, the Commission recommended the opening of negotiations in its annual report in October (Commission, 2009c, p. 19), leaving behind the shadow of the conflict that shook the country in 2001.

Notwithstanding these positive developments, the dispute with Greece over the constitutional name of the country delayed the opening of accession negotiations (Agnantopoulos, 2010). The Council took note of the Commission's recommendation, but decided to 'return to the matter during the next Presidency' (Council of the EU, 2009f) after Greece successfully blocked a decision on the opening of negotiations.[5] In line with the June 2008 Council Conclusions, the Council also reminded Macedonia's government that '[m]aintaining good neighbourly relations, including a negotiated and mutually acceptable solution on the name issue, under the auspices of the UN, remains essential' (Council of the EU, 2009f). Although a new cycle of negotiations was under way, with the support of the UN special representative Mathew Nimetz, no agreement had been achieved by the end of 2009.

Potential Candidate Countries

Serbia and Kosovo

Overall, 2009 was a positive year for Serbia's relations with the EU. Although war criminals Ratko Mladić and Goran Hadžić were still at large, co-operation with the ICTY was said to have further improved. For this reason, the Commission recommended the implementation of Serbia's Interim SAA with the EU and the Council confirmed this decision in December – the

---

[5] *European Voice*, 8 December 2009.

Netherlands had blocked the implementation of the agreement since its signature in April 2008 because of Serbia's non-co-operation with The Hague. Moreover, a major step in Serbia's path towards European integration was the Commission's decision to allow visa-free travel, ten years after the Kosovo war.

After its full deployment in 2008, the EU's rule of law mission, EULEX, continued to operate in Kosovo where the situation remained stable overall. Serbia signed a protocol on police co-operation with EULEX to share information on cross-border issues and the fight against organized crime. Kosovo's leaders, however, strongly opposed the signing of this agreement because it was said to undermine the sovereignty of the territory, and they walked out of the talks in the summer. The agreement also caused anger among the Kosovar population and led to several attacks on EULEX vehicles and buildings. The Kosovo issue also halted regional co-operation as Serbia continued to veto Kosovo's participation in regional initiatives.

Kosovo's first local elections since independence took place in November, with no major incidents reported. However, the elections revealed mounting tensions within the governing coalition between Prime Minister Hashim Thaci's Democratic Party of Kosovo (PDK) and President Fatmir Seijdiu's Democratic League of Kosovo (LDK). In Kosovo's annual report, the Commission pointed at problems with corruption, organized crime, political interference in the judiciary and high-level appointments in the administration, and the protection of minorities. The Commission also published a study on Kosovo that recommended several initiatives to improve the political and socio-economic situation in the territory, in particular, through visa liberalization and trade agreements, once the requirements were met (Commission, 2009d). The Council supported the implementation of these measures, 'without prejudice to Member States' positions on status' (Council of the EU, 2009f) – Spain, Romania, Slovakia, Greece and Cyprus had not recognized Kosovo as an independent country as of 31 December 2009.

Bosnia and Herzegovina, Albania and Montenegro

Overall, progress towards European integration in Bosnia was very limited during this period. Bosnian elites showed a growing reluctance to implement reforms despite repeated EU declarations urging them to do so. Short-term incentives such as visa liberalization also failed to promote reforms. In July, the Commission concluded that Bosnia had not met the benchmarks set in the 2008 road map, including the introduction of biometric passports, and was left without a visa-free agreement. The political situation also deteriorated in

2009. The inflammatory rhetoric by the Bosnian political leaders and lack of consensus damaged the functioning of Bosnian political institutions. In particular, challenges from the leadership of Republika Srpska against the legality and legitimacy of state-level bodies continued (Commission, 2009c, p. 29). Progress in the implementation of the police laws adopted in 2008 was very slow.

A new double-hatted High Representative/EU Special Representative (EUSR), Valentin Inzko, was appointed in March to replace Miroslav Lajčák. However, the authority of the High Representative, the main instrument of the international community to implement the Dayton agreement, has been increasingly challenged by domestic elites. The prospect of a closure of the Office of the High Representative (OHR) and its replacement by a reinforced, double-hatted, EUSR was ever more distant in 2009 despite pressure from the EU and the US. The Peace Implementation Council did not consider that Bosnia had fulfilled the five objectives and two conditions in its meeting of 18 November 2009 (PIC, 2009). To pressurize Bosnian authorities, the Commission's annual report stated for the first time that the EU would not consider an application for membership 'until the OHR [had] been closed' (Commission, 2009c, p. 29).

By the end of the year, the EU also increased its pressure on Bosnian political parties to agree to constitutional reform by linking this reform with the granting of candidate status by the EU. In its October report, the Commission warned Bosnia that the country 'will need to reform its constitutional framework to permit its institutions to function effectively before the Commission can recommend the granting of candidate country status. In particular, the country will need to be in a position to adopt, implement and enforce the laws and rules of the EU' (Commission, 2009c, p. 29). Notwithstanding this pressure, attempts to further constitutional reform, the so-called 'Butmir process', sponsored by the EU and the US failed in the autumn of 2009. The talks led by the Swedish foreign minister Carl Bilt and the US deputy secretary of state Jim Steinberg were criticized by some observers because they were badly prepared, inflamed the pro-independence rhetoric in Republika Srpska and further undermined the authority of the OHR.[6]

Given the lack of progress in the country, the mandate of the police mission (EUPM) was extended for another two years (2010–11). Similarly, and despite the fact that the security situation in the country was deemed 'stable' (Council of the EU, 2009f) and that contributing states faced increasing demands for troops in Afghanistan, EU Member States agreed to retain

---

[6] *European Voice*, 22 October 2009 and 17 December 2009.

EUFOR Althea, its military operation in Bosnia. The UN Security Council Resolution 1875 (2009) extended the mission's mandate until November 2010.

The SAA with Albania entered into force in April. At the end of the month, the Albanian government submitted a membership application to the EU. The Council tasked the Commission to submit a formal opinion on Albania's application in November. In the parliamentary elections that took place in June 2009, although 'tangible progress' was noted, Albania was still deemed some way short of meeting international standards. Problems included those identified by the OSCE election monitors included isolated acts of violence and irregularities with vote counting.[7] The ruling party of Prime Minister Sali Berisha, Albania's Democratic Party, won the elections by a narrow margin, but the results were contested by the opposition, the Socialist Party, for alleged irregularities. The newly elected parliament has since been boycotted by the Socialists who have refused to take up their seats and have asked for a recount of the election ballots. This has led to a stalemate in Albania's politics, threatening its membership perspective.[8] Echoing conclusions from previous years, the Commission's 2009 report also identified other areas where Albania needed to make progress, in particular, in the area of the rule of law (independence of the judiciary, corruption and the fight against organised crime) and freedom of expression (Commission 2009c, p. 14). Together with Croatia, Albania officially became a Nato member on 1 April 2009.

Montenegro's membership application, filed in December 2008, was also being considered by the Commission in 2009, with a decision expected in 2010. Visa liberalization was agreed for Montenegro at the end of the year. At the elections that took place in March, almost all international standards were met, although some shortcomings, in particular in relation to freedom of the media, were identified. Despite some progress in the implementation of the SAA, there remained problems regarding the implementation of judiciary reform, the fight against organized crime and corruption (Commission, 2009c, p. 14). In December, Montenegro was invited to join Nato's Membership Action Plan, a stepping stone to full membership.[9]

Iceland

One of the most significant developments in the EU's enlargement in 2009 had to do with Iceland's decision to apply for membership as a result of the

[7] *EUobserver.com*, 30 June 2009.
[8] *BalkanInsight.com*, 20 March 2010.
[9] *EUobserver.com*, 4 December 2009.

damaging effects of the crisis on the country's currency and financial sector. Following the collapse of the governmental coalition at the beginning of the year, new elections were held in April. The pro-European party, the Social Democratic Alliance, claimed victory and formed a government with the Left–Green Movement. One of the first decisions of the new government was to apply for EU membership in July and only a few days later, EU foreign ministers asked the Commission to draft an opinion on Iceland's application. The view from Brussels is that Iceland's negotiations will take much less time than those with any of the western Balkan countries, with some expecting Iceland to join with Croatia, probably in 2012. Iceland is a member of the European Free Trade Association (EFTA) and part of the European Economic Area established between the EU and the EFTA countries. Iceland is also an associated member of the Schengen Agreement. Hence, Iceland has implemented a significant amount of EU acquis. As the former Enlargement Commissioner Olli Rehn put it, 'the remaining distance to be covered will be shorter [for Iceland] than for other countries that do not have such strong ties with the EU' (Rehn, 2009). However, Rehn also warned in the same speech that despite Iceland's implementation record, 'the remaining distance may not necessarily be any easier' (Rehn, 2009) hinting at the problems that might arise in relation to fisheries policy and public opinion, which remains significantly Eurosceptic. Another issue that might strain EU–Icelandic relations refers to the collapse of the Icelandic bank Icesave. The UK and the Netherlands demanded that their nationals be reimbursed by Iceland to the tune of €3.9 billion, lost when the bank collapsed in the autumn of 2008. A deal was agreed for the repayment of these funds in October, but the overwhelming rejection of the agreement in a referendum in March 2010 means that the issue remains unresolved.

II. European Neighbourhood Policy

General Developments

After the innovations of the previous year, in which both the Union for the Mediterranean (UfM) and the Eastern Partnership (EaP) emerged as new directions for policy for the neighbourhood, 2009 represented a period of consolidation. The UfM largely settled into the pattern already established by its predecessor, the European Mediterranean Partnership, and so could be seen as largely a rebranding exercise rather than setting a substantive new direction for the EU's policy towards the Mediterranean basin. For the EaP, the focus was on establishing the structures and processes to facilitate activity and thereby to realize the political commitment given in the preceding year to a strand of the ENP specifically tailored to the EU's eastern neighbours.

The European Commission published its most recent assessment of the implementation of the European Neighbourhood Policy in April 2009, replicating the process conducted in 2006 and 2007 (Commission, 2009b). As with previous reports the Commission offered an overall assessment of policy implementation and specific analysis by sectors and by countries. The Commission's assessment was candid in highlighting that corruption remains pervasive across much of the region and that democratic reforms have slowed and human rights standards have slipped.

Eastern Partnership

In 2009, the proposal for an Eastern Partnership (EaP), originally presented by Poland and Sweden in May 2008, was taken further forward. At the 19–20 March 2009 meeting of the European Council, the EU's heads of state and government adopted a 'Declaration on the Eastern Partnership' (Council of the EU, 2009b) including setting the date for the launch summit of the EaP for 7 May 2009. The European Council endorsed the Commission's proposals on the scope and modalities of the EaP including funding of €600 million to cover the period to 2013 (Commission, 2008).

The Eastern Partnership launch summit on 7 May 2009 took place in Prague and brought together representatives of the Member States together with the presidents of Armenia, Azerbaijan, Georgia and Ukraine and representatives of the presidents of Belarus and Moldova. The summit declaration stressed that the intention would be to seek a 'more ambitious partnership' between the EU and the Eastern Partnership countries, this being realized through a specific eastern dimension of the wider European Neighbourhood Policy (Council of the EU, 2009c). The EaP replicates the ENP in being composed of both bilateral and multilateral arrangements. The key bilateral arrangement through which the EaP is to be realized is through new-style association agreements. The trade aspect of these agreements is intended to enact bilateral free trade areas between the EU and its partners and seek convergence with EU laws and standards. Other aspects of the agreements are to include 'Comprehensive Institution-Building Programmes' to improve administrative capability via the provision of training and technical assistance and increased co-operation on energy security issues through co-operation on stable and secure energy supply and transit in the long term and assistance with better regulation, energy efficiency and assisting the use of renewable energy sources. The EU also held out the promise of greater mobility via full visa liberalization (as a long-term goal and on a case-by-case basis) through visa facilitation and re-admission agreements.

The multilateral strand of the EaP is built around meetings of heads of state or government envisioned every two years taking place both in the EU and in the partner countries and annual meetings of ministers of foreign affairs. The organizing agenda for the multilateral strand of the EaP are four thematic platforms for which there would be 'Flagship Initiatives': democracy, good governance and stability; economic integration and convergence with EU sectoral policies; energy security; and contacts between people. These platforms are to provide the organizing structure for the business of the EaP. The initial meetings of the four thematic platforms took place in June 2009. A second round of platform meetings took place across October and November 2009 and at these meetings a set of core objectives was adopted for each of the platforms as well as a work programme covering the period from 2009–11.

The platforms are intended to operate as the key vehicle for progress in the multilateral strand of the EaP. Composed of senior officials the meetings of the platforms will take place at least twice yearly and oversee the implementation of the platform work programmes. The platforms, in turn, report to the annual meetings of ministers of foreign affairs – and sector-specific ministerial meetings are also envisioned. Alongside the establishment of the four platform work programmes the first six Flagship Initiatives have been established with three under way (on integrated border management; the Small and Medium Size Enterprise Facility; prevention and preparedness for natural and man-made disasters) and three to be enacted (regional energy markets and energy efficiency; the southern energy corridor; promoting good environmental governance).

The EaP is also intended to have both parliamentary and civil society dimensions. The Prague Summit encouraged the parliamentarians from the EU and the partner countries to take forward the European Parliament's proposal to establish an EU–Neighbourhood East Parliamentary Assembly (Euronest). The Euronest Parliamentary Assembly, which brings together the European Parliament and the parliaments of Armenia, Azerbaijan, Belarus, Georgia, Moldova and Ukraine, postponed its first meeting, which was due to take place in Brussels on 24 March 2009. The first meeting was cancelled as Belarus and the European Parliament failed to agree on the composition of the ten-member delegation representing the former. The source of disagreement was the European Parliament's proposal to invite representatives of the Belarusian opposition and non-governmental organizations to the Euronest meetings as observers because the Belarusian parliament is the only assembly in Europe in which none of the opposition parties are represented.

On the civil society dimension of the EaP, the European Commission's proposal for the establishment of an Eastern Partnership Civil Society Forum (CSF), made in its 2008 Communication and endorsed at the Prague Summit, held its first meeting on 16–17 November 2009 bringing together over 200 organizations of which over 140 were from EaP states and which produced a set of recommendations presented to the meeting of the Eastern Partnership Foreign Ministers meeting on 8 December 2009.

The €600 million in financing earmarked for the EaP falls within the pre-existing European Neighbourhood and Partnership Instrument (ENPI) and the rules guiding its programming and implementation are those set up in the ENPI Regulation. These resources are allocated for three main purposes (Commission, DG RELEX, 2009): support for partner country reforms through the implementation of Comprehensive Institution Building pro-grammes (approximately €175 million); Pilot regional development pro-grammes aimed at addressing regional economic and social disparities within partner countries (approximately €75 million); and implementation of the Eastern Partnership Multilateral dimension (approximately €350 million). The Prague summit declaration had also called for other donors including international financial institutions and the private sector to provide additional financing in support of projects and initiatives. In particular, the European Investment Bank and the European Bank for Reconstruction and Develop-ment (both represented at the summit) were urged to establish appropriate support for suitable investment projects facilitating reform and modernization and also to nurture the development of small and medium-sized enterprises.

Bilateral Relations

Belarus

As indicated above, Belarus was invited to join the EU for the formal launch of the EaP. This did not result in any significant *rapprochement* between the EU and Belarus and the relationship remains substantively unchanged from the preceding year. In a review of relations with Belarus in November 2009, the Council made clear that the human rights situation in Belarus, the lack of political reform allowing opposition and civil society organizations, alongside the absence of free and fair elections, all restrict a deepening of the relationship (Council of the EU, 2009e). Additionally, the EU continues to urge Belarus to abolish the death penalty. As illustra-tive of the stalemate in EU–Belarus relations the EU renewed the travel and other restrictions on named members of the regime first imposed in 2006 conducted under the CFSP with a new Common Position (2009/314/CFSP).

Moldova

EU–Moldova relations were affected by the political unrest and instability that convulsed Moldova following flawed parliamentary elections on 6–7 April 2009. Demonstrations called by opposition parties calling for a rerun of the election, claiming the governing Communist Party's electoral success to have been fraudulent, escalated into rioting with the presidential and parliament buildings attacked, and the latter subject to looting and arson. Government and opposition traded accusations on the degree to which agents provocateurs (and with the government claiming Romanian interference) were involved in the violence and the numbers killed and wounded in the government's attempt to re-establish order. The failure of the Moldovan parliament to elect a new president resulted in new elections scheduled for 29 July 2009. The EU directly involved itself in the electoral process with the Swedish Presidency sending Polish foreign minister Radek Sikorski as an envoy to Chisinau and with the blunt message that progress on relations through the Eastern Partnership, visa facilitation, economic assistance and a free trade zone were all conditional on free elections.

The opposition parties achieved a slim majority in parliament in the July elections and in August formed a new government organized as the Alliance for European Integration committed to furthering relations with the EU. Prime Minister Vlad Filat's first overseas visit was to Brussels in September, where he made clear that the new government sought a deepened relationship with the EU. The EU responded with the opening of negotiations for an Association Agreement on 12 January 2010. However, Moldova faced a deepening economic and budgetary crisis and the need to seek an IMF loan. The governing alliance's parliamentary power remained tenuous and lacked the three-fifths majority needed to replace President Vladimir Voronin who resigned in September 2009.

Ukraine

The negotiations with Ukraine for the Association Agreement that have been conducted since March 2007 continued into 2009. The Agreement is intended to replace the Partnership and Co-operation Agreement in force since 1998. Five negotiating rounds have been concluded on the Association Agreement and a third Joint Progress Report was issued in November 2009. A core aspect of the agreement is to be a Deep and Comprehensive Free Trade Area (DCFTA). The intention is for the agreement to be signed in 2010. Negotiations to be concluded include issues within the Chapter on Justice, Freedom and Security focusing on illegal employment; movement of persons; references to a visa-free travel regime; admission rules and judicial co-operation on civil matters. Further references to respect for the principles of independence, sovereignty, territorial integrity and inviolability of borders are to be finalized. For the DCFTA aspects of the agreement, work remains to be completed by Ukraine on regulatory approximation. The two sides agreed an 'Association Agenda' (the first of its kind) to replace the existing Action Plan at the EU Ukraine Co-operation Council on 16 June 2009 and which came into force following an exchange of letters on 23 November 2009. Alongside the JFS (Justice, Freedom and Security) Action Plan of 2007, the Association Agenda is intended to facilitate the entry into force of the Association Agreement. Ukraine was preoccupied with the campaign for presidential elections in the final months of 2009.

South Caucasus – Georgia, Armenia and Azerbaijan

The creation of the EaP provided an impetus for the push for negotiating Association Agreements with Georgia, Armenia and Azerbaijan and with draft mandates in preparation at the end of 2009. Although the EU has sought to treat the three countries collectively, Georgia's 2008 war with Russia has introduced an additional dimension to the relationship with the EU Monitoring Mission (EUMM) and EU Special Representative still *in situ*. The EU's assessment of all three states is that each continues to suffer from weak political systems and stressed economies (including Azberbaijan with a downturn in world oil prices). The EU's Action Plans for Armenia and Azerbaijan have failed to make any discernible impact on the ongoing dispute over Nagorno-Karabakh in 2009. The EU's aspiration for greater economic and political interdependence between the states of the south Caucasus remains unfulfilled.

North Africa

The EU's relationship with the states of north Africa stabilized in recent years with the agreement of Action Plans under the ENP and new funding arrangements established under the European Neighbourhood and Partnership Instrument (ENPI). Morocco remains the front-runner north African state in relations with the EU and with the first EU–Morocco summit scheduled to take place under the Spanish Presidency in March 2010 and tangible evidence of the 'advanced status' granted to Morocco in October 2008. Relations with Tunisia and Egypt continue to be routinely conducted through their ENP Actions plans and through the European Neighbourhood and Partnership Instrument.

EU–Libya relations did not move forward significantly in 2009. Libya remained outside the scope of the ENP and the UfM. Negotiations between the EU and Libya on a Framework Agreement, intended to open the way for the first substantive agreement that commenced in November 2008, had not been concluded. It was envisaged that this agreement would establish mechanisms for political dialogue and co-operation in the field of foreign and security policy, as well as for dialogue and co-operation on economic issues. It was to contain provisions for a free trade area (FTA). The agreement was expected also to foresee close co-operation on Justice, Freedom and Security issues as well as on many sectoral issues, in particular energy, transport, environment, industrial and enterprise policy, consumer protection, tourism and cultural heritage, agriculture and rural development, fisheries and maritime governance, social issues, science and technology, education and training. The European Commission was to prepare its first ever Country Strategy Paper for Libya, including a National Indicative Programme, covering the period from 2011 to 2013 to allow for Libya to receive ENPI funding. At present, EU-funded collaboration is limited to HIV/Aids prevention work and projects on illegal migration.

Middle East

The year began with Israel's military offensive 'Operation Cast Lead' in the Gaza Strip, worsening the already dire humanitarian situation on the ground. Despite several Council declarations calling for a ceasefire (Presidency of the EU 2008, 2009), individual Member State attempts to mediate in the conflict in the UN, and the sending of an EU delegation to the region at the beginning of January, the EU was unable to exercise any direct influence on the parties (Tocci, 2009). The war, which lasted over three weeks, left over 1,300 dead and devastating infrastructural damage. In response to the conflict, the EU committed €42 million in humanitarian aid. The Union also continued to be the largest donor in Palestine with €440 million from the Commission alone. However, the conflict highlighted once again the limitations of the EU's 'soft power' in the region, which has so far been unable to end the ' "destruction-reconstruction" cycle', as labelled by Commissioner Ferrero-Waldner (Ferrero-Waldner, 2009). During and after the conflict the EU offered to redeploy its border assistance mission, EUBAM Rafah, to support efforts to monitor the border with Gaza and to prevent arms smuggling, but to no avail – the mission has been on standby since 2007. The EU also extended the mandate of the police mission in the West Bank, EUPOL COPPS.

Declarations in 2009 reaffirmed the EU's vision for a two-state solution and its support for the establishment of 'an independent, democratic, contiguous and viable Palestinian state in the West Bank and Gaza, living side by side with Israel in peace and security' (Council of the EU, 2009a). In accordance with this policy, the EU condemned Israel's settlement expansion as well as illegal house demolitions and evictions of Palestinians from East Jerusalem which have been stepped up since 2008. Faced with mounting pressure from the US and the EU, Prime Minister Netanyahu announced a ten-month suspension of settlement construction at the end of November, a decision welcomed by the EU, but which was promptly rescinded by Israel. The EU also denounced the blockade of the Gaza Strip, which had disastrous humanitarian consequences on the population. The war in Gaza also increased the reluctance from the Commission and some Member States to upgrade EU relations with Israel, despite this move having been agreed in 2008.[10] Technical talks on the upgrade were suspended and at their annual summit in June the parties failed to make any progress on a new Action Plan. During the Swedish Presidency, EU relations with Israel reached a new low. At the December Council Conclusions, the Swedish Presidency pushed for a tough declaration on the Middle East recognizing Jerusalem as the capital of a Palestinian state. However, due to opposition from some Member States, the declaration was softened to '[i]f there is to be a genuine peace, a way must be found through negotiations to resolve the status of Jerusalem as the future capital of two states' (Council of the EU, 2009f, p. 9). As a necessary condition for the establishment of a Palestinian state, the EU also called the two Palestinian factions (Hamas in Gaza and Al Fatah in the West Bank) to move towards reconciliation (Council of the EU, 2009f, p. 10). However, the EU's refusal to engage with the Hamas government meant that the EU had no leverage on the parties and had to rely on the mediation efforts by Turkey and Egypt.

III. Norway and Switzerland

Norway's relationship with the EU was marked by its usual combination of close partnership allied with minor sectoral disputes in 2009. As illustrative was Norway's commitment of a frigate for six months to the EU's EUNAVFOR Somalia (Operation Atalanta) anti-piracy mission. And Norway also requested WTO dispute settlement consultations on the EU ban on trade in seal products. In the wider relationship a key strand was the negotiations, conducted alongside the other EEA states, for the EEA Financial Mechanisms, to cover the period from 2009 to 2014. Signed on 18 December 2009, Norway will provide approximately NOK 3 billion (€347 million) per year – a 22 per cent increase on the preceding five years – to reduce social and economic disparities and promote co-operation in Europe. The immediate

[10] *EUobserver.com*, 23 April 2009.

future of the relationship between the EU and Norway was reinforced by the Norwegian parliamentary elections of 14 September 2009 which resulted in the return to power of the coalition government led by Jens Stoltenberg of the Labour Party in alliance with the Socialist Left Party and the Centre Party. The partners presented their collective political platform for the period covering 2009–13. The platform categorically ruled out an application for EU membership. It also committed the government to the appointment of a public research-based committee (intended to have a broad range of expertise) to carry out a thorough and extensive review of the existing EEA Agreement and the consequences that the agreement has for all areas of Norwegian society.

The key issue of prominence in EU–Switzerland relations in 2009 was the issue of banking secrecy. The global financial crisis introduced a new impetus into the issue of banking secrecy which had previously been of concern because of its facilitation of tax evasion by EU Member State citizens. However, Switzerland was not alone in seeking to preserve its traditional banking secrecy with Austria and Luxembourg also under pressure by moves from both the OECD and the G20 to eliminate tax havens. As a consequence, moves by the European Commission to deepen co-operation against tax evasion, by allowing for bilateral information exchanges with third countries and to include Switzerland, were slowed down (see Howarth in this volume). Early 2010 also saw the EU Member States being drawn into a bilateral dispute between Switzerland and Libya, as a consequence of the former's membership of Schengen. The Libyan–Swiss dispute began in the summer of 2008 when a son of Muammar Gaddafi, Libya's leader, was arrested by police in Geneva. In response, Libya detained two Swiss businessmen and this then prompted the Swiss to bar Gaddafi, his family and top officials. Switzerland's membership of the Schengen agreement had the consequence of extending the travel restrictions to EU Member States.

Conclusions

The EU has given considerable attention to the architecture and the organiz-ing modalities of its relationships with its neighbours in recent years. As the events in 2009 demonstrated, EU membership continues to attract its neigh-bours, especially in times of financial difficulties, but progress towards acces-sion remains slow in many candidate and potential candidate countries. In relation to the ENP, the EU's relationships with its neighbours are now in a period of consolidation in which the broad strategy for the EU's 'near abroad' has been set and there is the onset of a degree of predictable routine. However, as events in Georgia in 2008 and those of Moldova in 2009 illustrate, the EU's neighbourhood remains a region in which political instability has the capacity to place the EU under pressure to deliver an effective policy response. Whether the global economic crisis will persist into 2010, and thereby further place neighbouring states' political systems under additional stress, cannot be discounted. It also remains to be seen how the EU's Lisbon Treaty arrangements for the conduct of its external action will impact on the formulation and conduct of policy towards the EU's neighbours.

Key Reading

For an assessment of the 2007 enlargement, see articles in the Special Issue of *Perspectives on European Politics and Society*, Vol. 10, No. 2. A number of articles have examined the EU's enlargement to the western Balkans and the conditions of success and failure of EU conditionality; in particular, see Noutcheva (2009), Freyburg and Richter (2010) and Renner and Trauner (2009). For other works that have analysed the EU's role in conflict management and transformation in its neighbourhood, see Gromes (2009) and the Special Issue of *Ethnopolitics*, Vol. 8, Nos. 3 and 4, edited by James Hughes. For a literature review of the EU's Mediterranean policies, see Holden (2009).

References

Agnantopoulos, A. (2010) 'The EU and Macedonia's Accession Process: Derailed or Delayed?'. *CFSP Forum*, Vol. 8, No. 2, pp. 7–13.

Commission of the European Communities (2006) 'Commission proposes renewed consensus on enlargement'. Press Release IP/06/1523, Brussels, 8 November.

Commission of the European Communities (2008) 'Communication from the Commission to the Council and the European Parliament. Eastern Partnership'. *COM*(2008) 823 final, Brussels, 3 December.

Commission of the European Communities (2009a) 'Communication from the Commission to the Council, the European Parliament, the European Economic and Social Committee and the European Central Bank. Five Years of an Enlarged EU – Economic Achievements and Challenges'. Brussels, 18 February.

Commission of the European Communities (2009b) 'Communication from the Commission to the European Parliament and the Council – Implementation of the European Neighbourhood Policy in 2008'. *COM*(2009) 188/3 Brussels, 23 April.

Commission of the European Communities (2009c) 'Communication from the Commission to the European Parliament and the Council. Enlargement Strategy and Main Challenges 2009–10'. *COM*(2009) 533, Brussels, 14 October.

Commission of the European Communities (2009d) 'Communication from the Commission to the European Parliament and the Council. Kosovo – Fulfilling its European Perspective'. *COM*(2009) 5343 Brussels, 14 October.

Commission of the European Communities DG RELEX (2009a) 'Vademecum on financing in the frame of the Eastern Partnership'. 16 December. Available at «http://ec.europa.eu/external_relations/eastern/docs/eap_vademecum_14122009_en.pdf».

Council of the EU (2009a) 'General Affairs and External Relations Council Conclusions on the Middle East Peace Process'. Brussels, 26 January.

Council of the EU (2009b) 'Presidency Conclusions'. Brussels European Council, 19–20 March, 7880/1/09.

Council of the EU (2009c) Joint Declaration of the Prague Eastern Partnership Summit, Prague, 7 May, 8435/09 (Presse 78).

Council of the EU (2009d) 'General Affairs and External Relations Council Conclusions on Enlargement'. Brussels, 27 July.

Council of the EU (2009e) 'Council Conclusions on Belarus, 2974th External Relations Council meeting'. Brussels, 17 November. Available at «http://www.consilium.europa.eu/uedocs/cms_Data/docs/pressdata/en/gena/111243.pdf».

Council of the EU (2009f) 'General Affairs and External Relations Council, 2984th Council meeting'. Brussels, 7–8 December.

Düzgit, S.A. and Tocci, N. (2009) 'Transforming Turkish Foreign Policy: The Quest for Regional Leadership and Europeanisation'. *CEPS Commentary*, Centre for European Policy Studies, 12 November.

Eurobarometer (2009) 'Views on European Union Enlargement'. February. Available at «http://ec.europa.eu/enlargement/pdf/press_corner/publications/eurobarometer_feb2009_analytical_report_20090506_en.pdf».

Ferrero-Waldner, B. (2009) 'European Union Pledges Support for Reconstruction of Gaza'. Speech by Commissioner for External Relations and ENP, Ferrero-Waldner, International Conference in support of the Palestinian economy for the reconstruction of Gaza, Sharm-el-Sheikh, 2 March.

Freyburg, T. and Richter, S. (2010) 'National Identity Matters: The Limited Impact of EU Political Conditionality in the Western Balkans'. *Journal of European Public Policy*, Vol. 17, No. 2, pp. 263–81.

Gromes, T. (2009) 'The Prospect of European Integration and Conflict Transformation in Bosnia and Herzegovina'. *Journal of European Integration*, Vol. 31, No. 4, pp. 431–47.

Holden, P. (2009) 'The European Union's Mediterranean Policy in Theory and Practice'. *Mediterranean Politics*, Vol. 14, No. 1, pp. 125–34.

Noutcheva, G. (2009) 'Fake, Partial and Imposed Compliance: The Limits of the EU's Normative Power in the Western Balkans'. *Journal of European Public Policy*, Vol. 16, No. 7, pp. 1065–84.

PIC – Peace Implementation Council (2009) 'Communiqué of the Steering Board of the Peace Implementation Council'. Sarajevo, 19 November.

Presidency of the EU (2008) 'Statement by the European Union on the Situation in the Middle East'. 30 December.

Presidency of the EU (2009a) 'Declaration by the Presidency on the Western Balkans, Gymnich meeting with the Western Balkans.' Hluboká nad Vltavou, 28 March.

Presidency of the EU (2009b) 'EU Presidency Statement on the Middle East'. Brussels, 13 January.

Rehn, O. (2009) 'The European Perspective of Iceland'. Speech at the University of Iceland, Reykjavik, 9 September.

Renner, S. and Trauner, F. (2009) 'Creeping EU Membership in South-East Europe: The Dynamics of EU Rule Transfer to the Western Balkans'. *Journal of European Integration*, Vol. 31, No. 4, pp. 449–65.

Schimmelfennig, F. and Sedelmeier, U. (2004) 'Governance by Conditionality: EU Rule Transfer to the Candidate Countries of Central and Eastern Europe'. *Journal of European Public Policy*, Vol. 11, No. 4, pp. 661–79.

Tocci, N. (2009) 'Lessons from Gaza: Why the EU Must Change its Policy'. *CFSP Forum*, Vol. 7, No. 2, pp. 7–9.

JCMS 2010 Volume 48 Annual Review pp. 205–223

Relations with the Rest of the World

DAVID ALLEN AND MICHAEL SMITH
Loughborough University

Introduction

In our review of 2008 (Allen and Smith, 2009), we drew attention to the looming presence of the international economic and financial crisis in the EU's international policies and policy-making. During 2009, this presence made itself felt very strongly, but it was not the only source of demands for adjustment and innovation in EU policies. The impact of the Obama presidency in the United States, of the continuing assertiveness of a number of emerging countries and of the internal debates about institutions that accompanied the final stages of ratification of the Lisbon Treaty all made for a challenging year (see Dinan in this volume), and one in which the definition of the EU's potential as a 'power' in international politics was a strong underlying theme (Grant, 2009). How could the EU make its presence felt in an increasingly multipolar or 'interpolar' world (Grevi, 2009)? Would Lisbon provide the basis for a new EU role in the changing world arena? Would there continue to be 'space' for the development of a distinctive EU approach to the problems confronting world politics and the global political economy? Whilst these questions would clearly not be answered definitively in the course of a year (and some would see them as questions for a 20-year period – see Grant, 2007), the following review gives important indications of some of the issues that the EU had to address in 2009.

I. General Themes

Foreign, Security and Defence Policy

Not for the first time is there much to report in the foreign and security policy issue area but, as so many times before, it is mainly of an institutional or procedural nature with little of real substance to comment upon. Thus on the very day that the Lisbon Treaty came into force (1 December) and as commentators poured over the credentials of the newly 'elected' (by the 27 EU heads of state and government) President of the European Council, Herman van Rompuy and the newly selected High Representative (otherwise known as the EU foreign policy chief or supremo), Catherine Ashton, the President of the United States, Barack Obama, announced that the United States was looking for Europeans to respond positively with both hard and soft power instruments to his long awaited and much anticipated decision to increase US troop levels in Afghanistan by over 30,000 men.[1] Whilst the last few weeks of 2009 saw a flurry of EU foreign policy institutional activity and anticipation, the EU maintained the stance that it has held ever since the much hailed election of President Obama, which is essentially one of collective silence and unwillingness to take initiatives or respond to them. Elsewhere in this contribution there is little specific to report about the substance of EU–China, EU–India, EU–Brazil or EU–Russia political and security relations or more generally about the EU's role in the rapidly evolving multipolar international political system. Instead we have just the long build-up to the ratification of the Lisbon Treaty with its attendant changes to the EU foreign policy-making procedures and the subsequent appointments mentioned above – both of which generated an underwhelming and disappointed response both inside and outside the EU.[2]

For much of 2009 the speculation was that Tony Blair, former UK prime minister, would be appointed to the newly created post of President of the European Council. Despite, or perhaps because of, the enthusiastic support of the UK government, it eventually became apparent that Blair was not acceptable partly because a majority of the EU Member States clearly did not want to appoint a 'big hitter' but preferred the idea of a low-key 'chair' for the European Council (arguably this was what the UK, at least, had in mind when it first supported the idea of replacing the rotating Presidency with an elected President (Wall, 2009; Stephens, 2009). Van Rompuy, the prime minister of Belgium, finally emerged as the joint choice of France and Germany possibly

---

[1] *European Voice*, 3 December 2009.
[2] See Barber's contribution to this volume. See also: *The Guardian*, 21 November 2009; *Financial Times*, November 2009; *Financial Times*, 21/22 November 2009; *Financial Times*, 23 November 2009; *The Guardian*, 26 November 2009; *European Voice*, 3 December 2009.

because his only known foreign policy stance was opposition to Turkish EU membership and possibly because he was a Belgian (so often their favoured country for sourcing and ensuring low-key appointments). Once van Rompuy was chosen it was necessary to 'balance' the appointment of a male, right-of-centre candidate from a small EU Member State with an (ideally) female, left-of-centre candidate from a large Member State. It was also necessary to appease the UK, for whom the foreign secretary, David Miliband, was the front-runner until he announced that he was not a candidate. Although otherwise unqualified, Catherine Ashton, who had replaced Peter Mandelson as the EU Trade Commissioner just a year earlier, met all the criteria mentioned above and was duly appointed and eventually confirmed early in 2010 by the European Parliament. Although an unlikely choice she had established a good record as a negotiator and she had an increasingly powerful ally in the Commission President Barroso who was himself reappointed for a second term. As a Vice-President of the Commission, Catherine Ashton will also head the new external relations 'team' at the Commission (although Barroso is also likely to maintain his keen interest and involvement in all aspects of external relations) which will consist of Štefan Füle from the Czech Republic (Enlargement and the European Neighbourhood Policy), Karel de Gucht from Belgium (Trade), Andris Piebalgs from Latvia (Development) and Kristalina Georgreva from Bulgaria (International Co-operation, Humanitarian Aid and Crisis Response). However Ashton's first major task, apart from chairing the Foreign Affairs Council and appointing her own people to chair the Political and Security Committee (but not COREPER) and some CFSP working groups will be to bring forward early in 2010 plans for the European External Action Service (EEAS).

The EEAS will eventually be staffed by officials drawn from the Commission, the Council and the EU Member States and it will be both an external diplomatic corps responsible for staffing the renamed European Union Delegations (previously European Commission Delegations) as well as the Brussels headquarters of the High Representative (a European Foreign Ministry in all but name). The EEAS is a huge and complex project that has been long anticipated with the Commission having begun an extensive training programme to give its own officials 'proper diplomatic skills'[3] and to bring them together with officials from the Member States and the Council to promote 'a shared diplomatic culture and an *esprit de corps*'. By the end of 2009, Ashton had faced her first rather difficult 'exchange of views' meeting with the European Parliament and van Rompuy had established that he saw himself more as a quiet chair of the European Council than as its external

---

[3] *European Voice*, 19 March 2009.

representative. However he had also made it clear that he intended to reduce the size of European Council meetings in future by limiting attendance to heads of state and government and thus usually excluding the foreign ministers (which will cause some problems for Member States with coalition governments). In addition the incoming Spanish Presidency made it clear that it did not foresee a swift end to the extensive role of the rotating Council Presidency in external affairs. There will be much to report on next year as the two new incumbents develop their roles. Ashton, in particular, has the near impossible task of combining the established role of High Representative which involves a great deal of travelling, with a huge bureaucratic/administrative role as a Commissioner and as head of the EEAS.

2009 was also an important year for the developing European security and defence policy (ESDP). Since it was established in 1999, there have been a total of 22 civilian and military ESDP missions, most of which have been on a relatively small scale and of limited duration. Thirteen of these missions were ongoing in 2009 including four police missions (Bosnia, the Congo, Palestine and Afghanistan – where the ambition is to train over 35,000 police officers), two justice and law missions (Kosovo and Afghanistan), a border monitoring mission at Rafah in Palestine, a monitoring mission in Georgia, security sector reform missions in the Congo and Guinea-Bassau, an anti-piracy mission off Somalia and a military mission in Bosnia. During 2009 the 3,700-strong EU force in Chad/Central African Republic handed over to the UN Minurcat mission in March with 2,000 of the EU troops joining the UN force. This high level of activity is beginning to become a problem for EU Member States whose armed and police forces as well as civilian workers are under considerable financial pressure in the wake of the financial crisis. It is significant that no new ESDP missions were initiated in 2009, although one new one was planned for Somalia in 2010.

The EU, of course, maintained its complex network of political dialogues with over 90 countries and it continued to try to use its 'soft power' to support democracy and to argue the case for human rights around the world. It played a major role (over 100 EU observers) in observing elections in Afghanistan and it welcomed the abolition of the death penalty in Togo whilst regretting its continued existence in the US, China, Thailand and Japan. However what it most conspicuously failed to do was to use its considerable foreign policy potential and resources to make a significant political impact on the world stage. The final ratification and the beginning of the implementation of the Lisbon Treaty is meant to initiate a new phase in the evolution of the EU as an international actor but at this point in time it is hard to see how the new arrangements are going to make the EU a more effective strategic actor in the rapidly evolving international system. With the Lisbon Treaty, and especially with the appointment of a successor to Javier Solana, armed with new powers and eventually with a significant new supporting infrastructure provided by the EEAS, the EU has sought to create the organizational basis for an enhanced role for the enlarged European Union. However whilst it may well have created the means for potentially projecting a collective, coherent and influential European voice in the world it is not at all clear that the Member States, in particular the larger ones, have the will to fulfil that potential.

The Common Commercial Policy

It was around the common commercial policy (CCP) that some of the most direct effects of the economic and financial crisis could be found during 2009. More accurately, it might be argued that the CCP during this year was surrounded by a series of threats and ominous developments, but that in formal policy terms it remained remarkably resilient. The key threat was that of protectionism – or more broadly 'economic nationalism' – as response to the crisis. This threat had two dimensions: on the one hand, it constituted a challenge within the Union itself, to maintain the open markets and non-discrimination that lie at the heart of the integration process, and on the other hand, it presented the challenge of maintaining multilateral processes and practices in a period when many countries saw them as desirable in the long term but not as an answer to their immediate problems.

The reshaping of multilateral institutions and of multilateral principles was thus at the core of the EU's international engagement during 2009. Most obviously, the emergence of the G20 of leading economies as a complement to and then as the replacement for the G7/8 challenged the Union to establish a central position within the new structures. The two key G20 meetings of 2009, in London during March and in Pittsburgh during September, presented a mixed picture. According to some commentators, the EU was 'absent' from the London G20 meeting,[4] with the key European roles being played by leading EU Member States, whilst the picture was little improved in Pittsburgh, where the search for a re-balancing of global trade structures was at the core of the discussions.[5] This was not the whole of the story, though, and it was clear over the course of the year that the EU, with its distinctive regulatory approach to international financial transactions, was at odds with the presumptions both of the United States and of emerging economies such as China. At the same time, the Union was active in pursuing regional trading arrangements such as its Free Trade Agreement with South Korea, which symbolized another key element in the lack of global consensus (see below). Ultimately, the year seemed to

[4] *The Guardian*, 26 March 2009.
[5] *Financial Times*, 21 September 2009.

demonstrate that the combination of internal tensions within the EU and external change in the global economy posed a large and growing challenge to the Union's role in the global political economy.

This uncertainty transmitted itself quite directly into the World Trade Organization negotiations under the Doha Development Round (DDA). These talks had been stalled effectively since 2005, with periodic attempts at revival, and during 2009 they again showed few signs of life. True, the completion of the DDA was central to the pronouncement made by the G20 at London and Pittsburgh, but little of this was translated into action in Geneva, where the talks are based. During the middle of the year, there was yet another attempt to revive the talks,[6] and during the autumn hopes were centred on a meeting due to take place in Geneva at the beginning of December.[7] For the EU, however, the timing was not good, since the December meeting precisely coincided with the departure of the Trade Commissioner, Catherine Ashton, for her new job as High Representative for Foreign and Security Policy (see above). In these circumstances, the hope for new momentum was stillborn, and the idea of EU activism was far-fetched. The EU was in fact more active in pursuing bilateral free trade agreements, reaching agreement with South Korea (see below) and initiating a process by which bilateral agreements with members of the Association of Southeast Asian Nations (ASEAN) could be pursued. Significantly, the latter process arose out of the failure of efforts to reach an inter-regional agreement with ASEAN.

During the year, a number of significant trade disputes continued to engage the attention of DG Trade, and in a couple of them there was real progress to report. The long-running dispute centring on the EU's banana regime, and relating to the preferential treatment accorded to bananas from African, Caribbean and Pacific (ACP) countries, was finally resolved with an agreement at the end of the year,[8] although this resolution in its turn created potential new difficulties for the ACP producers, addressed partly through transitional aid from the EU. The equally long-running dispute with the USA over hormone-treated beef was also largely resolved in the first half of 2009.[9] But the balance was redressed at least to some extent by new disputes or by the persistence of old ones: thus, the need to extend or drop the anti-dumping duties imposed during 2006 on shoe imports from China and Vietnam led to familiar tensions between importers, manufacturers and retailers before they were finally extended for 15 months late in the year,[10] whilst new disputes

---

[6] *Financial Times*, 26 May 2009.
[7] *Financial Times*, 3 September 2009.
[8] *European Voice*, 17 December 2009.
[9] *European Voice*, 7 May 2009.
[10] *Financial Times*, 23 December 2009.

arose with China over imports of metal wire and with the USA over imports of chicken washed in chlorine.[11] Considering the overall economic atmosphere, it might be argued that the number of new disputes was encouragingly small; but this might be countered by the argument that actually the real disputes and potential protectionism were happening through other, less transparent channels.

Development Co-operation Policy and Humanitarian Aid

Most aspects of EU spending have over the years incurred the wrath of the European Court of Auditors (COA) and this year in its annual report (European Court of Auditors, 2009) it drew attention to the fact that European Development Fund (EDF) payments were 'affected by a material level of error' despite the reform efforts initiated by the Prodi Commission when it set up the Europe Aid Co-operation Office back in 2001 and through it devolved responsibility for aid administration from Brussels to the overseas delegations.[12] Now in addition to responding to the COA criticisms, those responsible for development aid must deal with the consequences of the ratification of the Lisbon Treaty and the establishment of the EEAS. The EEAS will be separate from both Commission and the Council (under the leadership of the High Representative) and will staff the renamed EU delegations abroad who will now be responsible for the implementation of EU aid policies and expenditure. There are therefore fears that EU development aid in general may be in danger of becoming more a tool of European Foreign Policy than the focus of a drive to eradicate poverty and hunger from the world's poorest people with those non-EEAS members left in the Commission Development Directorate General effectively excluded, or at least placed at a distance, from the relevant foreign policy decision-makers. It remains to be seen how the role of the development Commissioner will evolve as Catherine Ashton defines her own role as High Representative/Vice-President of the Commission.

In 2009 the European Commission chastized the EU Member States for their ongoing failure to meet development aid targets. The EU Commissioner for Development, Karel De Gucht, reported that just five (Denmark, Luxembourg, the Netherlands, Sweden and Ireland) of the 27 EU Member States were likely to meet the target of spending 0.56 per cent of national income on development aid by 2010 and that of these Ireland was likely to join the 23 Member States failing to reach 0.7 per cent by 2015.[13]

---

[11] *European Voice*, 15 October 2009; *Financial Times*, 23 December 2009.
[12] *European Voice*, 19 November 2009.
[13] *European Voice*, 12 November 2009.

In addition to the €2.7 billion European Development Funding agreed in March 2009 for the countries of Africa, the Caribbean and the Pacific (ACP), the EU also provided humanitarian and disaster relief of over €900 million to 70 countries including the immediate release of 'fast track funding' where appropriate. Although the EU's offer of humanitarian relief is often referred to alongside development aid as example of its 'soft power' it remains an area of EU external activity mainly designed to improve the international environment rather than advance the EU's material interests. It is to be hoped that humanitarian aid and disaster relief will never be regarded as a tool of European Foreign Policy.

II. Regional Themes

Russia

The EU's relationship with Russia in 2009 got off to a predictably bad start following Prime Minister Putin's comments at the end of 2008 that 'the time of cheap energy resources, cheap gas is surely coming to an end.'[14] It became clear in January that this statement applied specifically to Ukraine with Russia threatening to cut off the supply of gas to Ukraine until it accepted both a significant increase in price and paid its outstanding gas debts to Russia. The EU's response at first was to view the breakdown of relations between Russia and Ukraine as none of its business – possibly because the EU Presidency had just been assumed by an inexperienced Czech Republic and possibly because stockpiles of gas in the EU were high. However 25 per cent of the EU's gas supply comes from Russia, 80 per cent of which is currently imported through pipelines that run through Ukraine, hence the EU soon found itself involved in attempts to mediate.

When this failed, the crisis escalated, Russia accused Ukraine of 'stealing' gas destined for western Europe and cut off the supply not just to Ukraine but also to the transit pipelines. Inside the EU the worst-hit countries were those like Greece, Bulgaria, Romania and Poland, which were most strongly dependent on Russian gas. Member States that were relatively unaffected like Germany and the UK then found themselves under pressure to assist their EU colleagues by exporting their own supplies and thus faced potential shortages themselves. As the costs of the lost exports began to hit Gazprom, and as the EU began to question more firmly the long-term wisdom of over-reliance on Russian gas and on Ukrainian pipelines, both sides saw advantages in reaching a settlement and by the end of January the crisis was over for another

[14] See Bajan Global Report, 28 December 2008, available at «http://bimchat.wordpress.com/2008/12/24/putin-no-more-cheap-gas/».

year. In 2004 the European Union had initiated what had been planned as annual meetings between the European Commission and the Russian leadership but these meetings had ceased after 2005. President Barroso's attempts to revive the meetings and to repair the damaged EU–Russia relationship by spearheading a mission to Moscow of EU Commissioners fell short of expectations when he argued in public with Prime Minister Putin over various human rights issues and comments that he had made during the gas crisis about the sincerity and reliability of Russian and Ukrainian negotiators.[15]

Later, at the first 2009 EU–Russia summit, which was held rather bizarrely in Khabarovsk in Siberia apparently because Václav Klaus, the Czech President, had never been there before, Russia unsuccessfully, and some might think provocatively, asked the EU to help Ukraine pay off its gas debts.[16] At the second summit, held in Stockholm in November, one of the few tangible results was an agreement on an Enhanced European Early Warning System designed to anticipate possible future disruptions to gas supplies. It remains to be seen whether this new system will prevent further repetition of what has become a regular source of conflict at the start of each year, but Russian willingness to participate in such a system indicates a concern to maintain EU confidence in the security of the gas supply from Russia as does Russia's increased interest in the construction of new pipelines to the EU that avoid Ukraine.

Apart from the limited success of the formal meetings discussed above, EU–Russia relations remain bedevilled by the EU's general inability to forge a strategy for Russia[17] as well as its specific inability to develop and maintain either a common energy policy (Bailes, 2009, p. 30) or a clear view of Ukraine's membership prospects. In May the EU's launch of its Eastern Partnership failed to reassure either Russia or Ukraine whilst Russia's further activities in both South Ossetia and Abkhazia appeared to breach the agreement negotiated by the EU at the end of the Georgian intervention in 2008 (see Whitman and Juncos, this volume). Finally, Russia mystified the EU by stating that it now wished to apply for membership of the World Trade Organization not in its own right but as a part of a customs union with Belarus and Kazakhstan.

Africa

Faced with a growing Chinese interest in Africa, the EU has both increased its interest in trilateral EU–China–Africa co-operation and sought to enhance

---

[15] *Global Post*, 6 February 2009, available at «http://www.globalpost.com/dispatch/european-union/090206/chilly-visit-moscow».
[16] *Financial Times*, 25 May 2009.
[17] *The Guardian*, 5 February 2009.

further the EU–African relationship. To this end, the EU's Political and Security Committee held its first-ever joint meeting with counterparts from the African Union in Addis Ababa to discuss election-related violence, unconstitutional government change and the conflicts in Somalia and Sudan. With regard to Somalia, plans were made for a military training mission designed to produce an army and a police force capable of dealing on land with the bases used by the pirates that another ESDP mission (EURONAVFOR–Operation Atalanta) is confronting at sea off the Horn of Africa. The decision to launch the military training mission was made in November, but implementation was scheduled for May 2010.[18]

In the Sudan, concern was expressed about delays in implementing the 2007 Comprehensive Peace Agreement (CPA) that both the US and the EU have invested heavily in. The CPA was designed to lead to a census, elections and eventually in 2011 a referendum on independence for southern Sudan, but there are growing fears that the EU needs to do more to maintain the necessary momentum for what would be an exceptional peaceful transfer of authority. The indictment of the president of Sudan by the International Criminal Court (ICC) in some ways made matters worse because Sudan will not sign the EU Cotonou Agreement which would release significant funds for southern Sudan because signature of Cotonou requires recognition of the ICC.

In September an EU troika delegation was the first from the EU to visit Zimbabwe since 2002.[19] Although it was able to report some progress by the unity government of Robert Mugabe and Morgan Tsvangirai towards the objectives laid out in the September 2008 Global Political Agreement, it was clear that many problems remained. The troika thus recommended and the Council then confirmed (Council of Ministers, 2010) that targeted sanctions should remain in place whilst EU humanitarian assistance would remain at an average of €79 million a year with a small additional injection of €7.5 million for an education sponsorship fund.

Asia

One of the key features of the 'new multipolarity' which can be discerned during 2009 is the growing role – and growing assertiveness – of China (Clegg, 2009; Deng, 2008). This has been true for some years in the global political economy, but it has become markedly more apparent in the areas of diplomacy and security, and particularly in Chinese–American relations. During 2009, the EU found itself in the middle of this process, but arguably with little leverage over the ways in which the Chinese chose to assert

[18] *European Voice*, 12 November 2009.
[19] *The Guardian*, 14 September 2009.

themselves and so there was considerable uncertainty about the future of the EU–China 'strategic partnership' (Cameron, 2009; Grant and Barysch, 2008; Jing Men, 2008; Smith and Xie, 2009). At the top level, there was a 'thaw' in the relations between Brussels and Beijing, which had been distinctly icy in the later part of 2008 because of the frictions over Tibet (see Allen and Smith, 2009); Chinese prime minister Wen Jiabao visited Brussels in January, and in addition to the conclusion of an agreement on the safeguarding of intellectual property and reduction of counterfeiting, this visit resulted in the setting of a broad agenda for the rest of 2009.[20] Key to this agenda were two events during May and June: first, the convening of the EU–China High Level Economic and Trade Dialogue, and second, the resumption of EU–China Summit meetings, which was carried further with a second summit in October. Chinese and EU officials were also brought into intensive contact with each other during the G20 meetings in London and Pittsburgh. The issue was not really whether the EU–China dialogue could be restored; rather, it was whether the EU could wield any autonomous influence on Chinese policies given the changing global context and the increasingly abrasive relations between China and the USA. A much-cited and controversial analysis of the EU's China policies published during the year pointed not only to the EU's lack of external leverage but also to the lack of internal consensus on how to deal with China (Fox and Godement, 2009), and this provided a strong leitmotif for the current phase of EU–China relations.

More specific policy areas provided additional evidence for the EU's difficulties in dealing with China. Although there was a continuation of co-operation in matters of intellectual property (see above) and customs co-operation, there were a number of continuing disputes about EU anti-dumping measures on such items as metal wire, candles and shoes (see above). More significantly, the EU faced major difficulties in dealing with China's stance on global warming, in the context of the approaching Copenhagen Conference; the assertive nature of Chinese policy and their resistance to any binding commitments constituted a major roadblock to the EU's aims,[21] and in the event constituted a major obstacle to any kind of ambitious agreement. European leaders were frank in their disappointment at the Copenhagen outcome, but it was difficult to see how they could exert additional leverage as discussions moved on towards the Cancun Conference of Parties scheduled for December 2010.

EU relations with south Asian countries have become markedly more prominent in recent years, especially in the case of India. During 2009,

[20] *European Voice*, 29 January 2009; *Financial Times*, 31 January 2009.
[21] *Financial Times*, 18 March 2009, 2 June 2009, 11 June 2009, 13 June 2009.

negotiations continued over elements of the projected 'strategic partnership' with India, but they continued to meet obstacles, particularly through the reluctance of the Indian government to include any mention of non-economic issues and through their resistance to linkage between trade issues and the environment; the EU–India Summit held in early November thus had little significant progress to report.[22] On the more positive side of the ledger, India showed more interest than previously in a Doha Round agreement, but this had little eventual effect on the prospects for the Geneva WTO talks (see above). With other south Asian countries, the record was decidedly mixed during 2009: the first summit meeting between the EU and Pakistan took place in June,[23] and there was growing EU interest in foreign policy issues linking Afghanistan and Pakistan for obvious security reasons,[24] but at the same time relations with Burma (Myanmar) remained tense, particularly after the middle of the year when further measures were taken by the regime against Aung San Suu Kyi. As a result, EU sanctions against Burma were extended and widened, but there was increasing debate about the effectiveness of Union policies and some support for a policy of 'engagement' which might pay better dividends.[25] Sri Lanka attracted the EU's attention in particular because of the ending of the war between the government and Tamil rebels, and because of apparent human rights violations during the process; as a result, the EU threatened to withdraw its 'GSP Plus' trade preferences for the Colombo government, although by the end of the year it appeared that these preferences might be extended with careful monitoring of the situation in Sri Lanka.[26]

Latin America

It is fair to say that 2009 was a relatively fallow year in relations between the EU and Latin America – perhaps reflecting the marginal status of the continent in a number of the key issues confronting not only the EU but also the global political economy during the year. Nonetheless, in October the Commission presented proposals for a strengthening of the EU–Latin America partnership (Commission, 2009). The EU's encounters with its key Latin American partner – Brazil – intensified during the year, mainly in the context of the G20 and other multilateral institutions dealing with the financial crisis. The EU–Brazil summit in October focused on broader regional development

---

[22] *European Voice*, 5 November 2009.
[23] *European Voice*, 4 June 2009.
[24] *European Voice*, 22 October 2009.
[25] *The Guardian*, 2 June 2009; *European Voice*, 27 September 2009, 3 December 2009.
[26] *Financial Times*, 30 September 2009, 20 October 2009; *The Guardian*, 11 September 2009. 'GSP Plus' extends additional trade preferences to EU partners, on condition of 'good governance'.

issues as part of the broader development of the 'strategic partnership' between the two. EU–Brazil contacts were not always comfortable, though, as for example when the Brazilians took an assertive stance in the Copenhagen environment conference. Otherwise, the EU continued its pursuit of a trade agreement with the Andean Group (Colombia, Ecuador and Peru), completing five rounds of negotiations, and of an association agreement with a number of central American countries that will include a free trade agreement (Commission, 2010, p. 74). Perhaps more significantly in the political sphere, there were new contacts with Cuba: Commissioner Ferrero-Waldner visited Havana in July 2009[27] and it was reported that the Spanish government would use its Presidency of the Union in early 2010 to promote bilateral contacts with Cuba, despite worries that this might compromise the EU's position on human rights.[28]

The United States, Japan and Other Industrialized Countries

One of the most obvious challenges posed to the EU at the global (and at the bilateral) level during 2009 was that generated by the new Obama administration in Washington; in turn, this linked with continuing issues about the nature of EU–US institutional frameworks and policy co-ordination (Peterson and Steffenson, 2009; Smith, 2009). As noted in the 2008 *JCMS Annual Review*, Obama had been 'Europe's candidate' to succeed George W. Bush, but it was clear that Obama had more than Europe to worry about when he took office. It was also unclear whether the EU could assert itself and make itself a matter of priority for the administration, given the insistent demands of US–China relations and more global issues. One way of doing this would have been to make the EU an essential partner in confronting not only the global financial and economic crisis but also the continuing pressures of conflict in Afghanistan and the pursuit of counter-terrorism strategy, but as Dominique Moïsi argued in January 2009 it was far from clear that the EU was capable of uniting in such an effort.[29] In the diplomatic and security realms, the administration adopted what might be described as a pragmatic adjustment to multipolarity, recognizing the limitations of US power and the need for collaboration with other regional and global forces. This did not give top priority to the EU: as European political leaders scrambled to be the first to meet Obama or get a visit from Hillary Clinton, the new secretary of state, it was notable that on both fronts they came second to China. Given also the strength of domestic pressures in the USA itself, it was clear that gaining

---

[27] *European Voice*, 30 July 2009.
[28] *European Voice*, 3 December 2009.
[29] *Financial Times*, 8 January 2009.

Washington's attention would be a major task, and a number of commentaries during the year reflected the general uncertainty about this issue (De Vasconcelos and Zaborowski, 2009a,b; Niblett, 2009).

When Washington's attention on diplomatic and security matters was gained, it was not clear that the Europeans could meet the challenge that was laid down by the president. Three issues came to predominate: Guantanamo, Afghanistan (increasingly linked to Pakistan) and Iran. The question of whether EU Member States could reach a common position on how to respond to US requests that they receive former Guantanamo detainees as that facility was closed down preoccupied EU Member States for much of the early part of the year.[30] Eventually an agreement was reached during June, by which Member States would exchange information about the process and in which it was central that the US Congress had agreed to provide financial support for resettlement of detainees.[31]

When it came to Afghanistan, the key issue was the extent to which EU Member States (via Nato) would commit themselves to further military involvement in support of the US 'surge' that took place in the second half of the year; the often tense negotiations on this topic were not fully resolved until late in the year, and even then tensions persisted, exacerbated in September by mutual recriminations between the US and Germany over the bombing of a convoy and civilian deaths in Afghanistan itself.[32] By the end of the year, the EU had moved towards a strategy for Afghanistan focused strongly on state building rather than counter-terrorism, and it was not clear how this would relate to the evolving US position.[33]

The shifting nature of US policy was also apparent in the case of Iran, where the Obama administration adopted a more pragmatic and flexible approach, at least initially, than that of its predecessor.[34] By contrast, the 'EU3' (Britain, France and Germany) had begun working on more severe sanctions to be implemented if Iran failed to comply with previous demands.[35] Minds were focused in June by the contested Iranian election result, after which the EU played a notably 'harder' role than the United States,[36] and later by Iranian claims that they were rapidly increasing the rate at which they were enriching uranium and therefore in principle moving towards a position where they could construct a nuclear device. In the autumn a new dimension became apparent, with an offer to reprocess Iranian uranium in which the US

---

[30] *European Voice*, 15 January 2009, 20 May 2009.
[31] *The Guardian*, 5 June 2009, 16 June 2009.
[32] *Financial Times*, 8 September 2009.
[33] *Financial Times*, 27 October 2009.
[34] *The Guardian*, 15 April 2009.
[35] *Financial Times*, 26 February 2009.
[36] *Financial Times*, 23 June 2009.

was joined by France and Russia (but not by the EU collectively). The new engagement of Russia and also China, especially after the renewed fears that Iran would muster a nuclear capability, meant that by the end of 2009 a new set of players was likely to be involved in any subsequent developments.[37]

The development of the economic relationship with the USA posed its own challenges which were considerably sharpened by the financial crisis. One of the underlying tensions in transatlantic relations arose from the divergent approaches of continental Europeans on the one side and the US and the UK on the other to the support of threatened banks and other financial institutions. A dramatic – and ironic – articulation of this in early 2009 was by the Czech prime minister Mirek Topolánek, who in a speech to the European Parliament described the US and British approach as 'the road to hell',[38] reflecting his view that massive intervention was a betrayal of the kind of 'Anglo-Saxon' capitalism that the US and the UK should pursue, but tensions were also evident in French and German views on the morality of capitalism and the need for greater regulation.[39] More specifically, all EU Member States – and the EU collectively – were disturbed by the inclusion in the US stimulus package of 'Buy American' (and later 'Drive American' and 'Hire American') clauses, designed to make sure that US firms were the major beneficiaries.[40] The EU was provoked into threatening litigation, especially on government procurement, emphasizing the potential effects on world trade in general as well as on European interests.[41] This issue, as noted at the beginning of this article and above, linked strongly with more general differences of EU and US positions on the management of the world economy, and also with the pressures exerted by powerful US domestic forces.

At the same time as these broad, almost philosophical issues were debated across the Atlantic, a series of more specific trade disputes persisted.[42] The dispute between the EU and the US over the regulation of online gambling, in which American authorities were seen as discriminating against European companies, continued, as did that over the US subsidization of bio-diesel exports (in which the EU retaliated by imposing duties on US products), and they were joined by the dispute over chlorine-treated chickens noted earlier in this article. Reference was made earlier in this article to the two 'success stories' of hormone-treated beef and bananas; but although they were effectively resolved during 2009, they had been around since the early to

---

[37] *Financial Times*, 1 December 2009.
[38] *Financial Times*, 26 March 2009.
[39] *The Guardian*, 9 January 2009.
[40] *Financial Times*, 4 January 2009, 14 February 2009, 4 August 2009.
[41] *European Voice*, 26 February 2009.
[42] See the excellent Special Report in *European Voice*, 2 April 2009.

mid-1990s, so this was not necessarily an encouraging sign. There continued to be tensions over 'security-related' issues of commercial activity: in one such case, the EU was split over how to accord the US access to details of bank transfers via the SWIFT system, when the relevant data were moved from the US to Switzerland,[43] and in another case, there was residual tension over the ways in which the US system of electronic visa waivers (ESTA) was to be administered, and in particular over whether a fee would be charged to those using it.[44]

A key feature of EU–US relations during the year was the build-up to and the outcome of the Copenhagen Conference on global warming, which had as its key aim the negotiation of a new climate change regime to succeed the Kyoto Protocol. Whereas under George W. Bush there had been active hostility to environmental regulation, the EU's expectation was that under the Obama administration, there would be a new openness to multilateral solutions. Thus, there was evidence that EU leaders envisaged an 'alliance' with the US as Copenhagen approached.[45] But as the year progressed, two features became clearer: first, that the EU was less likely to gain the attention of, and leverage over, the US than was China, and second, that US domestic forces would be a potent obstacle to any hopes in the administration of more flexibility. As a result, preparations for the negotiations followed an uncertain course, with some elements of a game of 'chicken'; and the EU was faced with a situation in which any offers or concessions it might make on emissions targets or other commitments were inevitably conditional on what might or might not be offered by others. The endgame of the Copenhagen negotiations in mid-December saw the EU being effectively marginalized – in an area where they had hitherto claimed leadership of the international effort – by horse-trading between the US, China and a number of other emerging economies. The result – a less than binding set of commitments to less than precise targets and modalities – was in many ways a defeat for the EU's conception of international collective action and governance, and resulted in an extended post mortem.[46]

Whilst relations with the United States were often a source of tensions during 2009, those between the EU and Canada seemed to reach a new level. Central to this was the initiation of negotiations for a free trade agreement – to be precise, a Comprehensive Economic and Trade Agreement (CETA). These were foreshadowed early in the year, and followed on from a far-reaching 'open skies' agreement reached in the previous year (see Allen and

[43] *European Voice*, 16 April 2009, 30 July 2009.
[44] *European Voice*, 8 January 2009, *Financial Times*, 11 November 2009.
[45] *The Guardian*, 29 January 2009.
[46] *Financial Times*, 23 December 2009.

Smith, 2009) although they did not start until the autumn. Interestingly, the process also included participation from the Canadian Provinces, which have a significant economic role.[47] Not all was sweetness and light in EU–Canadian relations, and in particular the CETA negotiations were threatened on the one hand by efforts in the European Parliament to take measures against the Canadian seal trade and on the other by the Canadians' decision to impose visa requirements on Czech citizens; but the sense of momentum was palpable.

Finally, relations with the two established advanced industrial powers of east Asia, Japan and South Korea, presented a study in contrasts during 2009. Relations with Japan continued along their established path, with the summit in April covering a wide range of industrial and commercial areas;[48] major initiatives were not contemplated given the approaching Japanese elections. Meanwhile, relations with South Korea took a major step forward with the conclusion of negotiations for a free trade agreement and its approval by the Council in July.[49] A key area of tension around these negotiations was the fears of EU car manufacturers that Korean products (both cars and car parts) would gain free access to the EU without reciprocal access being given to EU products, and this will remain a key test of the effectiveness of the agreement. The agreement itself will also be accompanied by a 'framework agreement for a strategic partnership', adding South Korea to a growing list of strategic partners identified by the Union.[50]

Conclusions

What is clear from this study of the EU's external political, economic and security activities in 2009 is that at present, despite its considerable economic capability, the EU struggles to 'punch its weight' in the world in a co-ordinated and coherent manner and is therefore by no means either ready or able to take its (much anticipated) place in the evolving system of major powers. It remains to be seen whether the impetus provided by the ratification of the Lisbon Treaty can be used to create a more effective and wide-ranging EU contribution to a rapidly changing world order, where the challenge is as much to the EU's established roles as it is to potential new areas of engagement and influence.

[47] *European Voice*, 15 September 2009.
[48] *European Voice*, 30 April 2009.
[49] *European Voice*, 16 July 2009.
[50] *European Voice*, 8 October 2009.

Key Readings

Commission (2010) provides a useful, but less extensive than in previous years, survey of the external relations of the EU (Chapter 3, 'The EU as a World Player', pp. 55–71). *European Voice* (Volume 15, 2009) provides a sound summary of recent developments as does the *CFSP Forum* which is published bi-monthly by FORNET («http://www.fornet.info/CFSPforum.html0») and contains numerous articles on all aspects of CFSP and ESDP activities.

References

Allen, D. and Smith, M. (2009) 'Relations with the Rest of the World'. *JCMS*, Vol. 47, s1, pp. 213–33.

Bailes, A. (2009) 'External Security Policies and the European Model'. In Tsoukalis, L. (ed.) *The EU in a World in Transition: Fit for What Purpose?* (London: Policy Network).

Cameron, F. (2009) 'The Development of EU–China Relations'. In Taneja, P., Wiessala, G. and Wilson, J. (eds) *The European Union and China: Interests and Dilemmas* (Amsterdam: Rodopi).

Clegg, J. (2009) *China's Global Strategy: Towards a Multipolar World* (London: Pluto).

Commission of the European Communities (2009) 'EU–Latin America: Global Players in Partnership'. Communication from the Commission. *COM*(2009)495, 30 September.

Commission of the European Communities (2010) 'General Report on the Activities of the European Union 2009'. European Commission, Brussels.

Council of Ministers (2010) 'Council Conclusions on Zimbabwe'. 2996th Foreign Affairs Council Meeting, Brussels, 22 February.

Deng, Y. (2008) *China's Struggle for Status: The Realignment of International Relations* (Cambridge: Cambridge University Press).

De Vasconcelos, A. and Zaborowski, M. (eds) (2009a) *European Perspectives on the New American Foreign Policy Agenda* (Paris: EU Institute for Security Studies).

De Vasconcelos, A. and Zaborowski, M. (eds) (2009b) *The Obama Moment: European and American Perspectives* (Paris: EU Institute for Security Studies).

European Court of Auditors (2009) 'Annual Report on the Implementation of the Budget 2008'. OJC 2009C, 269/01.

Fox, J. and Godement, F. (2009) *A Power Audit of EU–China Relations* (London: European Council on Foreign Relations).

Grant, C. (2007) *Preparing for the Multipolar World: European Foreign and Security Policy in 2020* (London: Centre for European Reform).

Grant, C. (2009) *Is Europe Doomed to Fail as a Power?* (London: Centre for European Reform).

Grant, C. and Barysch, K. (2008) *Can Europe and China Shape a New World Order?* (London: Centre for European Reform).

Grevi, G. (2009) 'The Interpolar World: A New Scenario'. Occasional Paper (Paris: EU Institute for Security Studies), June.

Men, J. (2008) 'EU–China Relations: From Engagement to Marriage?' EU Diplomacy Paper (Bruges: Department of International Relations and Diplomacy Studies, College of Europe).

Niblett, R. (2009) 'Ready to Lead? Rethinking America's Role in a Changed World'. Chatham House Report (London: Royal Institute of International Affairs), February.

Peterson, J. and Steffenson, R. (2009) 'Transatlantic Institutions: Can Partnership be Engineered?' *British Journal of Politics & International Relations*, Vol. 11, No. 1, pp. 25–45.

Smith, M. (2009) 'Transatlantic Economic Relations in a Changing Global Political Economy: Achieving Togetherness but Missing the Bus?' *British Journal of Politics & International Relations*, Vol. 11, No. 1, pp. 94–107.

Smith, M. and Xie, H. (2009) 'The European Union's "Strategic Partnership" with China: How Much Strategy? How Much Partnership?' Paper presented at the UACES Annual/Research Conference, Angers, France, September.

Stephens, P. (2009) 'Europe does Not Need a Big Shot'. *Financial Times*, 27 October, p. 13.

Wall, S. (2009) 'Council President an Ill-Defined Role'. *European Voice*, Vol. 15, 15 October, p. 15.

The EU Economy: The Euro Area in 2009*

DERMOT HODSON
Birkbeck College, University of London

Introduction

The year 2009 may well have been one to forget for the euro area but it was undoubtedly one to remember for scholars of economic and monetary union (EMU). Although it lacked the high drama of 2007, which saw euro area money markets freeze following the collapse of the US sub-prime mortgage market (Verdun, 2008), and the suspense of 2008, which brought euro area banks to the brink after the demise of Lehman Brothers (Quaglia *et al*, 2009; Verdun, 2009), there was no shortage of action as the real effects of the global financial crisis continued to unfold.

For economists, 2009 provided an opportunity to observe at close quarters the euro area's response to a large symmetric shock with significant asymmetric effects. The euro area as a whole remained in recession as world trade experienced its worst slump since World War II and credit shortages squeezed firms and consumers. No euro area member escaped this recession but economies with a heavy reliance on exports (for example, Germany) and those facing significant financial losses (for example, Ireland) or sharp falls in housing prices (for example, Spain) experienced tougher times than most (Commission, 2009).

For those with an interest in euro area governance, 2009 shed further light on EMU's experimental approach to policy-making (Hodson, 2010). European

* Thanks to Nat Copsey and Tim Haughton for helpful comments on an earlier draft. The usual disclaimer applies.

Central Bank (ECB) watchers watched Frankfurt turn to unconventional monetary policies once interest rates could fall no further. Students of the Stability and Growth Pact saw widespread breaches of EMU's fiscal rules as government borrowing in the euro area soared. Followers of EU financial market policy were faced with the most ambitious attempts yet to give the Community a stronger say over prudential supervision. Experts on external representation encountered repeated efforts by euro area members to reach a co-ordinated position on international issues.

This article explores these and other themes in its overview of developments in the euro area in 2009. Section I presents some stylized facts concerning the economic situation in the euro area. Section II looks at the key steps taken by the ECB over the course of the year. Section III discusses decisions taken in the context of the Stability and Growth Pact. Section IV explores the EU's response to the de Larosière Report on the future of financial supervision. Section V explores the euro area's international role in 2009.

I. The Economic Situation in the Euro Area in 2009

Gross domestic product (GDP) fell by 4.0 per cent in real terms in 2009 as the global financial crisis continued to bite (see Table 1). Perhaps the most visible impact of the crisis was a serious shortfall in external demand, with total exports from the euro area to the rest of the world falling by 14.2 per cent in 2009 compared with a modest increase of 1.0 per cent in 2008.[1] The worsening international outlook discouraged investment, as did credit shortages and a slowdown in the construction sector, with the result that total investment in the euro area fell by 10.7 per cent in 2009, compared with a drop of 0.4 per cent in 2008. Consumption was altogether more resilient, falling by 1.0 per cent in the private sector and rising by 2.0 per cent in the public sector. The latter was due, in part, to fiscal stimulus packages implemented by several Member States in 2008 and 2009 (see below).

Although all euro area countries experienced negative growth in 2009, some were harder hit than others. Cyprus fared best, recording a fall in real GDP of just 0.7 per cent thanks to its limited exposure to toxic assets and stringent approach to financial supervision. Ireland fared worst, contracting by 7.5 per cent due, *inter alia*, to its reliance on a financial sector that incurred large losses during the crisis and a sharp correction in property

---

[1] The data referred to in this section are, unless otherwise, stated based on the European Commission's Autumn 2009 Economic Forecast. Full text available at «http://ec.europa.eu/economy_finance/ publications/publication16055_en.pdf». Full details of all steps taken under the Stability and Growth Pact in 2009 are available at «http://ec.europa.eu/economy_finance/sgp/deficit/countries/index_en.htm».

Table 1: Real GDP Growth (% Annual Change) – Euro Area (2005–10)

	2005	2006	2007	2008	2009^e	2010^f
Belgium	1.8	2.8	2.9	1.0	−2.9	0.6
Germany	0.8	3.2	2.5	1.3	−5.0	1.2
Ireland	6.2	5.4	6.0	−3.0	−7.5	−1.4
Greece	2.2	4.5	4.5	2.0	−1.1	−0.3
Spain	3.6	4.0	3.6	0.9	−3.7	−0.8
France	1.9	2.2	2.3	0.4	−2.2	1.2
Italy	0.7	2.0	1.6	−1.0	−4.7	0.7
Cyprus	3.9	4.1	4.4	3.7	−0.7	0.1
Luxembourg	5.4	5.6	6.5	0.0	−3.6	1.1
Malta	4.1	3.8	3.7	2.1	−2.2	0.7
Netherlands	2.0	3.4	3.6	2.0	−4.5	0.3
Austria	2.5	3.5	3.5	2.0	−3.7	1.1
Portugal	0.9	1.4	1.9	0.0	−2.9	0.3
Slovenia	4.5	5.8	6.8	3.5	−7.4	1.3
Slovakia	6.5	8.5	10.4	6.4	−5.8	1.9
Finland	2.8	4.9	4.2	1.0	−6.9	0.9
Euro area	1.7	3.0	2.8	0.6	−4.0	0.7

Source: Commission (2009), p. 188, Table 1.
Note: Estimates are denoted by *e* and forecasts by *f*.

prices following the end of a prolonged boom. Slovakia, which became the 16th country to join the euro area in January 2009, lagged not far behind with a growth rate of −5.8 per cent, reflecting its high degree of economic openness at a time of heightened instability in the international economy.

Among the larger euro area members, France outperformed Germany, with real GDP in the former contracting by 2.2 per cent compared with 5.0 per cent in the latter. Franco–German growth divergences in 2009 were rooted to some degree in differing growth strategies. France, with its reliance on domestic demand, avoided the worst of the global downturn in trade. According to the Commission's estimates, falling net exports from France to the rest of the world reduced the real GDP growth rate by just 0.1 percentage point in 2009. The corresponding figure for Germany stood at 3.4 percentage points, reflecting the limits of the country's export-driven growth model. The corollary of this point, however, is that the German economy is expected to recover fairly rapidly as global trade resumes, with real GDP forecast to rise by 1.2 per cent in 2010. A German recovery will help to lift the euro area's economic fortunes, although the latter is expected to grow by just 0.7 per cent in 2010. Economic recovery is thus expected to

Table 2: Unemployment (% of the Civilian Labour Force) – Euro Area (2005–10)

	2005	2006	2007	2008	2009^e	2010^f
Belgium	8.5	8.3	7.5	7.0	8.2	9.9
Germany	10.7	9.8	8.4	7.3	7.7	9.2
Ireland	4.4	4.5	4.6	6.0	11.7	14.0
Greece	9.9	8.9	8.3	7.7	9.0	10.2
Spain	9.2	8.5	8.3	11.3	17.9	20.0
France	9.3	9.2	8.4	7.8	9.5	10.2
Italy	7.7	6.8	6.1	6.8	7.8	8.7
Cyprus	5.3	4.6	4.0	3.6	5.6	6.6
Luxembourg	4.6	4.6	4.2	4.9	6.2	7.3
Malta	7.2	7.1	6.4	5.9	7.1	7.4
Netherlands	4.7	3.9	3.2	2.8	3.4	5.4
Austria	5.2	4.8	4.4	3.8	5.5	6.0
Portugal	7.7	7.8	8.1	7.7	9.0	9.0
Slovenia	6.5	6.0	4.9	4.4	6.7	8.3
Slovakia	16.3	13.4	11.1	9.5	12.3	12.8
Finland	8.4	7.7	6.9	6.4	8.5	10.2
Euro area	9.0	8.3	7.5	7.5	9.5	10.7

Source: Commission (2009), p. 199, Table 23.
Note: Estimates are denoted by e and forecasts by f.

take hold in the euro area in 2010 but the signs suggest that it could be a long and drawn-out affair.

The recession has inevitably taken its toll on the euro area labour market. Unemployment rose from 7.5 per cent of the civilian labour force in 2008 to 9.5 per cent in 2009 and is expected to increase further in 2010 (see Table 2). Aggregate trends, once again, mask considerable cross-country differences. Unemployment in Spain rose from 11.3 per cent in 2008 to 17.9 per cent in 2009 and is forecast to reach 20 per cent in 2010. The reasons for this dramatic increase in the rate of joblessness are not yet clear – Spain's real GDP fell by less than the euro area average in 2009 – but labour laws that leave a significant share of the workforce on easy-to-cancel temporary contracts and a collapse in the construction industry are prime suspects. The unemployment rate in Germany, in contrast, was surprisingly stable in 2009, rising by just 0.4 percentage points compared with 2008. One explanation is that Germany had adjusted to the crisis by cutting the numbers of hours worked rather than the number of workers employed (Commission, 2009). The fact that German unemployment looks set to increase to 9.2 per cent in 2010 suggests, however, that firms may have merely postponed labour market adjustment by hoarding labour in the early stages of the crisis.

Table 3: Inflation Rates (% change on preceding year) – Euro Area (2005–10)

	2005	2006	2007	2008	2009[e]	2010[f]
Belgium	2.5	2.3	1.8	4.5	0.0	1.3
Germany	1.9	1.8	2.3	2.8	0.3	0.8
Ireland	2.2	2.7	2.9	3.1	−1.5	−0.6
Greece	3.5	3.3	3.0	4.2	1.2	1.4
Spain	3.4	3.6	2.8	4.1	−0.4	0.8
France	1.9	1.9	1.6	3.2	0.1	1.1
Italy	2.2	2.2	2.0	3.5	0.8	1.8
Cyprus	2.0	2.2	2.2	4.4	0.8	3.1
Luxembourg	3.8	3.0	2.7	4.1	0.0	1.8
Malta	2.5	2.6	0.7	4.7	2.0	2.0
Netherlands	1.5	1.7	1.6	2.2	1.1	0.9
Austria	2.1	1.7	2.2	3.2	0.5	1.3
Portugal	2.1	3.0	2.4	2.7	−1.0	1.3
Slovenia	2.5	2.5	3.8	5.5	0.9	1.7
Slovakia	2.8	4.3	1.9	3.9	1.1	1.9
Finland	0.8	1.3	1.6	3.9	1.8	1.6
Euro area	2.2	2.2	2.1	3.3	0.3	1.1

Source: Commission (2009), p. 195, Table 16.
Note: Estimates are denoted by e and forecasts by f.

Fears of stagflation (falling economic growth and rising inflation) in the euro area in 2008 were replaced by worries over deflation (sustained falls in price levels) in 2009 (Table 3). High energy and food prices saw the rate of inflation rise from 2.1 per cent in 2007 to 3.3 per cent in 2008 creating an uncomfortable tension between the pursuit of price stability and the promotion of economic recovery. Energy and, to a lesser extent, food price rises abated in 2009, helping to ease inflationary pressures. This development, coupled with downward pressure on producer prices, caused the rate of inflation in the euro area to fall to a historic low of 0.3 per cent in 2009. Several euro area members experienced zero or negative rates of inflation in 2009, raising concerns that disinflation could give way to deflation. Inflationary pressures are forecast to pick up again in 2010, however, which suggests that this scenario is unlikely to materialize.

The euro area witnessed a reversal of fiscal fortunes in 2009 as the financial crisis started to weigh on public finances (Table 4). Italy and Portugal posted budget deficits below 3 per cent of GDP in 2008, the first time that all euro area members met the Stability and Growth Pact's rules on short-term government borrowing since the single currency entered circulation in 2002. By 2009, all but three euro area members, Cyprus, Finland and Luxembourg, exceeded the 3 per cent of GDP reference value, reflecting the heavy toll taken on euro area

Table 4: Net Lending (+) or Net Borrowing (−) General Government Balance (% of GDP) – Euro Area (2005–10)

	2005	2006	2007	2008	2009[e]	2010[f]
Belgium	−2.7	0.3	−0.2	−1.2	−5.9	−5.8
Germany	−3.3	−1.6	0.2	0.0	−3.4	−5.0
Ireland	1.7	3.0	0.3	−7.2	−12.5	−14.7
Greece	−5.2	−2.9	−3.7	−7.7	−12.7	−12.2
Spain	1.0	2.0	1.9	−4.1	−11.2	−10.1
France	−2.9	−2.3	−2.7	−3.4	−8.3	−8.2
Italy	−4.3	−3.3	−1.5	−2.7	−5.3	−5.3
Cyprus	−2.4	−1.2	3.4	0.9	−3.5	−5.7
Luxembourg	0.0	1.3	3.7	2.5	−2.2	−4.2
Malta	−2.9	−2.6	−2.2	−4.7	−4.5	−4.4
Netherlands	−0.3	0.5	0.2	0.7	−4.7	−6.1
Austria	−1.6	−1.6	−0.6	−0.4	−4.3	−5.5
Portugal	−6.1	−3.9	−2.6	−2.7	−8.0	−8.0
Slovenia	−1.4	−1.3	0.0	−1.8	−6.3	−7.0
Slovakia	−2.8	−3.5	−1.9	−2.3	−6.3	−6.0
Finland	2.8	4.0	5.2	4.5	−2.8	−4.5
Euro area	−2.5	−1.3	−0.6	−2.0	−6.4	−6.9

Source: Commission (2009), p. 206, Table 37.
Note: Estimates are denoted by *e* and forecasts by *f*.

public finances by the global financial crisis. Countries on the geographical periphery of EMU were hardest hit with Spain, Greece and Ireland posting double-digit deficits and Portugal lagging not far behind.

The rapid rise in government borrowing in euro area members is due to a variety of reasons. Countries such as Ireland have faced a perfect storm of rising expenditure on troubled banks and falling tax revenues due not only to swings in the automatic stabilizers but also to the end of a decade-long housing boom during which the state had come to rely on stamp duties (Commission, 2009). These developments have left little room for a fiscal stimulus in Member States such as Ireland but the same is not true of all euro area countries. Fiscal stimulus measures in Germany were valued at 1.5 per cent of GDP in 2009 and 2.0 per cent of GDP in 2010, which lagged behind only China, Saudi Arabia and the USA among G20 members (IMF, 2009).

II. Euro Area Monetary Policy in 2009

Having waited until October 2008 to cut interest rates in response to the global financial crisis – the US Federal Reserve began to ease monetary policy in September 2007 – the ECB made up for lost time in 2009. The euro area monetary authority announced four interest rates cuts between January and May 2009, taking the interest rate on the main refinancing operations from 2.50 per cent to a historic low of 1 per cent. Conventional monetary policies have been accompanied by unconventional measures. The latter have included allowing banks to use a wider range of assets as collateral when borrowing from the Eurosystem and a switch from variable to fixed rate tenders for the Bank's main refinancing operations, thus providing banks with unlimited liquidity at very low interest rates (ECB, 2009).

In June 2009 the ECB unveiled a plan to purchase €60 billion in euro-denominated covered bonds, long-term debt security backed by mortgages or public sector loans. This was a fairly modest sum when compared with the US Federal Reserve's $800 billion credit easing programme and the Bank of England's £200 billion Asset Purchase Facility. The ECB's covered bond scheme was also more modest in its ambitions since it could only be used to purchase one class of private sector asset. The Fed's credit easing programme, in contrast, has been used to purchase, *inter alia*, debt securities backed by car loans, credit cards, and student loans debt and mortgage-backed securities held by federal agencies. Similarly, the Bank of England's Asset Purchase Facility is used to purchase private sector assets and government bonds.

The specific character of the ECB's covered bond scheme may have been an attempt on the part of the euro area monetary authority to safeguard its independence. Minegishi and Cournède (2010), for example, suggest that the ECB was less exposed than other central banks to the interest rate risk associated with exit strategies from unconventional monetary policies. The US Federal Reserve, they suggest, stands to make significant losses as it divests itself of long-dated assets such as Treasury securities, agency bonds and mortgage-backed securities if, as expected, market interest rates rise in the coming years. Under some scenarios, such losses could compromise the perceived independence of the Fed, especially if a capital injection from the government was necessary. This risk is lower for the ECB, the authors argue, not only because the sums spent on covered bonds were comparatively low but also because the maturity on this particular class of asset is typically lower than that on mortgage-backed securities and gilts.

The ECB's approach to unconventional monetary policy in 2009 may also have reflected an understanding of underlying approaches to corporate governance in a monetary union dominated by, what proponents of the Varieties of Capitalism would refer to as, co-ordinated market economies (see Hall and Soskice, 2001; Hancké *et al.*, 2007). For its part, the ECB justified its covered bond scheme on the grounds that it provides direct support to banks, which in turn provide 70 per cent of financing for corporations in the euro area. This figure stands at just 20 per cent for the USA, reflecting the reliance of corporations in liberal market economies on more diverse sources of finances (Hall and Soskice, 2001). This, Trichet (2009) implied, is why the USA's credit easing approach offers support for the financial system at large by purchasing treasury securities, agency bonds and mortgage-backed securities.

III. The Stability and Growth Pact in 2009

The fact that the Stability and Growth Pact was not suspended in 2009 comes as a surprise for scholars of EU governance. Rules-based approaches to fiscal policy have fallen by the wayside during the global financial crisis – see Hodson and Mabbett (2009) on the suspension of the UK fiscal code of conduct – but the Stability and Growth Pact somehow still seems to retain the support of Member States. This is all the more surprising when it is recalled that the slowdown in economic growth and upturn in government borrowing that precipitated the suspension of the Stability and Growth Pact in November 2003 were of a much lower order of magnitude than that witnessed as a result of the global financial crisis.

Some scholars would explain the Stability and Growth Pact's longevity by virtue of fact that the EU's fiscal rules are no longer binding since the reforms of March 2005. These reforms, sold by EU authorities as a means of enhancing the economic rationale underpinning the Pact, were widely dismissed at the time as a political fudge. Feldstein (2005), for one, argued that 'the Council [had] specified exceptions to the interpretation of these rules that made them effectively meaningless' and concluded that 'there is no longer any restraint on individual country deficits' (Feldstein, 2005, p. 9).

These doubts have not yet been borne out during the global financial crisis. There is no evidence to suggest that EU policy-makers have turned a blind eye to budget deficits in excess of 3 per cent of GDP in spite of the exceptional nature of the crisis. In keeping with Article 126(3) TFEU (ex 104) the Commission has prepared a report on all Member States that have breached the reference value and in no case has the EU executive failed to follow up with an Article 126(5) recommendation to the Council on the existence of an excessive deficit, in spite of the exceptional nature of the financial crisis. EU finance ministers have, for their part, endorsed all Commission recommendations concerning the existence of an excessive deficit under Article 126(6) and issued recommendations to the Member States concerned to bring their excessive budget deficits to an end.

Once Ecofin has endorsed the European Commission's proposal on the existence of an excessive deficit, it falls to the former to issue a recommendation for corrective action under Article 126(7). Under the code of conduct underpinning the Stability and Growth Pact, Member States facing special circumstances can be given longer than normal to correct their excessive deficits. Whereas the meaning of special circumstances had originally been left undefined, the revised Pact instructs EU authorities to take account of the same set of exceptionality clauses that apply to decisions over the existence of an excessive deficit. In principle, this makes it easier for ECOFIN to given an extension to Member States facing an excessive deficit, with the code of conduct stating that countries facing special circumstances should, as a rule, be given three rather than two years after the deficit is identified to reduce their borrowing below 3 per cent of GDP (ECOFIN, 2009a, p. 8).

These provisions were used to full effect in April 2009, for example, when Ecofin gave France and Spain until 2012 rather than 2011 to correct their excessive deficits. This decision was consistent with the March 2005 reform of the Stability and Growth Pact, in so far as Ecofin's decision was based on a recommendation from the European Commission that deemed special conditions existed in France and Spain. Ecofin also decided at this time that Ireland faced special circumstances, although the decision to grant a deadline of 2013 rather than 2011, though it was in line with the letter of the Stability and Growth Pact, went beyond the norms laid down in the code of conduct for corrective excessive deficits. Similar leeway was shown when Ecofin decided in November 2009 to allow Germany, Austria, the Netherlands, Slovenia, Slovakia and Portugal until 2013 to correct their excessive deficits.

The revised Stability and Growth Pact introduced an additional degree of flexibility by allowing Member States that face 'unexpected adverse economic events with major unfavourable consequences for government finances' to repeat a step under Article 126(7) or Article 126(8) of the excessive deficit procedure providing they have undertaken 'effective action' in line with earlier recommendations. This provision was put into effect in November 2009, when Ecofin concluded that Ireland, Spain and France had taken effective action but faced extraneous problems 'due to the economic environment'. Ireland's deadline for correcting its excessive deficit was extended from 2013 to 2014, while the deadline for both France and Spain was extended from 2012 to 2013.

If the global financial crisis has been the sternest test yet of the revised Stability and Growth Pact then the EU's response to fiscal developments in Greece has been the most difficult part of this test. Greece's fiscal problems came to light in October 2008 when the government informed Eurostat that its budget deficit in 2007 would be 3.5 per cent of GDP and not, as had been indicated in April 2008, 2.8 per cent of GDP. This news dealt a severe blow to the credibility of EU fiscal surveillance, not least because Ecofin had voted in June 2007 to abrogate an excessive deficit procedure against Greece, in part, on the understanding that the deficit for that year would be reduced to 2.4 per cent. It also reignited concerns over the credibility of Greek statistics, which had surfaced periodically during the first ten years of EMU (see Savage, 2005).

Although the deterioration of Greek public finances compromised the credibility of the Stability and Growth Pact, it also showed Member States' determination to enforce the EU's fiscal rules. In April 2009, EU finance ministers, acting on a recommendation from the European Commission, once more declared Greece to be in a state of excessive deficit, giving the Greek government until 2010 to correct its excessive deficit. The leniency shown to France, Spain and Ireland at this time was not extended to Greece. The official reason given for this decision was that the deterioration in public finances in Greece stemmed not from extraneous circumstances but from a failure to consolidate public finances during a period of buoyant economic growth.

This situation went from bad to considerably worse in October 2008 when the newly elected government of George Papandreou revised the expected budget deficit for 2009 from 3.7 per cent to 12.7 per cent, citing higher public expenditure by the previous administration. This announcement fuelled financial market concerns about Greece's creditworthiness, as reflected in the widening spread (i.e. the interest rate differential) between Greek and German ten-year bonds and in the decision by Standard and Poor's to down-grade Greece's sovereign credit rating in December 2009.

The Greek fiscal crisis asked serious questions about the fiscal foundations of EMU, with some commentators predicting that a Greek default could spill over into Portugal, Spain and elsewhere. EU authorities sought to allay such concerns by pressing ahead with the excessive deficit procedure against Greece, this being one of the few courses of action readily available to restore confidence in the euro area economy. On 2 December 2009, Ecofin, acting on a recommendation from the European Commission, adopted a decision under Article 126(8) establishing that Greece had undertaken inadequate action in response to its earlier recommendation. This was followed on 16 February 2010 by a decision under Article 126(9) giving notice to Greece to undertake specific measures to eliminate its excessive deficit by 2012. If the choice of deadline signalled a less stringent interpretation of the revised Stability and Growth Pact than had hitherto been the case – the European Commission was arguing as late as November 2009 that Greece could not be granted an extension without undertaking effective action – the specific measures enacted by the Council are among the most stringent ever contained in a document on EU fiscal surveillance.

To understand this point, compare the Article 126(9) recommendation issued against Greece in February 2005 (Ecofin, 2005) with the one issued in February 2010 (Ecofin, 2010). The former simply called on the Greek government to ensure 'a rigorous implementation of the 2005 budget' and the need for 'measures of a permanent nature leading to a correction in the deficit of at least 0.6 of a percentage point of GDP' but said nothing about specific tax and expenditure decisions. The latter, in contrast, identified specific decisions to be taken by the Greek government and higher taxes on alcohol and fuel. Such measures were not devised from scratch – they were mostly taken from the 2010 update to Greece's stability programme – but they represent an unprecedented degree of involvement by the EU in the fiscal affairs of a sovereign country.

In summary, a paradox of 2009 is that despite widespread breaches in EMU's fiscal rules, Member States resorted to the most stringent interpretation yet of the Stability and Growth Pact. The reforms of March 2005 allowed for greater flexibility but the European Commission and the Ecofin did not, as some predicted, use this flexibility to ignore blatant breaches of the EU's fiscal rules. This is especially true in the case of Greece, which faced the harshest penalties yet imposed under the Stability and Growth Pact. It remains to be seen whether the Stability and Growth Pact will see out the global financial crisis. The EU's initial efforts to promote fiscal consolidation in Greece failed to reassure financial markets, paving the way for a joint bail-out by the EU and the International Monetary Fund (IMF) in 2010 in a move that may lead to a radical rethink of fiscal governance in the euro area.

IV. The Future of Financial Supervision

Under the EU's current legal framework, the responsibility for financial supervision in the euro area falls not to the Eurosystem but to the individual Member States. The Eurosystem is required under the Treaty to contribute to 'the smooth conduct of policies pursued by the competent authorities relating to the prudential supervision of credit institutions and the stability of the financial system' (Article 127 TFEU). To this end, the ECB monitors and regularly reports on financial stability in the euro area.

National supervisors have also agreed to co-ordinate their supervisory practices in the context of the Lamfalussy Process (Quaglia, 2008). More specifically, the so-called 'level 3 committees' – the Committee of European Banking Supervisors, the Committee of European Securities Regulators and the Committee of European Insurance and Occupational Pensions Supervisors – encourage consistency in the transposition of framework principles and implementation measures and a convergence in supervisory practices by fostering co-operation between officials from the Commission and national regulators.

As in other political systems, there has been much soul searching in the EU on the future of financial supervision in the light of the global financial crisis. A major milestone in the European debate was the publication in February 2009 of the de Larosière report, which presented the findings of a high-level group on EU financial supervision convened by the President of the European Commission, José Manuel Barroso, and chaired by a former governor of the *Banque de France*, Jacques de Larosière. The report called for the creation of two new Community bodies, a European Systemic Risk Council (ESRC) to ensure financial stability in the EU as a whole and a European System of Financial Supervisors (ESFS) to ensure closer co-ordination between national supervisors (De Larosière Group, 2009).

A striking feature of the de Larosière report was its plea for a supranational approach to financial supervision in a domain where Member States have been reluctant to resort to the traditional community method of decision-making. Significantly, the ESRC would be chaired by the President of the ECB, giving Frankfurt a much greater say in macro-prudential supervision than has hitherto been the case. The plan would also extend the ECB's reach beyond the euro area since the ESRC would include all Member States of the ECB General Council, i.e. ECB Executive Board members and the national central bank governors of all 27 EU Member States. The de Larosière report remained a little vague about the precise powers of the ESRC, beyond saying that it should take charge of an 'early warning mechanism' that would allow it to issue recommendations and opinions in the event of threats to financial stability.

The de Larosière Group's support for a supranational approach to financial supervision was also reflected in its plans for the ESFS. This new institution would bring together three new community bodies, which would replace the level three Lamfalussy committees. The Committee of European Banking Supervisors would be replaced by the European Banking Authority, the Committee of European Securities Regulators would become a European Securities Authority, and the Committee of European Insurance and Occupational Pensions Supervisors would be replaced by the European Insurance Authority. Whereas the Lamfalussy process depended on soft, non-binding forms of co-ordination between national authorities, the de Larosière report argued that the ESFS should have recourse to hard law measures. The group's most significant proposal in this respect was that the ESFS should have the authority to conduct legally binding mediation in the event of disagreement between national supervisors.

The European Council in March 2009 welcomed the de Larosière report as a 'basis for action' but Member States soon rowed back on the idea of delegating such significant powers over the macro and micro aspects of prudential supervision to the Community level (European Council, 2009a). The Ecofin Council in June 2009 noted the unease of some Member States with the idea of giving the ESFS legally binding powers of mediation (Ecofin, 2009b). The European Council in June 2009 also bowed to opposition from the UK and others towards giving the ECB a say over financial stability beyond the euro area. The conclusions of this summit consequently stated that the chair of the ESRC should be chosen from the ECB General Council, which in effect opens to the door to the appointment of a national central bank governor from outside the euro area (European Council, 2009b).

The European Commission's formal proposals for the creation of the European Systemic Risk Board (ESRB), as it was renamed, and ESFS took on board these and other concerns. On the governance of the ESRB, the Commission conceded that the chair should be drawn from the ECB General Council. The Commission also diluted de Larosière's ideas for the ESFS by, *inter alia*, insisting that this body should be allowed to settle disagreements between national authorities only as a last resort. These proposals on financial supervision walk a fine line between arguments for and against greater EU involvement in this field. On the one hand, the plans promise the most significant transfer of economic competence to the EU level since the launch of EMU in 1999. On the other hand, the proposals reflect EU Member States' reticence about investing too much power in a single Community body.

In December 2009, EU finance ministers opened negotiations with the European Parliament over the Commission's proposals on EU financial supervision. The stage is set in 2010 for a showdown between minimalist and maximalist visions of the proposed institutional reforms. The opening salvo in this showdown was fired in December 2009 by the co-ordinators for the European People's Party, the Progressive Alliance of Socialists and Democrats, the Alliance of Liberals and Democrats for Europe and the Greens, who publicly warned EU Finance Ministers against further diluting the proposals presented in the de Larosière report (Gauzès *et al.*, 2009).

V. The Euro Area as a Global Actor

From the need for co-ordinated action to unfreeze international money markets to the challenge of designing regulatory reforms in a world of capital mobility, the global financial crisis has created a set of policy challenges that Europeans cannot hope to meet by themselves. The crisis thus provides a

critical test case of EU Member States' ability to engage in collective diplomacy on the international economic stage. There were numerous opportunities
for such co-ordination in 2009 but none attracted more attention than the G20
summit in April, which brought the leaders of the world's major industrialized
and developing countries to London to seek a global solution to a global crisis.

The fact that the London summit took place at all was due, in no small
measure, to the EU's agenda-setting powers on the international stage. French
President Nicolas Sarkozy was the guiding spirit in this regard, using France's
Presidency of the EU in the second half of 2008 to make the case for a summit
of world leaders in response to the financial crisis. Sarkozy was the first world
leader to issue such a call, suggesting in a speech to the UN General Assembly in September 2008 that leaders of the Group of Eight (G8) should meet
with their counterparts from 'some emerging economies' (Sarkozy, 2008).
Sarkozy returned to the United States in October 2008, armed with a mandate
from the European Council and accompanied by Commission President
Barroso, for talks with President George W. Bush on a worldwide solution to
the crisis. This meeting was significant as it paved the way for the summit of
G20 leaders in Washington in November 2008, which in turn laid the ground-
work for more detailed discussions of policy responses to the crisis at the G20
summit in London.

EU Member States maintained a fairly united front in London. The heads
of state and government agreed on a 'line to take' on international financial
issues at the Spring European Council in Brussels in March 2009 (see European Council, 2009a, Annex I) and EU Member States of the G20, France,
Germany, Italy and the United Kingdom joined by representatives of the
Council Presidency and the ECB worked closely together to co-ordinate their
positions. Although much was made of Sarkozy's threat to walk out of the
summit if sufficient progress was not made, he and other EU leaders were
broadly supportive of the summit's outcome, which included an agreement to
strengthen and provide additional resources to international financial institutions, such as the IMF and World Bank and to clamp down on tax havens
(Black, 2009).

Opinion is divided on whether the G20 summit in London in April 2009
went far enough and whether it will achieve its stated aims (see Kirton and
Guebert, 2009). The summit nonetheless stands as an instance in which EU
Member States showed themselves capable of collective action on the world
stage when the need arises. What is not known at this stage is whether
EU Member States can continue to co-ordinate their efforts at international
diplomacy in this way once the financial crisis abates. The detailed 'agreed
language' adopted by heads of state and government in advance of the G20
summit in Pittsburgh in September 2009 suggests that it might (European

Council, 2009c). Angela Merkel's remarks in advance of this summit, which implied that the UK and others had sought to detract from debates over financial regulation by focusing on macroeconomic imbalances, suggests that it might not (Luce *et al.*, 2009).

While the European Council was ever present on the international stage in 2009, the Eurogroup was, at times, conspicuous by its absence. The euro area's fragmented system of external representation is partly to blame here. The EU delegation to the G20 does not normally include the Eurogroup President, in contrast to, for example, meetings of the Group of 7(G7) finance ministers, where the elected representative of euro area finance ministers is a full participant. The Eurogroup President, Jean-Claude Juncker, also faced stiff competition from French president Sarkozy in the battle to speak for the euro area during the financial crisis.

In a speech to the European Parliament in July 2008, Sarkozy outlined plans for strengthening the Eurogroup, including the creation of a permanent secretariat independent of the European Commission and a structured dialogue between euro area finance ministers and the ECB (Sarkozy, 2008). This was followed in October 2008 by reports that the French president was seeking to assume the chair of the Eurogroup following the end of Juncker's term of office (Erlanger, 2008). In the end, Sarkozy's putsch came to nothing, allowing Jean-Claude Juncker to seek and win a third term as Eurogroup President in January 2009. The entry into force of the Lisbon Treaty in December 2009 brought a premature end to this term of office but Juncker was reappointed for a fourth term in January 2010. Although this decision leaves the Luxembourg prime minister in charge of the Eurogroup until 2012 at the earliest, it remains to be seen whether euro area finance ministers can reclaim the initiative over euro area economic governance that they ceded to the heads of state and government during the global financial crisis.

Conclusions

There is, as the playwright Alan Bennett wrote, no period so remote as the recent past. There can, in other words, be no guarantee that what appears significant about the year gone by will still do so with the benefit of hindsight. This crucial caveat notwithstanding, there was much to observe in 2009 to inform political economy understandings of the euro area. This was, above all, the year in which the financial crisis got real for the euro area, with falling investment and the slump in world trade weighing on the real economy and causing the worst recession of modern times. The recession bore all the hallmarks of a symmetric shock with asymmetric effects, with all Member

States affected but some paying a higher price than others for their exposure to global trade, toxic assets and bursting property bubbles. The response of euro area authorities to these developments was predictable in some respects and surprising in others.

In the monetary sphere, the ECB's cautious response to interest rate cuts was true to form for a central bank with an overriding interest in price stability although it moved fairly rapidly once the inflationary pressures of 2008 subsided. The Bank proved less reticent than anticipated about embracing unconventional monetary policies, although its covered bond scheme to provide emergency credit to euro area banks was modest in scale and less ambitious than the actions of other central banks.

In the financial sphere, the de Larosière report's blueprint for the future of prudential supervision in the EU was surprisingly supranational, calling as it did for the creation of new community bodies to prevent a recurrence of the excessive risk taking that precipitated the financial crisis. The Member States' response to these plans was predictably intergovernmental, seeking as it did to limit the powers of the Community in general and the ECB in particular.

In the fiscal sphere, the Stability and Growth Pact proved to be surprisingly resilient in 2009. The European Commission and Econfin prosecuted all Member States that posted budget deficits in excess of 3 per cent in spite of the exceptional nature of the crisis. Greece has been hardest hit by these sanctions as EU authorities have sought, with limited success thus far, to reassure markets that a sovereign default is not inevitable.

In the sphere of external relations, 2009 was a year in which EU Member States found their voice on the world stage. Although they did not always say the same thing, Member States did pursue their collective interests, driving the agenda that led to the landmark summit of the G20 in London and putting up a fairly united front at the summit itself. If the EU was the winner from this exercise then the euro area may have been the loser insofar as the Eurogroup President was effectively sidelined in the G20's important discussions on the future of global governance.

References

Black, I. (2009) 'G20 summit: Sarkozy Praises Brown and Obama for Roles in "Historic" Outcome'. *The Guardian*, 2 April.

Commission of the European Communities (2009) 'Economic Forecast Spring 2009'. European Economy, No. 3, Office for Official Publications of the EC, Luxembourg.

De Larosière Group (2009) 'The High Level Group on Financial Supervision in the EU'. Available at «http://ec.europa.eu/economy_finance/focuson/crisis/documents/de_larosiere_report_en.pdf».

Econfin (2005) 'Council Decision of 17 February 2005 Giving Notice to Greece to Take Measures for the Deficit Reduction Judged Necessary in Order to Remedy the Situation of Excessive Deficit'. OJ L 153/29, 16 June.

Econfin (2009a) 'Specifications on the Implementation of the Stability and Growth Pact and Guidelines on the Format and Content of Stability and Convergence Programmes'. Available at «http://ec.europa.eu/economy_finance/sgp/pdf/coc/ 2009-11-19_code_of_conduct_(consolidated)_en.pdf»

Econfin (2009b) '2948th Economic and Financial Affairs Council Meeting'. Press Release 168, Nr. 10737/09, 9 June, Luxembourg.

Econfin (2010) 'Council Decision of 16 February 2010 Giving Notice to Greece to Take Measures for the Deficit Reduction Judged Necessary in Order to Remedy the Situation of Excessive Deficit'. OJ L 83/13, 30 March.

Erlanger, S. (2008) 'Sarkozy Boldly Attacks Financial Crisis, but Europe Wants Results'. *New York Times*, 30 October.

European Central Bank (2009) 'The Implementation of Monetary Policy since August 2007'. Monthly Bulletin 07/09, ECB, Frankfurt a.M., pp. 75–90.

European Council (2009a) 'Presidency Conclusions'. 18–19 June 2009, 11225/2/09 Rev 2, Brussels.

European Council (2009b) 'Presidency Conclusions 19/20 March 2009'. 7652/1/08 Rev., Brussels.

European Council (2009c) 'Agreed Language for the Pittsburgh G-20 Summit'. Informal Meetings of the Heads of State and Government, 17 September, Brussels. Available at «http://www.consilium.europa.eu/uedocs/cms_data/docs/ pressdata/en/ec/110166.pdf».

Feldstein, M. (2005) 'The Euro and the Stability Pact'. National Bureau for Economic Research Working Paper, No. W11249, April.

Gauzès, J.P., Bullmann, U., Goulard, S. and Giegold, S. (2009) 'Financial Supervision: European Parliament Will Not Agree to Water Down the New European Authorities'. Press Release 2 December, European Parliament, Brussels.

Hall, P. and Soskice, D. (eds) (2001) *Varieties of Capitalism: The Institutional Foundations of Comparative Advantage* (Oxford: Oxford University Press).

Hancké, B., Rhodes, M. and Thatcher, M. (eds) (2007) *Beyond Varieties of Capitalism: Conflict, Contradictions and Complementarities in the European Economy* (Oxford: Oxford University Press).

Hodson, D. (2010) 'Economic and Monetary Union as an Experiment in New Modes of EU Policy-Making'. In Wallace, H., Pollack, M. and Young, A. (eds) *Policy-Making in the European Union* (Oxford: Oxford University Press), pp. 157–80.

Hodson, D. and Mabbett, D. (2009) 'UK Economic Policy and the Global Financial Crisis: Paradigm Lost?' *JCMS*, Vol. 47, No. 5, pp. 1041–61.

International Monetary Fund (2009) 'Note to the Group of Twenty'. Available at «http://www.imf.org/external/np/g20/pdf/020509.pdf».

Kirton, J. and Guebert, J. (2009) 'A Summit of Substantial Success: The Performance of the G20 in Washington in 2008'. G20 Research Group, Toronto. Available at «http://www.g8.utoronto.ca/g20/analysis/2008performance090307.pdf».

Luce, E., Giles, C. and Guha, K. (2009) 'Tensions over IMF Threaten to Mar G20'. *Financial Times*, 24 September.

Minegishi, M. and Cournède, B. (2010) 'Monetary Policy Responses to the Crisis and Exit Strategies'. OECD Economics Department Working Paper No. 753 (Paris: OECD).

Quaglia, L. (2008) 'Committee Governance in the Financial Sector'. *Journal of European Integration*, Vol. 30, No. 3, pp. 565–80.

Quaglia, L., Eastwood, R. and Holmes, P. (2009) 'The Financial Turmoil and EU Policy Co-operation'. *JCMS AR*, Vol. 47, No. s1, pp. 1–25.

Sarkozy, N. (2008) Speech to the European Parliament. Strasbourg, 21 October.

Savage, J.D. (2005) *Making the EMU: The Politics of Budgetary Surveillance and the Enforcement of Maastricht* (Oxford: Oxford University Press).

Trichet, J.-C. (2009) 'The ECB's Enhanced Credit Support'. Keynote address, University of Munich, Munich, 13 July.

Verdun, A. (2008) 'Economic Developments in the Euro Area'. *JCMS AR*, Vol. 46, No. s1, pp. 215–31.

Verdun, A. (2009) 'Economic Developments in the Euro Area'. *JCMS*, Vol. 47, s1, pp. 233–57.

JCMS 2010 Volume 48 Annual Review pp. 243–266

The EU Economy: Member States Outside the Euro Area in 2009*

RICHARD CONNOLLY
University of Birmingham

Introduction

As 2009 began, the world economy found itself in the midst of the worst economic downturn since the Great Depression of 1929–33. The global financial crisis, which began in the summer of 2007, and which brought financial markets to the brink of collapse in the late summer of 2008, quickly exerted an extraordinarily negative effect on economic activity worldwide, even outside those countries located at the epicentre of the financial crisis. International trade fell at a historically unprecedented rate. Asset prices across a wide range of classes plummeted. Commodity prices – which only six months before had reached record highs – followed suit. The international banking system survived only through the provision of unprecedented levels of government assistance, resulting in a rapid reduction in credit provision as banks sought to rebuild capital levels. Economic output collapsed as new orders were frozen, investment plans postponed and firms began to shed labour rapidly. Across the world, private sector demand – consumption and investment – contracted sharply. By March, the global economic situation was so dire that some analysts were inclined to make unfavourable comparisons with the early stages of the Great Depression (Eichengreen and O'Rourke, 2009). All economies within the non-euro area were affected by

* I am indebted to Silvana Malle for her insightful comments, as well as to the editors, Nathaniel Copsey and Tim Haughton. The usual disclaimers apply.

the sudden slowdown in global economic activity, with some experiencing recessions that were among the most severe in the world.

In response, monetary policy was promptly loosened across the world. Central banks slashed interest rates; cheap and widely accessible liquidity was provided to an ailing financial sector; impaired assets, such as mortgage-backed securities, were taken from the fragile balance sheets of financial corporations and transferred to rapidly expanding public sector balance sheets. Governments also increased spending levels to combat the contraction in private demand, resulting in a deterioration of budget balances across the world. As well as relying on the traditional automatic stabilizers, governments also propped up sectors considered systemically important, including both the automotive ('cash for clunkers' schemes) and banking sectors (capital injections). In some countries, the International Monetary Fund (IMF) rushed to provide financial support, attaching far less stringent conditions than in previous crises. By the middle of the year, these actions resulted in the stabilization of the international financial system, a rebound in asset and commodity prices, an upturn in international trade and, most importantly, a resumption of economic growth in most major economies. In short, a second depression appeared to have been averted by the end of 2009. However, despite the apparent return of the global economy from the brink of disaster, the crisis continued to exert a deeply negative influence over the economies of the non-euro area.

While the remedial action described above prevented economic catastrophe, it did not solve the fundamental problem: that of a persistent global imbalance between countries that were net savers – the most notable of which were China, Japan, Germany and most oil exporters, and countries that were net spenders, including the USA, the UK, Spain and other countries located on the geographical periphery of the European Union (Eichengreen, 2007; Wolf, 2009). Surplus countries tended to have export-oriented growth models and comparatively deficient domestic demand; deficit countries tended to be reliant on credit-fuelled consumption for economic growth due to relatively low domestic savings. Consequently, the surplus economies acted as 'vendor financiers', effectively lending money to consumer economies to purchase their goods. For a while this relationship generated booming global economic growth: world GDP growth averaged close to 5 per cent annually over 2004–07, the strongest four consecutive years of global growth since the early 1970s.

However, persistent current account surpluses in the export-oriented countries resulted in the accumulation of large stocks of debt in the deficit countries, eventually triggering a severe financial crisis (McKinsey Institute, 2010). The presence of large stocks of debt across some of the world's largest economies suggests that it might be accurate to describe the current downturn as a 'balance sheet recession' (Koo, 2008). This describes a situation where over-indebted private sector agents (household and corporate) concentrate on debt repayment and raising savings rates with potentially deflationary consequences. This is for three reasons. First, because firms and households do not wish to borrow, the supply of credit stops growing. Second, as private sector agents repair their balance sheets, conventional monetary policy becomes less effective; banks are unable to transmit lower interest rates because of the reluctance of the private sector to borrow. Finally, as private sector balance sheets improve, only persistent government deficits can counteract the deflationary effects of the contraction in private sector demand. For some, this explains what occurred in Japan during its 'lost decade' (for example, Wood, 2006; Koo, 2008). If this is indeed what is unfolding now, it would imply a considerably lower future level of consumption in advanced economies, with important implications for export-oriented economies dependent on external demand. This also suggests that deficient domestic demand may afflict any economy that suffers from excessive indebtedness, as is the case in a number of the non-euro area economies.

This article assesses how the broader trends in the global economy outlined above affected the performance of the EU economies outside the euro area in 2009. Although each of the economies covered here experienced the crisis in a different way, two main trends are evident. First, countries dependent on external capital inflows or domestic credit were most exposed to the contraction of cross-border capital flows and tightening credit conditions. Second, a high degree of openness to trade further amplified the exposure of economies to the crisis (Goldstein and Xie, 2009). Where an economy was placed on these two measures explained the majority of variation in the impact of the crisis. Section I gives an overview of key economic performance indicators. Sections II and III summarize key developments in each of the 11 economies. The final section provides a brief summary and suggests key issues for the year ahead.

I. Economic Performance Outside the Euro Area: Main Economic Indicators

Economic Growth

Nearly all the countries covered here are estimated to have suffered a deeper recession than the euro area average (Table 1). Indeed, the recessions in Latvia and Lithuania were among the most severe in the world. Only in Poland did the economy register a positive rate of growth. However, what was particularly

Table 1: Real GDP Growth (% Annual Change) – Non-Euro Area (2005–10)

	2005	2006	2007	2008	2009[e]	2010[f]
Bulgaria	6.2	6.3	6.2	6.0	−5.9	−1.1
Czech Republic	6.3	6.8	6.1	2.5	−4.8	0.8
Denmark	2.4	3.3	1.6	−1.2	−4.5	1.5
Estonia	9.4	10.0	7.2	−3.6	−13.7	−0.1
Latvia	10.6	12.2	10.0	−4.6	−18.0	−4.0
Lithuania	7.8	7.8	9.8	2.8	−18.1	−3.9
Hungary	3.5	4.0	1.0	0.6	−6.5	−0.5
Poland	3.6	6.2	6.8	5.0	1.2	1.8
Romania	4.2	7.9	6.3	6.2	−8.0	0.5
Sweden	3.3	4.2	2.6	−0.2	−4.6	1.4
UK	2.2	2.9	2.6	0.6	−4.6	0.9
Euro area	1.7	3.0	2.8	0.6	−4.0	0.7

Source: Commission (2009, p. 188, Table 1).
Note: Estimates are denoted by *e* and forecasts by *f*.

striking for the economies covered in this article was the sharp turnaround of fortunes, as economies that had previously enjoyed fast rates of growth quickly swung into deep recession in 2009. The tendency towards trade openness and the receptiveness to capital inflows certainly helped generate high levels of pre-crisis growth; these same factors, however, caused the severity of the downturn to be much sharper. The swing in economic fortunes between 2007 and 2009 is described in Figure 1. While the travails of the Baltic economies are perhaps well known, the shift from growth to recession was also comparatively severe in Bulgaria, Romania and, to a lesser extent, the Czech Republic. Among the advanced economies, the relative change in fortunes for Sweden and the UK was also noteworthy as both economies saw a more precipitous peak-to-trough drop than both the United States and the euro area average.

Employment

The effect of this turnaround in economic output on labour markets was certainly considerable, although perhaps not as great as some initially feared (Table 2). While unemployment increased in every one of the non-euro area Member States, the sharpest increases were observed in the Baltic economies. Here, the level of unemployment roughly tripled between 2007 and 2009. While no country escaped rising unemployment, Denmark and Poland fared best, recording only modest increases. Unfortunately, because unemployment is a lagging indicator, unemployment levels are forecast to continue to rise in nearly all countries well into 2010, and perhaps beyond. Because most of the

Figure 1: Economic Growth Slowdown in Non-Euro Area and Other Groups, 2007–09

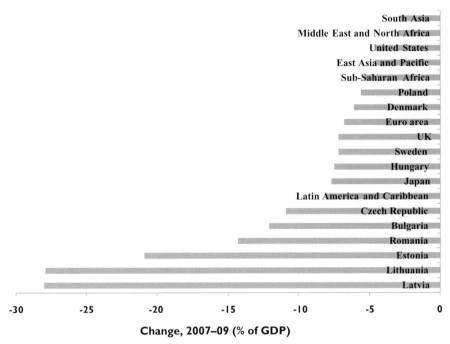

Change, 2007–09 (% of GDP)

Source: EU Member States from Commission (2009); other data taken from World Bank (2010).

economies covered here are open, trade-oriented economies, a sustained and broadly based recovery across the region will be required to generate sufficient external and internal demand to increase labour capacity utilization. Notwithstanding the general downward trend in employment levels, it is worth noting that unemployment rates have not quite plumbed the depths that some feared. A combination of flexible labour markets, increased discretionary public sector spending and surprisingly buoyant external demand (often helped by government policies elsewhere) have all helped to prop up employment levels. However, a quick and robust recovery is vital if permanent losses to potential output are not to occur.

Inflation

The deterioration in labour markets has contributed to a dramatic decline in the rate of inflation (Table 3). The decline has been most precipitate in the Baltic economies and Bulgaria where the contraction in cross-border capital

Table 2: Unemployment (% of the Civilian Labour Force) – Non-Euro Area (2005–10)

	2005	2006	2007	2008	2009ᵉ	2010ᶠ
Bulgaria	10.1	9.0	6.9	5.6	7.0	8.0
Czech Republic	7.9	7.2	5.3	4.4	6.9	7.9
Denmark	4.8	3.9	3.8	3.3	4.5	5.8
Estonia	7.9	5.9	4.7	5.5	13.6	15.2
Latvia	8.9	6.8	6.0	7.5	16.9	19.9
Lithuania	8.3	5.6	4.3	5.8	14.5	17.6
Hungary	7.2	7.5	7.4	7.8	10.5	11.3
Poland	17.8	13.9	9.6	7.1	8.4	9.9
Romania	7.2	7.3	6.4	5.8	9.0	8.7
Sweden	7.4	7.0	6.1	6.2	8.5	10.2
UK	4.8	5.4	5.3	5.6	7.8	8.7
Euro area	9.0	8.3	7.5	7.5	9.5	10.7

Source: Commission (2009, p. 199, Table 23).
Note: Estimates are denoted by *e* and forecasts by *f*.

Table 3: Inflation Rateᵃ (% change on preceding year) – Non-Euro Area (2005–10)

	2005	2006	2007	2008	2009ᵉ	2010ᶠ
Bulgaria	6.0	7.4	7.6	12.0	2.4	2.3
Czech Republic	1.6	2.1	3.0	6.3	0.6	1.5
Denmark	1.7	1.9	1.7	3.6	1.1	1.5
Estonia	4.1	4.4	6.7	10.6	0.2	0.5
Latvia	6.9	6.6	10.1	15.3	3.5	−3.7
Lithuania	2.7	3.8	5.8	11.1	3.9	−0.7
Hungary	3.5	4.0	7.9	6.0	4.3	4.0
Poland	2.2	1.3	2.6	4.2	3.9	1.9
Romania	9.1	6.6	4.9	7.9	5.7	3.5
Sweden	0.8	1.5	1.7	3.3	1.9	1.7
UK	2.1	2.3	2.3	3.6	2.0	1.4
Euro area	2.2	2.2	2.1	3.3	0.3	1.1

Source: Commission (2009, p. 195, Table 16).
Notes: ᵃ Harmonized index of consumer prices. Estimates are denoted by *e* and forecasts by *f*.

flows forced a sudden narrowing of extreme current account deficits. As previously abundant credit quickly became scarce, prices dropped. Furthermore, the downward base effects of record commodity prices in the summer of 2008 also exerted a deflationary effect on import prices as commodity prices saw a correlated decline to levels approximating 25 per cent below peak by March. As commodity prices picked up again into the summer, along with a more general upturn in economic activity, inflation began to rise again.

Exchange rate movements are also important in determining prices: deflation is less severe where the nominal exchange rate has depreciated significantly, as has been the case in Poland, Romania, Sweden and the UK; where fixed exchange rates are present, as in the Baltic economies and Bulgaria, outright deflation is a far bigger danger. At this stage, deflation induced by deficient demand – both internal and external – is the immediate danger, both in Europe and across the world. This is unlikely to be helped on the supply side due to the presence of potentially excessive capacity across a number of sectors.

Private Sector Financial Balances

In order to appreciate the sources of the deflationary tendencies in the economies under review here, it is instructive to note the change in private sector financial balances that occurred between 2007 – the last year before the financial crisis began to affect the real economy – and 2009. The private sector balance measures the extent to which aggregate spending corresponds with aggregate income in the private sector. As is evident in Figure 2, a considerable shift towards income exceeding expenditure has occurred in the

Figure 2: Change in Private Sector Financial Balance,[a] 2007–09 (% of GDP) – Non-Euro Area

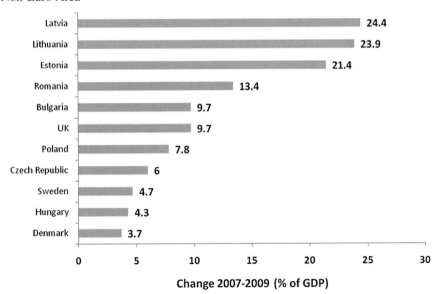

Sources: Commission (2009); author's calculations.
Note: [a] The Private Sector Financial Balance is the difference between private income and private spending. It can be written as: Private Sector Financial Balance = Government Balance + Current Account Balance.

private sector of each of the economies of the non-euro area Member States. Indeed, this shift is almost perfectly correlated with the severity of the output swing that occurred in the same period (described in Figure 1).[1] This shift has occurred as households moved to repay debt amid tightening credit conditions and a worsening economic outlook, and firms cut investment expenditure. Unless this shift towards private sector saving is counterbalanced by either: (a) an increase in net external demand; or (b) a corresponding public sector deficit, there is a likelihood of a severe deflationary spiral. This has certainly been the case in the Baltic economies and Romania, where the room for discretionary public sector spending has, for different reasons, been constrained, and where dampened external demand has been insufficient to compensate for the savage cut in private sector spending.

Public Finances

Given the acute shift towards saving relative to income that has occurred in the private sectors of the countries covered here, it is perhaps unsurprising that government balances have tended to take a corresponding turn for the worse (Table 5). The recession caused tax revenues to shrink at the same time as governments increased spending to counteract flagging private demand. Indeed, if governments had not increased spending, the likelihood is that recessions in each country would have been deeper than they already are. As Table 4 illustrates, countries that previously ran government surpluses, such as Bulgaria, Denmark, Estonia and Sweden, are all now running deficits. The largest changes in government balances have occurred in Latvia and the UK. Nearly all government balances are forecast to deteriorate over the course of 2010.

   Increased flows of government borrowing are resulting in a significant expansion of stocks of government debt across the non-euro area Member States, mirroring similar tendencies elsewhere in the world. The situation has taken a sharp turn for the worse in those countries running the largest annual deficits; the stock of Latvian government debt is forecast to have nearly quadrupled between 2005 and 2009, while that of the UK is forecast to have roughly doubled over the same period. A build-up of government debt is quite normal in the aftermath of both a financial crisis and recessions more generally, although perhaps not at the levels observed in Latvia and the UK (Reinhart and Rogoff, 2009; IMF, 2009). What is perhaps most striking about this particular episode is the fact that nearly all advanced economies, and many of the major emerging economies, are increasing their debt burdens simultaneously. Consequently, the volume of government bonds being floated on international

---

[1] There is a Pearson's *r* correlation coefficient of 0.96 for the sample of countries covered in this article.

Table 4: Net Lending (+) or Net Borrowing (−), General Government Balance (% of GDP) – Non-Euro Area (2005–10)

	2005	2006	2007	2008	2009^e	2010^f
Bulgaria	1.9	3.0	0.1	1.8	−0.8	−1.2
Czech Republic	−3.6	−2.6	−0.7	−2.1	−6.6	−5.5
Denmark	5.2	5.2	4.5	3.4	−2.0	−4.8
Estonia	1.6	2.3	2.6	−2.7	−3.0	−3.2
Latvia	−0.4	−0.5	−0.3	−4.1	−9.0	−12.3
Lithuania	−0.5	−0.4	−1.0	−3.2	−9.8	−9.2
Hungary	−7.9	−9.3	−5.0	−3.8	−4.1	−4.2
Poland	−4.1	−3.6	−1.9	−3.6	−6.4	−7.5
Romania	−1.2	−2.2	−2.5	−5.5	−7.8	−6.8
Sweden	2.3	2.5	3.8	2.5	−2.1	−3.3
UK	−3.4	−2.7	−2.7	−5.0	−12.1	−12.9
Euro area	−2.5	−1.3	−0.6	−2.0	−6.4	−6.9

Source: Commission (2009, p. 206, Table 37).
Note: Estimates are denoted by e and forecasts by f.

capital markets may soon exceed the appetite of investors, at least at prevailing prices. If this causes interest rates to rise in the future, governments with large stocks of debt may find themselves forced to divert increasing amounts of resources simply to service existing debt. As it stands now, it is noteworthy that while stocks of government debt have increased in every country covered here after 2008, the levels of debt forecast for 2010 are still below the euro area average. Indeed, stocks of government debt tend to be much lower across central and eastern Europe, with the notable exception of Hungary.

Competitiveness

This general presence of growing stocks of debt in the public sector, and the legacy of large stocks of private sector debt accumulated during the pre-crisis 'boom' years (in for example, the Baltic economies, Bulgaria, Denmark and the UK), raises the question of just how such a debt overhang can be reduced in the future. As long as the private sector continues to reduce its expenditure (Figure 2), government expenditure is likely to exceed income unless economies are able to generate sufficient growth from trade. As such, the issue of competitiveness has again come to the fore. As Table 6 illustrates, several economies suffered a considerable erosion of competitiveness before the crisis unfolded: Bulgaria, Estonia, Latvia and Romania all saw unit labour costs rise sharply prior to 2008. For these countries, and many others across the world, a depreciation of the Real Effective Exchange Rate (REER) might

Table 5: Gross General Government Debt (% of GDP) – Non-Euro Area (2005–10)

	2005	2006	2007	2008	2009ᵉ	2010ᶠ
Bulgaria	29.2	22.7	18.2	14.1	15.1	16.2
Czech Republic	29.7	29.4	29.0	30.0	36.5	40.6
Denmark	37.1	31.3	26.8	33.5	33.7	35.3
Estonia	4.6	4.5	3.8	4.6	7.4	10.9
Latvia	12.4	10.7	9.0	19.5	33.2	48.6
Lithuania	18.4	18.0	16.9	15.6	29.9	40.7
Hungary	61.8	65.6	65.9	72.9	79.1	79.8
Poland	47.1	47.7	45.0	47.2	51.7	57.0
Romania	15.8	12.4	12.6	13.6	21.8	27.4
Sweden	51.0	45.9	40.5	38.0	42.1	43.6
UK	42.2	43.2	44.2	52.0	68.6	80.3
Euro area	70.1	68.3	66.0	61.5	78.2	84.0

Source: Commission (2009, p. 208, Table 42).
Note: Estimates are denoted by *e* and forecasts by *f*.

Table 6: Real Effective Exchange Rate (% change on preceding year) – Non-Euro Area (2005–10)

	2005	2006	2007	2008	2009ᵉ	2010ᶠ
Bulgaria	−1.0	3.3	11.5	13.3	11.1	2.5
Czech Republic	4.8	5.6	3.4	13.8	−3.9	2.6
Denmark	0.5	1.2	3.2	5.9	4.2	0.4
Estonia	1.1	7.8	14.2	10.5	−0.9	−3.5
Latvia	7.8	13.2	23.0	19.1	−7.0	−8.8
Lithuania	3.2	7.8	3.0	5.1	4.1	−2.7
Hungary	3.1	−5.7	8.9	1.7	−9.7	4.8
Poland	11.0	1.1	3.7	12.5	−18.9	2.3
Romania	33.0	6.9	19.3	1.5	−5.8	5.3
Sweden	−3.8	−1.5	3.9	−2.7	−7.2	2.9
UK	−0.5	1.5	2.9	−13.6	−10.5	−1.8
Euro area	−2.0	−0.4	1.8	3.9	4.5	1.7

Source: Commission (2009, p. 203, Table 32).
Note: Estimates are denoted by *e* and forecasts by *f*.

offer the quickest route to a restoration of robust economic growth. Indeed, it is striking that Poland's resilience during the crisis was aided by a rapid depreciation of the REER, largely caused by a sharp fall in the złoty in the first half of 2009. However, for those countries that are part of ERM II (Bulgaria and the Baltic states), nominal exchange rate depreciation is not an option; instead, a restoration in competitiveness can occur only through a fall in labour costs. This will be made particularly difficult by the existence of large stocks of private sector debt, due to the fact that real wage deflation will increase the real debt burden.

II. Economic Developments in the Old Euro-Outsiders

The economies of the old euro-outsiders differ from the new euro-outsiders in that they are all established high-income economies. All experienced deep recessions over the course of 2009. There are, however, significant differences among them. For example, Sweden and Denmark were part of the group of persistent surplus economies described in the introductory section. They were both relatively dependent on exports for growth in the pre-crisis years and so proved susceptible to the slump in international trade. The UK, on the other hand, was one of the largest deficit economies. As a result, the drop in international trade was less important for the UK; instead, the contraction in credit caused a slump in private consumption.

United Kingdom

After over a decade of what Mervyn King described as 'Non-Inflationary Constant Expansion' (NICE), the UK economy stopped growing in Q2 of 2008, and entered its deepest post-war recession thereafter. Only in the final quarter of 2009 did the economy stop contracting, although the margin of error attached to preliminary estimates suggests that even this may not mark the end of the recession. Overall, real GDP is estimated to have fallen by 4.6 per cent in 2009 and by nearly 7 per cent from the second quarter of 2008. This has wiped out over five years of GDP growth. Furthermore, the rapid depreciation of the pound that has occurred over the last two years has considerably reduced the dollar (and euro) value of the UK economy, and curtailed consumer purchasing power. Unemployment continues to rise, while investment has slumped at an alarming rate. And all this has occurred despite the unprecedented efforts of the Bank of England and a record peacetime government budget deficit. The poor performance of the UK economy is a result of a number of imbalances that had been accumulating during the boom years, most notably in the household and financial sectors.

An expansion of the financial sector helped boost UK growth during the pre-crisis boom. Through a record expansion of credit to the private sector, it helped generate a sustained rise in house prices and a prolonged increase in private consumption. This injection of credit helped mask the fact that productivity levels in the UK had not really improved (relative to its peers) for some time. Furthermore, the effect of this financial sector-generated boom on government revenues, which has subsequently proven to be illusory, caused the government to enter the economic crisis with only limited discretionary fiscal capacity. As house prices declined from the beginning of 2008 into the first half of 2009,[2] the fragility of household balance sheets was exposed; saddled with unprecedented levels of debt, and facing the prospect of a prolonged rise in unemployment and years of below-trend growth, the UK consumer quickly began to reduce consumption and raise perilously low savings rates. As a result, private consumption – which accounts for around 60 per cent of domestic demand – dropped by 3.3 per cent in 2009, while fixed investment shrank by 15.9 per cent over the same period.

Policy intervention since the onset of the crisis can be broken down into two components. The first, monetary policy, has aimed at restoring financial stability through the provision of cheap and accessible liquidity to the banking system. As well as reducing the base short-term interest rate to nearly zero, the Bank of England also embarked on the radical step of injecting £200 billion into the financial system – known as quantitative easing (QE) – in an effort to hold down interest rates and increase the flow of credit to the private sector. Low interest rates also relieved pressure on the heavily indebted household sector as the cost of mortgage repayments was slashed. Despite these efforts, the growth of the money supply remained muted.

The second component of government intervention was fiscal policy. Perhaps most importantly, the purchase of equity stakes in some of the UK's ailing, but systemically important, banks helped stave off insolvency fears. A temporary cut in the VAT rate also helped buoy domestic demand, and high government spending that had already been planned in the pre-crisis period was maintained. However, aside from the VAT cut, discretionary government spending was quite limited due to an already large public spending schedule.

The effect of the sudden and sharp contraction in domestic demand caused a significant rise in the unemployment rate, which climbed from 4.8 per cent in 2005 to an estimated 7.8 per cent in 2009. This was forecast to rise further to 8.7 per cent in 2010, which would be likely to exert a prolonged drag on private consumption. In addition, the sharp depreciation of the pound (it dropped roughly 25 per cent in trade-weighted terms from 2007 to 2009)

---

[2] In fact, according to data from the Bank of England, house prices began to rise again throughout the second half of 2009 (Bank of England, 2009). While this has caused optimism in some quarters, it is likely that these rises are temporary and largely attributable to: (a) an exceptionally small volume of transactions, as vendors refuse to sell below the 2007 price; and (b) the effects of low interest rates that enable even distressed homeowners to maintain repayments. Given the credit constraints on the demand side, any future increase in the supply of homes on the UK housing market is likely to result in a resumption of a decline in prices. Any resumption of the decline in house prices will also be likely to further impair the balance sheet of the banking sector.

caused inflationary pressures to emerge despite anaemic domestic demand. While it was hoped that this depreciation might provide a boost to competitiveness and help induce a shift towards export-oriented growth, the evidence in 2010 suggested that this process would take a long time.

Finally, as the stock of government debt ballooned over the course of the crisis (it nearly doubled in the space of only two years), all political parties agreed that spending would have to drop over the medium to long term. Given the weakness of domestic demand, while net exports are yet to make a positive contribution to growth in 2010, any contraction in public spending is likely to increase the probability of a 'double-dip' recession. With this in mind, economic policy, especially the timing of any withdrawal of fiscal and monetary stimuli, will be fraught with danger for years to come.

Denmark

As in the UK, the global recession compounded a recession that was already under way in the Danish economy. After a decade of sustained growth, a burst real estate bubble and rising inflation caused the economy to contract by 1.2 per cent in 2008. The effects of dwindling world trade were transmitted to the Danish economy in the early part of 2009, and exacerbated an already sharp reduction in private consumption, which declined by as much as 4.5 per cent in 2009. However, because the contraction in domestic demand was so sharp, imports fell faster than exports, meaning that net exports still made a positive contribution to GDP in 2009. To offset the slump in domestic demand, the Danish government promptly intervened to cut taxes, increase wages and release pension funds. Consequently, real incomes actually rose during 2009, although this was not enough to prevent a deep recession that caused unemployment almost to double, rising from 3.3 per cent in 2008 to 5.8 per cent in 2009.

This swing in consumer sentiment was primarily caused by the accumulation of a large stock of private sector debt that eventually resulted in a reversal of a prolonged house price boom. Thus, by 2008, the stock of private sector credit in Denmark reached 218 per cent of GDP, compared to 213 per cent in the UK and 129 per cent in Sweden (World Bank, 2010). This expansion of credit caused the house price growth to increase by an average of 9.3 per cent between 1994 and 2007. This compares to average annual house price growth over the same period of 9.1 per cent in the UK and 7.4 per cent in Sweden (OECD, 2010). As a result, several banks failed in early 2009, and the Danish government was forced to enact two bank rescue packages.

Fortunately, while the private sector had been running persistent deficits, the government had, in contrast to the UK, operated a counter-cyclical fiscal policy, and had accumulated several years of budget surpluses. This meant that it entered the crisis with a comparatively modest stock of government debt (33.3 per cent of GDP in 2008) and plenty of room to initiate what was an impressive array of discretionary measures to stimulate the economy. As a result, the budget swung from a surplus of 3.4 per cent in 2008 to a deficit of −2.0 per cent in 2009. While this has exerted only modest pressure on the stock of government debt – it was forecast to rise to 33.5 per cent in 2011 – the severe contraction of private demand, caused by impaired balance sheets in the financial and household sectors, suggests that government spending may have to exceed income for some time to come if the economy is to recover.

Sweden

Like Denmark and the UK, the Swedish economy contracted rapidly during the end of 2008 and the first half of 2009. As a small, open economy with an export structure oriented towards capital goods and transport equipment, the slump in international trade caused exports to make a negative contribution to GDP in 2009, despite a significant depreciation of the krona; this was in stark contrast to previous years when Sweden's export performance underpinned a period of brisk economic expansion. However, as in Denmark and the UK, it was the sharp seizure of domestic demand that explains the severity of the recession. Private consumption fell by 1.3 per cent, while investment shrank by 17 per cent. Only an aggressive loosening of fiscal and monetary policy prevented a deeper recession.

While the private sector credit expansion was not as large as in Denmark and the UK, a number of financial vulnerabilities were present. First, the household sector remains overleveraged; although the ratio of private sector debt to GDP was not as high as in the UK or Denmark, household debt was 160 per cent of disposable income in 2009, and was forecast to rise throughout 2010 because of unusually low interest rates. This helped reverse a decline in house prices that had started in 2007. Second, the health of the banking sector remained contingent on events in the Baltic economies. The relatively sound capital provision in the Swedish banking sector enabled it to absorb rising non-performing loans (NPLs) in the depression-stricken Baltic economies in 2009. Any unanticipated losses seemed likely to constrain the capacity of the banking system to supply domestic demand for credit in the event of a recovery.

As in Denmark, government prudence in the pre-crisis period enabled the Swedish government to enact a number of discretionary fiscal measures to combat the recession, including measures that amounted to 1.5 per cent of

GDP in 2009, and an additional 1 per cent for 2010. These measures were primarily aimed at mitigating the rise in unemployment, which was 6.1 per cent in 2007, and was forecast to peak at over 10 per cent in 2010. Fortunately, with a modest stock of government debt (38 per cent of GDP in 2008), the Swedish government retained the capacity to offset any future persistence of deficient domestic demand.

III. Economic Developments in the New Euro-Outsiders

Unlike the old euro-outsiders, the new euro-outsiders are among the poorest economies in the EU. The last two decades involved a huge effort in achieving the transition from planned to market economies, a process that was largely complete by 2000. Subsequently the main challenge was to boost productivity levels, and as a result, raise living standards. This process took longer. In order to achieve this aim, most economies of the region liberalized trade and capital accounts. Consequently, the years preceding the crisis were characterized by fast growth rates of exports and capital inflows. Although this growth model performed well prior to the crisis, the crisis tended to punish economies that were either export-oriented or those that exhibited financial vulnerabilities (Connolly, 2009; Goldstein and Xie, 2009; Aslund, 2009). Many of the old euro-outsiders displayed both of these features, rendering them particularly susceptible to the effects of the financial crisis.

Poland

Poland was the only country from within the EU to post positive economic growth in 2009. Indeed, economic activity accelerated in the final quarter of the year, registering a provisional rise in real GDP of 1.7 per cent, up from 0.1 per cent, 0.5 per cent and 0.5 per cent, respectively, in the preceding three quarters. This comparatively strong performance was due to a number of factors. First, Poland was a relatively closed economy compared to its regional neighbours. With a ratio of exports to GDP of 40 per cent, the health of the domestic Polish market was of greater importance than external events. Second, the health of the domestic economy was helped by the relatively limited importance of the financial sector to pre-crisis economic growth: while domestic credit to the private sector had grown over the previous decade, particularly lending to households for mortgages, the overall stock of private sector debt stood at only 55 per cent of GDP (EBRD, 2009). Third, the depreciation of the złoty, which was down 41 per cent against the euro over the period August 2008–February 2009, helped net exports make a positive contribution to GDP growth, despite the general fall in external demand.

Fourth, expansionary fiscal measures (including a reduction in income tax rates) helped cushion private consumption. Finally, an investment-focused recovery plan, combined with the timely inflow of EU funds, helped mitigate the slump in investment that accompanied tighter credit conditions. Notwithstanding Poland's relatively strong performance in 2009, it should be noted that the economy has still experienced a significant slowdown compared to the pre-crisis trend rate of growth (5.1 per cent over the 2003–08 period).

While the effects of the crisis on the financial sector in Poland were muted when compared to many of its neighbours, the crisis has caused increased risk aversion in the banking sector. This has resulted in a tightening of credit conditions, particularly to the corporate sector. However, the demand for credit among firms is also likely to be lower, particularly as there is thought to be considerable underutilization of production capacity. In the household sector, tighter lending conditions, as well as a rise in unemployment, have dampened the previously steady demand for credit.

Unemployment, which abated after reaching nearly 20 per cent in 2003, is also rising again as the rate of economic growth has slowed, and was forecast to touch 10 per cent in 2010. Combined with a slowdown in real wage growth and a higher degree of precautionary saving, the prospects for consumption in Poland are subject to significant downside risks. Furthermore, further appreciation of the currency could also erode Poland's current competiveness and reduce the positive impact of net exports. However, any appreciation of the złoty will at least dampen inflation which was forecast to rise in most of its neighbours. In short, while sensible macroeconomic policies, and not a little good fortune, helped cushion Poland from the wider economic crisis, the recovery in Poland will not be without risks.

Hungary

Hungary entered 2009 in poor shape. Lax fiscal policy prior to 2006 caused a sharp increase in budget deficits and public debt levels. As a result, fiscal policy was reversed in mid-2006 as efforts were made to repair the government balance sheet. Relatively restrained private demand during the same period further dampened economic growth in Hungary; modest but positive growth rates were recorded in 2007 and 2008 only because of strong export growth. Thus, the rapid downturn in world trade that occurred in 2008–09 weakened the only sector of the Hungarian economy that had generated robust growth in recent years. Although exports continued to be the only component of GDP that was positive in 2009, this was due to imports falling even faster. The government, constrained by its pre-crisis policy of fiscal consolidation, and by its commitments to the EU, IMF and World Bank, did not move to offset weakening domestic demand and the fall in external demand. As a result, output which was anaemic prior to the crisis, fell by an estimated 6.5 per cent in 2009.

Unlike many of the other economies covered in this article, the Hungarian public sector was the primary source of financial vulnerabilities. However, private sector credit also grew in recent years, reaching nearly 70 per cent of GDP by 2008 (EBRD, 2009). The majority of this debt was built up in the corporate sector to mask years of slow productivity growth. And while the volume of household sector debt was reasonably low when compared to many of its peers, the fact that a large proportion of it was denominated in foreign currencies (primarily euro) caused the real debt burden of Hungarian households to shoot up in the early part of 2009 as the forint depreciated at an alarming rate.

In short, impaired balance sheets across sectors have caused a particularly severe recession in Hungary. Indeed, because of the absence of significant discretionary fiscal measures, the contraction of economic activity is not forecast to end until the end of 2010. Thus, any recovery is likely to be based on weak domestic foundations and will be exposed to any potential negative external developments. In the context of deficient domestic demand, the current rate of unemployment (10.5 per cent in 2009) was forecast to rise over 2010.

Czech Republic

Real GDP in the Czech Republic grew by an average of 5 per cent over 2003–09. This enabled per capita income to converge with the EU average, rising from 73 per cent of the EU average in 2003, to 80 per cent in 2008. This strong performance was helped by sensible macroeconomic and structural policies, and reinforced by a vibrant export sector. Credit growth, while considerable, was congruent with the Czech Republic's trajectory of convergence. However, as a small, open economy, the collapse in external demand that followed the financial crisis exerted a dampening effect on output. Growth slowed at the end of 2008 and was estimated to have contracted by 4.8 per cent in 2009. Although the export channel was the primary driver of the recession in the Czech Republic, the worsening of the general economic outlook saw the supply and demand for credit tighten, inward foreign investment flows fall, and the reining in of fixed investment more widely (estimated to have fallen 7.2 per cent in 2009).

Financial vulnerabilities were quite limited in the Czech Republic because of prudent regulation, a strong domestic deposit base that reduced the dependence on external capital flows, and a comparatively low exposure to foreign currency-denominated loans. This has resulted in only a mild shock to the balance sheets of the Czech private sector. Furthermore, while the government had previously run a pro-cyclical fiscal policy, the comparatively modest size of pre-crisis budget deficits (well below 3 per cent for a number of years), and a similarly modest stock of gross government debt (around 30 per cent of GDP in 2008), ensured that the government could initiate a number of discretionary measures to offset the external demand shock. The government adopted two stimulus packages, including measures to support employment, a cut in social security contributions, and a boost to public investment. Consequently, public consumption helped prevent unemployment from rising above 7 per cent in 2009, a level comparable to that of 2005. With balance sheets largely healthy across the Czech economy, future prospects are closely tied to fluctuations in external demand. With many 'cash for clunkers' schemes across the EU due to expire later this year, the prospects for Czech export performance remained uncertain.

The Baltic Economies

This section deals with the three Baltic economies collectively. As well as their geographic proximity, these three economies all displayed similar economic characteristics, both prior to the crisis and in their performance during 2009.

After stellar growth rates in the 2000s, all three of the Baltic economies suffered a severe contraction of economic activity in 2009 that was comparable in scale to that experienced in the 'transition depression' of the early 1990s. Indeed, 2009 was the single worst year of economic performance for all three economies since independence. All three economies experienced an acute withdrawal of private demand: in 2009, private consumption fell by approximately a fifth, while fixed investment collapsed by around 35 per cent in all three cases. This compounded an already sharp contraction of economic activity that occurred in 2008. Estonia, the best-performing Baltic economy in 2009, experienced a decline in real GDP of an estimated 13.7 per cent; Latvia and Lithuania saw declines of 18 and 18.1 per cent, respectively. As a result of this sharp retrenchment of private demand, current account deficits that were previously excessively large quickly narrowed; all three current accounts swung into surplus in 2009. Consequently, while export volumes collapsed amid the slump in international trade, the faster contraction in imports caused net exports to be the only positive component of GDP in 2009. Unemployment, perhaps the most useful indicator of the human cost of a recession, roughly tripled in all three economies. Inflation, which was beginning to overheat in the region prior to the crisis, plummeted, with Latvia experiencing outright deflation in 2009.

As small, open economies that experienced huge inflows of foreign capital in the pre-crisis period, the severity of the recession in the Baltic countries appeared over-determined. Indeed, both Estonia and Latvia had already succumbed to macroeconomic imbalances before the crisis; both had moved into recession in early 2008. Private sector indebtedness had reached dangerous levels: stocks of private sector debt had roughly tripled, while external debt – primarily borrowed from Swedish banks – exceeded GDP in all three countries. As credit dried up from the end of 2008, and as the true extent of the economic catastrophe became apparent, house prices, which had ballooned in recent years and helped feed a feeling of growing prosperity, were brought crashing down: in 2009 alone, prices are estimated to have fallen by between 30 per cent in Estonia, and 50 per cent in Latvia (Latvian Statistical Office, 2010; Estonian Statistical Office, 2010).

As the huge burden of debt caused private sector demand to shrivel over the course of 2009, the governments of the three economies faced a similar quandary: should they abandon their fixed currency regimes and increase government spending to offset dwindling private demand? Or should they adhere to their fixed currency regimes, but amplify the immediate effects of the recession in the short run by refusing to increase discretionary spending? So far, despite significant public unrest, particularly in Latvia, all three governments have opted for the latter. There are two main reasons for this course of action. First, elementary macroeconomic theory would suggest that fiscal expansion is less effective in small, open economies as the positive effects are likely to spill over abroad and reduce the domestic multiplier effect. Second, and perhaps more importantly, governments in all three countries have reiterated their desire to achieve membership of the euro area in the future; as such, they recognize that failure to adhere to the ERM II regime will set them back in achieving this aim. In 2009, Baltic governments remained steadfast in this aim.

By precluding the option of currency devaluation, the Baltic economies faced the long, and probably arduous, task of restoring competiveness if they were to effect a shift away from consumption-based growth to a model that would be more oriented towards exports and (non-residential) investment. Rapid wage inflation in the pre-crisis period resulted in the erosion of what were previously very competitive labour costs. Barring an unexpected and unprecedented increase in total factor productivity, only a protracted episode of wage deflation could now claw back lost competiveness. This process had begun in all three economies, but needed to continue for a considerable period of time. This was likely to compound what was already an exceptionally nasty recession. On the positive side, a dampening of previously overheating economies would at least help the governments of the Baltic countries satisfy the convergence criteria set out for aspiring euro area economies.

Bulgaria

In the five years prior to the onset of the global recession the Bulgarian economy had grown at an average annual rate of 6 per cent. This strong performance was underpinned by large inflows of foreign direct investment (which helped fund an expanding current account deficit), robust domestic investment, and an expansion of domestic consumption, fuelled in large part by external borrowing. However, net exports were not an important component of the Bulgarian growth model; thus, Bulgaria's exposure to the global recession was primarily related to its dependence on external capital rather than a drop in external demand for Bulgarian goods. The seizure of cross-border capital flows that occurred around the turn of the year caused the Bulgarian economy to contract by an estimated 5.9 per cent in 2009. Investment collapsed by 21.1 per cent in 2009, while private consumption was reined in by 5.7 per cent. As the demand for imports declined, the current account deficit narrowed and net exports made a positive contribution to GDP for the first time in years.

This shift to export-oriented growth, albeit forced, was fortunate due to the limited capacity of the Bulgarian government to provide discretionary fiscal support to offset the collapse in investment and private consumption. Because of its currency board arrangement, which pegs the lev to the euro, the Bulgarian government was unable to enact any significant expansion of public borrowing. Thus, while the stock of gross government debt was extremely low (estimated to be just 15.1 per cent in 2009), Bulgaria's membership of ERM II implied that a shift to export-oriented growth remained the most likely route to economic growth for as long as credit conditions remain tight. Indeed, with the level of total external debt already in excess of 100 per cent of GDP, it was unclear as to whether the Bulgarian economy had the capacity to absorb further inflows of lending.

If Bulgaria was to make a permanent switch towards a more export-oriented growth model, an increase in competiveness was required. Persistent and high wage inflation during the pre-crisis period eroded Bulgaria's competitive position; double-digit Real Effective Exchange Rate appreciation from 2007 until late 2009 was much higher than that of its neighbours. Because of the currency board, the only way of achieving a more competitive export sector was either through enormous, and as yet unseen, productivity increases, or through a significant bout of domestic wage deflation. The latter seemed more likely at this stage. However, a high level of indebtedness in the household and corporate sectors made wage deflation an expensive course of action as it would have caused a real increase in their respective debt burdens. Indeed, the wage deflation route was further complicated by the fact that a number of other economies, from within the euro area and outside, were also likely to be adopting similar deflationary measures. As such, the path towards a strong and sustainable recovery was fraught with difficulty.

Romania

After several years of very strong economic performance, the Romanian economy experienced a violent reversal of fortunes in 2009; real GDP turned sharply from growth of 6.2 per cent in 2008 to a contraction of an estimated 8 per cent in 2009. The years before 2009 were characterized by signs of considerable overheating and unsustainable fiscal and external imbalances: the current account deficit hit 13.6 per cent in 2007 with inflation rising to 7.9 per cent in 2008. Like Bulgaria, the pre-crisis boom was primarily associated with a rapid expansion of investment and a credit-fuelled expansion of private consumption. And like Bulgaria, over-indebted corporate and household sectors were reliant on short-term external funding. As the global credit crunch reached its nadir in early 2009, fixed investment declined by 12.3 per cent, with only stronger than anticipated FDI inflows preventing an even larger collapse. Consumers sharply reined in spending, forcing a savage 12.3 per cent contraction in private consumption. As in Bulgaria, the sharp retrenchment in domestic demand resulted in a narrowing of the current account deficit and the return of a positive contribution of net exports to GDP.

While the similarities with Bulgaria are stark, it was also important to note that, unlike Bulgaria, years of pro-cyclical budgetary policy caused gross government debt to nearly double between 2007 and 2009, albeit from a low base of 12.6 per cent. Furthermore, with a more flexible exchange rate regime than Bulgaria, the lei suffered a severe depreciation, plummeting more than 30 per cent from its 2007 peak at the beginning of the year. In the absence of fiscal credibility, and in the face of increasing doubts about the sustainability of Romania's balance of payments position, the government sought external financial support. A combined action by the EU, the European Investment Bank, the European Bank of Reconstruction and Development, the IMF and the World Bank provided €20 billion of medium-term financial assistance. While this achieved the aim of short-term stabilization, it imposed constraints on the capacity of the government to counteract the negative effects of the collapse in domestic demand. Consequently, unemployment rose 6.4 per cent in 2007, to an estimated 9 per cent in 2009.

Several key differences exist between Bulgaria and Romania that suggest that the latter may be better placed for a sustainable recovery. First, the stock of private sector debt was much smaller than in Bulgaria. Romania had an external debt to GDP ratio of less than 50 per cent, compared to over 100 per cent in Bulgaria; and the stock of private sector debt was less than 40 per cent in Romania, compared to around 75 per cent in Bulgaria. Second, a flexible exchange rate would enable Romania to restore lost competiveness without resorting to potentially painful domestic wage deflation, particularly now that previously loose income policies in the public sector have been tightened.

Conclusions

The effects of the global financial crisis nearly caused economic catastrophe in 2009. In the first three months of the year the levels of global output, international trade and most stock market indices were plummeting at a faster rate than in the 1930s. However, the magnitude of the monetary and fiscal response by governments across the world was enough to avert immediate disaster. As output stabilized, and then grew in the second half of the year, attention shifted from staving off immediate dangers to a debate on the timing and speed of the withdrawal of government support, better known as 'exit strategies'. Higher than forecast rates of growth in China, India and Brazil, as well as a return to growth in the world's largest economy, the USA, gave some cause for at least cautious optimism that the end of the Great Recession was imminent.

As this article has illustrated, the performance of the non-euro area economies during 2009, and during the Great Recession more generally, can largely be explained by where an economy stood in terms of its level of debt, and by the degree of trade dependency. The best performer – Poland – had relatively low levels of debt, and was not as dependent on trade as many other countries from within the non-euro area. By contrast, economies that exhibited signs of both excessive debt and high trade dependence tended to experience relatively severe recessions. The three Baltic economies, characterized by extremely high levels of private sector debt and high levels of trade openness, suffered among the worse recessions in the world during 2009. While this simple explanation does help explain the majority of variation in performance across the non-euro area economies in 2009, several further observations can be made.

First, the benefits of government intervention – both monetary and fiscal – in mitigating the worst effects of the crisis were clear. While the recession was severe for many countries, the experience of the Baltic states, where offsetting government support was minimal, demonstrated that it might have been far worse if governments had not stepped in to put a floor on the contraction in domestic demand. Indeed, Poland, with its lower trade openness and debt levels, still required timely and significant fiscal intervention to stave off recession.

Second, flexible exchange rates appeared to be preferable to fixed exchange rates, in the short term at least. Those countries with fixed or semi-fixed exchange rates – the Baltic states, Bulgaria and to a lesser extent Romania – certainly performed worse than those without. This was almost certainly linked to the constraints imposed on government spending by their exchange rate regimes. This policy choice of extreme short-term pain was motivated by the prospect of long-term gain in the form of eventual euro area membership. However, putting to one side the issue of whether this would be politically feasible in the light of the euro area's existing problems, the strength of the euro relative to other currencies suggested that any restoration of competitiveness would have to occur through domestic deflation, an ominous prospect given the high levels of foreign currency denominated debt that existed in the fixed exchange rate economies.

Looking ahead to 2010, international trade was expected to increase as the world economy emerged from the Great Recession. However, the overhang of debt in many cases left open the prospect of a prolonged 'balance sheet' recession, implying years of sub-trend private demand. This would leave many economies even more dependent on external demand, and, in a number of countries, would likely presage a significant rise in levels of government debt. This increase was already causing concerns over the long-term sustainability of increasing sovereign debt levels. Should these concerns translate into higher bond yields, financing costs would increase further across the economy. Such an eventuality had the potential to reverse the gains made in the second half of 2009, and perhaps even plunge the world economy back into recession. Unfortunately, the widespread deficiency of domestic demand was likely to require continued offsetting of public sector support, particularly if international trade failed to accelerate quickly to pre-crisis levels.

In short, the effects of the global economic crisis looked likely to be felt for years beyond 2009. For the majority of countries covered in this article, the risks for the future remain firmly to the downside. Policy-makers – both in the non-euro area Member States and beyond – seemed destined to be walking a fiscal tightrope for many years to come, signalling a new era of economic instability. As a result, dealing with long-term challenges, such as the fiscal costs associated with ageing populations, economic competition from the rapidly expanding Asian economies, and continued slow productivity growth, looked likely to prove even more difficult.

References

Aslund, A. (2009) 'The East European Financial Crisis'. CASE Working Papers No. 395 (Warsaw: CASE).

Bank of England (2009) 'Financial Stability Report: December'. No. 26 (London: Bank of England).

Commission of the European Communities (2009) *European Economic Forecast: Autumn 2009* (Brussels: ECFIN).

Connolly, R. (2009) 'Financial Vulnerabilities in Emerging Europe: An Overview'. *Bank of Finland Institute for Transition Online Research*, No. 3.

Estonian Statistical Office (2010) Statistics Database. Available at «http://www.stat.ee/?lang=en».

Eichengreen, B. (2007) *Global Imbalances and the Lessons of Bretton Woods* (Cambridge, MA: MIT Press).

Eichengreen, B. and O'Rourke, K.H. (2009) 'A Tale of Two Depressions'. 18 June. Available at «http://www.voxeu.org/index.php?q=node/3421».

European Bank for Reconstruction and Development (2009) *Transition Report 2009: Transition in Crisis* (London: EBRD Press).

Goldstein, M. and Xie, D. (2009) 'The Impact of the Financial Crisis on Emerging Asia'. Peterson Institute Working Paper Series No. 09–11 (Washington, DC: Peterson Institute.

International Monetary Fund (2009) *World Economic Outlook* (New York: IMF).

Koo, R. (2008) *The Holy Grail of Macroeconomics: Lessons from Japan's Great Recession* (Singapore: Wiley Press).

Latvian Statistical Office (2010) Statistics Database. Available at «http://www.csb.gov.lv/?lng=en».

McKinsey Global Institute (2010) 'Debt and Deleveraging: The Global Credit Bubble and its Economic Consequences'. Available at «http://www.mckinsey.com/mgi/publications/debt_and_deleveraging/index.asp».

OECD (2010) *World Economic Outlook* (Paris: OECD Press).

Reinhart, C. and Rogoff, K. (2009) *This Time is Different: Eight Centuries of Financial Folly* (Princeton, NJ: Princeton University Press).

Wolf, M. (2009) *Fixing Global Finance: How to Curb Financial Crises in the 21st Century* (New Haven, CT: Yale University Press).

Wood, C. (2006) *The Bubble Economy: Japan's Extraordinary Speculative Boom of the '80s and the Dramatic Bust of the 1990s* (New York: Equinox Publishing).

World Bank (2010) *World Bank Development Indicators* (Washington, DC: World Bank). Available at «http://esds.ac.uk».

JCMS 2010 Volume 48 Annual Review pp. 267–274

Chronology: The European Union in 2009

FABIAN GUY NEUNER
University of Birmingham

At a Glance

Presidencies of the EU Council: Czech Republic (1 January–30 June) and Sweden (1 July–31 December).

January

1	The Czech Republic takes over the Council Presidency.
1	Slovakia becomes the 16th country to adopt the euro on the currency's tenth anniversary.
1	Russia halts natural gas exports to Ukraine after failed payment negotiations provoking several days of serious supply shortages across eastern Europe.
8	Bank of England cuts interest rates to 1.5 per cent making this the lowest rate since the institution's inception.
12	Extraordinary meeting of the Energy Council urges Russia to resume gas supplies.
18	The gas dispute between Russia and Ukraine is resolved after the countries' leaders negotiate a new ten-year contract.
20	Barack Obama is inaugurated as president of the United States.
20	Ecofin discusses restoring growth and re-emphasizes the need for structural reforms.
21	Israel completes withdrawal from Gaza strip after a three-week military operation.

21	Commission adopts EU Maritime Transport Strategy 2018.
21	The European Central Bank cuts interest rates in the euro area from 2.5 per cent to 2 per cent in the light of the recession.
26	Icelandic prime minister Geir Haarde resigns after government and the country's financial systems collapse.

February

1	Jóhanna Sigurðardóttir takes over as prime minister of Iceland.
5–6	European University-Business Forum discusses link between higher education and business and how they can collaborate better.
8	Swiss vote in a referendum in favour of extending freedom of movement of persons within the EU to Bulgaria and Romania.
8	Liechtenstein parliamentary election sees Patriotic Union become largest party in the *Landtag*.
9	French President Sarkozy announces €6.5 billion bail-out for French automotive industry which attracts criticism from a range of EU leaders.
18	Czech parliament (lower house) ratifies the Lisbon Treaty.
19	Internal Market Scoreboard is released. On the whole Member States are praised for high implementation rate of internal market rules.
22	Berlin Summit sees Europe's G20 leaders agree on a joint strategy to tackle the financial crisis in the run-up to the April G20 Summit.
23	Commission adopts a strategy for the prevention of environmental and man-made disasters.
25	The Commission receives recommendations for tighter financial oversight from a group of financial experts chaired by Jacques de Larosière.
26	Former Serbian president Milan Milutinović is acquitted by the International Criminal Tribunal for the Former Yugoslavia on charges of war crimes.

March

| 1 | Informal EU summit discusses the implementation of the 'Economic Recovery Plan'. |
| 2 | 'EU Enlargement – 5 Years After' Conference concludes that eastern enlargement had positive effect on all EU Member States. |

5	Commission presents joint report on Social Protection and Social Inclusion outlining the need for active inclusion strategies.
11	The European Central Bank further cuts interest rates to 1.5 per cent.
19–20	European Council focuses on economic recovery through fiscal stimulus and the single market. Further consideration is given to energy security, climate change and the Eastern Partnership.
22	Gjorge Ivanov elected president of Macedonia.
23	The EP and the Czech Presidency strike a deal on the third energy liberalization package.
24	Czech Prime Minister Mirek Topolánek's government loses a vote of no confidence, following which he announces his resignation. The European Commission pronounces its confidence in the Czech Presidency's ability to continue fulfilling its role.

April

1	Stabilization and Association Agreement with Albania enters into force.
1	Albania and Croatia join Nato.
1–2	First European Consumer Summit.
2	G20 Summit in London sees leaders of most industrialized countries pledge €832 billion to overcome global financial crisis. The Summit is partly overshadowed by demonstrations and clashes between activists and the police on London's streets.
4	George Abela sworn in as president of Malta following an indirect election held in January.
4	Ivan Gašparovič re-elected president of Slovakia.
4	Anders Fogh Rasmussen elected Secretary General of Nato during the Strasbourg-Kehl summit which also marked the organization's 60th anniversary.
5	Informal EU–US Summit.
8	The European Central Bank further cuts interest rates to 1.25 per cent.
25	Icelandic parliamentary election in the wake of the country's financial turmoil sees victory for the Social Democratic Alliance.

26	Andorran parliamentary election won by the Social Democratic Party.
28	EU–Russia Permanent Partnership Council on Energy makes progress towards an energy dialogue.
28	Albania formally applies for EU membership.
29	Commission adopts '2009 Ageing Communication' aimed at tackling the demographic challenges facing Europe. This includes projections to increase age-related expenditure by 4.75 per cent of GDP by 2060.
30	Extraordinary meeting of health ministers discusses a joint response to the A/H1N1 influenza virus.

May

1	Fifth anniversary of 2004 enlargement.
4	EU–Japan Summit in Prague.
6	Czech parliament (upper house) ratifies the Lisbon Treaty.
6	EU–Canada Summit sees the launch of the Comprehensive Economic Partnership Agreement with a view to enhance trade relations.
7	Launch of the Eastern Partnership in Prague.
7	Employment Summit proposes actions to fight unemployment and create new jobs. Recommendations include both EU and national-level initiatives to increase mobility and entrepreneurship amongst young people.
8	Southern Corridor Summit moves on discussions of energy security and the development of closer links between the EU and the Southern Caucasus, Central Asia and the Middle East.
13	European Commission fines computer chip manufacturer Intel €1.06 billion (the highest-ever fine for anti-competitiveness practices).
13	The European Central Bank cuts interest rates to 1 per cent.
14–15	Brussels Economic Forum.
17	European Commissioner Dalia Grybauskaitė is elected as first female president of Lithuania.
20	EU–China Summit in Prague.
21–22	EU–Russia Summit in Khabarovsk.
23	Horst Köhler is re-elected president of Germany in an indirect election.

June

1	General Motors files for bankruptcy.
4–7	European Parliament elections take place across Europe. The election returns clear gains for the centre-right and the turnout reaches an all-time low of 43.2 per cent.
7	Jean-Claude Juncker's Christian Social People's Party expands its majority in the Luxembourg election.
7	Danes vote in favour of a referendum to change the rules of accession to the throne. The new ruling introduces equal primogeniture thus preventing males from having precedence over females in the line of succession.
17	Informal EU–Jordan Summit discusses the Middle East peace process.
17	First EU–Pakistan Summit. Topics covered included security, regional co-operation, energy and trade.
18–19	European Council. Discussions focus on economic recovery, the future of the Lisbon Treaty and co-operation on climate change in the run-up to the Copenhagen Summit. Further consideration was given to tackling illegal immigration, transatlantic relations and the Middle East Peace Process.
21	Consequent upon a referendum in 2008 Greenland establishes self-government in key areas including the judiciary and the police force.
23	EU–OPEC Energy Dialogue in Vienna.
28	Prime Minister Sali Berisha's Democratic Party of Albania remains the strongest party following the Albanian parliamentary election.
30	German Federal Constitutional Court's ruling on the compatibility of the Lisbon Treaty with the German Basic Law.
30	Turkey opens the Taxation accession negotiation chapter making it the 11th of the 35 chapters to be opened.

July

1	Sweden takes over the EU Council Presidency.
1	EU roaming regulation enters into force and leads to a significant reduction in roaming costs for mobile phone services.
5	Boyko Borisov's Citizens for European Development of Bulgaria Party wins the parliamentary election in Bulgaria.

8–10	G8 Summit in L'Aquila.
14	Polish MEP Jerzy Buzek (European Peoples Party) elected President of the European Parliament with 86 per cent of the votes.
23	Iceland formally applies for EU membership.

August

| 18 | Representatives of Germany's leading parties agree on proposals on how the Lisbon Treaty can be implemented in accordance with German law. |
| 20 | European Observation Mission monitors the Afghan presidential election. |

September

1	Due to EU regulations the first stage in the phasing out of uneconomical light bulbs begins.
11	EU–South Africa Summit. The discussions are concentrated around global responses to climate change and economic recovery.
14	Jens Stoltenberg's Red–Green coalition wins Norwegian parliamentary election.
16	José Manuel Barroso's nomination for a second term as President of the European Commission is approved by the European Parliament.
17	Informal meeting of EU heads of state and government agrees joint approach for Pittsburgh G20 Summit.
17–18	Ministerial conference on the Baltic Sea Strategy.
21	UK House of Commons speaker Michael Martin resigns over his handling of the parliamentary expenses scandal.
23	Commission adopts financial supervision package. The package includes the creation of a European Systemic Risk Board (ESRB) and a European System of Financial Supervisors (ESFS) which will set out to strengthen financial monitoring on both a system and an individual institution level respectively.
24–25	The G20 Summit in Pittsburgh concentrates discussions on securing future economic sustainability after the crisis. The group agrees to make the G20 the key forum for economic co-operation thus including major developing nations in discussions that had previously been restricted to the G8 nations.

27	José Sócrates' Socialist Party wins the Portuguese legislative election despite losing 24 seats.
27	The German federal election returns a clear victory for the centre-right which leads to Chancellor Angela Merkel's Christian Democratic Union entering into a coalition with the Free Democratic Party.
30	Commission presents a strategy aimed at enhancing EU–Latin American relations.

October

3	Ireland votes in favour of the Lisbon Treaty in a second referendum.
4	Greek legislative election sees George Papandreou lead the Socialist Party (PASOK) to victory by winning 58 additional seats in the parliament.
10	Polish President Lech Kaczyński ratifies the Lisbon Treaty.
15	EU–Korea Free Trade Agreement is signed thereby laying the foundation for the second largest free trade area after NAFTA.
21	Irish parliament (lower house) ratifies the Lisbon Treaty.
22	Irish parliament (upper house) ratifies the Lisbon Treaty.
29–30	European Council discusses the implementation of the Lisbon Treaty in the light of the final national ratifications, a joint approach to the Copenhagen Climate discussions and the Baltic Sea Strategy.

November

3	Czech President Václav Klaus ratifies the Lisbon Treaty after the Czech Constitutional Court deems that the Treaty is compatible with Czech law removing the final obstacle for the Treaty to be able to enter into force.
3	EU–US Summit in Washington sees discussions around economic recovery, energy security and foreign policy. Outcomes include the creation of an EU–US Energy Council and a declaration on non-proliferation and disarmament.
6	EU–India Summit.
9	Germany celebrates the 20th anniversary of the fall of the Berlin Wall.
16–17	Third Equality Summit.
16–18	World Summit on food security in Rome.
18	EU–Russia Summit in Stockholm.

20	Belgian prime minister, Herman van Rompuy, is appointed first permanent President of the EU Council and Catherine Ashton, the British Trade Commissioner, is appointed High Representative for Foreign Affairs at a meeting of the European Council.
22	Romanians vote in a referendum in favour of moving from a bicameral parliament to a unicameral one with a maximum of 300 seats.
27	José Manuel Barroso announces his proposed line-up and portfolio distribution for the Barroso II Commission.
29	Swiss vote in a referendum in favour of banning any future construction of minarets.
30	EU–China Summit.

December

1	The Lisbon Treaty comes into force.
3	Rail passenger regulation enters into force.
6	Traian Băsescu is re-elected president of Romania.
7–18	United Nations Climate Change Conference in Copenhagen.
8	First meeting of foreign ministers as part of the Eastern Partnership.
10–11	European Council finalizes the 'Stockholm Programme' for 2010–14 aimed at expanding the area of freedom, security and justice. Other topics covered were financial supervision and evaluating the Lisbon strategy.
19	Visa-free travel across the EU is extended to citizens of Serbia, Macedonia and Montenegro.
19	Copenhagen Accord signed. The agreement fostered an understanding to keep temperature rises below 2 degrees Celsius but failed to propose clear emission reduction targets.
21	Croatia makes progress towards EU membership by closing its 17th accession negotiation chapter.
21	Turkey opens the environment accession negotiation chapter making it the 12th of the 35 chapters to be opened.
22	Serbia formally applies for EU membership.
22	Uwe Corsepius confirmed as Secretary General of the EU Council for 2011–15.

Index

Note: Italicized page references indicate information contained in tables.